Carnegie Commission on Higher Education
Sponsored Research Studies

BRIDGES TO UNDERSTANDING:
INTERNATIONAL PROGRAMS OF AMERICAN
COLLEGES AND UNIVERSITIES
Irwin T. Sanders and Jennifer C. Ward

GRADUATE AND PROFESSIONAL EDUCATION,
1980:
A SURVEY OF INSTITUTIONAL PLANS
Lewis B. Mayhew

THE AMERICAN COLLEGE AND AMERICAN
CULTURE:
SOCIALIZATION AS A FUNCTION OF HIGHER
EDUCATION
Oscar and Mary F. Handlin

RECENT ALUMNI AND HIGHER EDUCATION:
A SURVEY OF COLLEGE GRADUATES
Joe L. Spaeth and Andrew M. Greeley

CHANGE IN EDUCATIONAL POLICY:
SELF-STUDIES IN SELECTED COLLEGES AND
UNIVERSITIES
Dwight R. Ladd

STATE OFFICIALS AND HIGHER EDUCATION:
A SURVEY OF THE OPINIONS AND
EXPECTATIONS OF POLICY MAKERS IN NINE
STATES
Heinz Eulau and Harold Quinley

ACADEMIC DEGREE STRUCTURES:
INNOVATIVE APPROACHES
PRINCIPLES OF REFORM IN DEGREE
STRUCTURES IN THE UNITED STATES
Stephen H. Spurr

COLLEGES OF THE FORGOTTEN AMERICANS:
A PROFILE OF STATE COLLEGES AND
REGIONAL UNIVERSITIES
E. Alden Dunham

FROM BACKWATER TO MAINSTREAM:
A PROFILE OF CATHOLIC HIGHER
EDUCATION
Andrew M. Greeley

THE ECONOMICS OF THE MAJOR PRIVATE
UNIVERSITIES
William G. Bowen
(Out of print, but available from University Microfilms.)

THE FINANCE OF HIGHER EDUCATION
Howard R. Bowen
(Out of print, but available from University Microfilms.)

ALTERNATIVE METHODS OF FEDERAL
FUNDING FOR HIGHER EDUCATION
Ron Wolk

INVENTORY OF CURRENT RESEARCH ON
HIGHER EDUCATION 1968
Dale M. Heckman and Warren Bryan Martin

The following technical reports are available from the Carnegie Commission on Higher Education, 1947 Center Street, Berkeley, California 94704.

RESOURCE USE IN HIGHER EDUCATION:
TRENDS IN OUTPUT AND INPUTS, 1930–1967
June O'Neill

TRENDS AND PROJECTIONS OF PHYSICIANS
IN THE UNITED STATES 1967–2002
Mark S. Blumberg

MAY 1970:
THE CAMPUS AFTERMATH OF CAMBODIA
AND KENT STATE
Richard E. Peterson and John A. Bilorusky

The following reprints are available from the Carnegie Commission on Higher Education, 1947 Center Street, Berkeley, California 94704.

ACCELERATED PROGRAM OF MEDICAL EDUCATION, *by Mark S. Blumberg, reprinted from* JOURNAL OF MEDICAL EDUCATION, *vol. 46, no. 8, August 1971.*

SCIENTIFIC MANPOWER FOR 1970–1985, *by Allan M. Cartter, reprinted from* SCIENCE, *vol. 172, no. 3979, pp. 132–140, April 9, 1971.*

A NEW METHOD OF MEASURING STATES' HIGHER EDUCATION BURDEN, *by Neil Timm, reprinted from* THE JOURNAL OF HIGHER EDUCATION, *vol. 42, no. 1, pp. 27–33, January 1971.*

REGENT WATCHING, *by Earl F. Cheit, reprinted from* AGB REPORTS, *vol. 13, no. 6, pp. 4–13, March 1971.*

WHAT HAPPENS TO COLLEGE GENERATIONS POLITICALLY?, *by Seymour M. Lipset and Everett C. Ladd, Jr., reprinted from* THE PUBLIC INTEREST, *no. 24, Summer 1971.*

AMERICAN SOCIAL SCIENTISTS AND THE GROWTH OF CAMPUS POLITICAL ACTIVISM IN THE 1960s, *by Everett C. Ladd, Jr., and Seymour M. Lipset, reprinted from* SOCIAL SCIENCES INFORMATION, *vol. 10, no. 2, April 1971.*

THE POLITICS OF AMERICAN POLITICAL SCIENTISTS, *by Everett C. Ladd, Jr., and Seymour M. Lipset, reprinted from* PS, *vol. 4, no. 2, Spring 1971.*

THE DIVIDED PROFESSORIATE, *by Seymour M. Lipset and Everett C. Ladd, Jr., reprinted from* CHANGE, *vol. 3, no. 3, pp. 54–60, May 1971.*

JEWISH AND GENTILE ACADEMICS IN THE UNITED STATES: ACHIEVEMENTS, CULTURES AND POLITICS, *by Seymour M. Lipset and Everett C. Ladd, Jr., reprinted from* AMERICAN JEWISH YEAR BOOK, *1971.*

THE UNHOLY ALLIANCE AGAINST THE CAMPUS, *by Kenneth Keniston and Michael Lerner, reprinted from* NEW YORK TIMES MAGAZINE, *November 8, 1970 .*

PRECARIOUS PROFESSORS: NEW PATTERNS OF REPRESENTATION, *by Joseph W. Garbarino, reprinted from* INDUSTRIAL RELATIONS, *vol. 10, no. 1, February 1971.*

. . . AND WHAT PROFESSORS THINK: ABOUT STUDENT PROTEST AND MANNERS, MORALS, POLITICS, AND CHAOS ON THE CAMPUS, *by Seymour Martin Lipset and Everett C. Ladd, Jr., reprinted from* PSYCHOLOGY TODAY, *November 1970.**

DEMAND AND SUPPLY IN U.S. HIGHER EDUCATION: A PROGRESS REPORT, *by Roy Radner and Leonard S. Miller, reprinted from* AMERICAN ECONOMIC REVIEW, *May 1970.**

RESOURCES FOR HIGHER EDUCATION: AN ECONOMIST'S VIEW, *by Theodore W. Schultz, reprinted from* JOURNAL OF POLITICAL ECONOMY, *vol. 76, no. 3, University of Chicago, May/ June 1968.**

INDUSTRIAL RELATIONS AND UNIVERSITY RELATIONS, *by Clark Kerr, reprinted from* PROCEEDINGS OF THE 21ST ANNUAL WINTER MEETING OF THE INDUSTRIAL RELATIONS RESEARCH ASSOCIATION, *pp. 15–25.**

NEW CHALLENGES TO THE COLLEGE AND UNIVERSITY, *by Clark Kerr, reprinted from Kermit Gordon (ed.),* AGENDA FOR THE NATION, *The Brookings Institution, Washington, D.C., 1968.**

PRESIDENTIAL DISCONTENT, by Clark Kerr, reprinted from David C. Nichols (ed.), PERSPECTIVES ON CAMPUS TENSIONS: PAPERS PREPARED FOR THE SPECIAL COMMITTEE ON CAMPUS TENSIONS, American Council on Education, Washington, D.C., September 1970.*

STUDENT PROTEST—AN INSTITUTIONAL AND NATIONAL PROFILE, by Harold Hodgkinson, reprinted from THE RECORD, vol. 71, no. 4, May 1970.*

WHAT'S BUGGING THE STUDENTS?, by Kenneth Keniston, reprinted from EDUCATIONAL RECORD, American Council on Education, Washington, D.C., Spring 1970.*

THE POLITICS OF ACADEMIA, by Seymour Martin Lipset, reprinted from David C. Nichols (ed.), PERSPECTIVES ON CAMPUS TENSIONS: PAPERS PREPARED FOR THE SPECIAL COMMITTEE ON CAMPUS TENSIONS, American Council on Education, Washington, D.C., September 1970.*

*The Commission's stock of this reprint has been exhausted.

The Nonprofit Research Institute

ITS ORIGIN, OPERATION, PROBLEMS, AND PROSPECTS

by *Harold Orlans*

Program on Technology and Society,
Harvard University

Ninth of a Series of Profiles Sponsored by
The Carnegie Commission on Higher Education

MC GRAW–HILL BOOK COMPANY

New York   St. Louis   San Francisco   Düsseldorf
London   Sydney   Toronto   Mexico   Panama
Johannesburg   Kuala Lumpur   Montreal
New Delhi   Rio de Janeiro   Singapore

*The Carnegie Commission on Higher Education,
1947 Center Street, Berkeley, California 94704,
has sponsored preparation of this profile as a
part of a continuing effort to obtain and present
significant information for public discussion.
The views expressed are those of the author.*

THE NONPROFIT RESEARCH INSTITUTE
Its Origin, Operation, Problems, and Prospects

Library of Congress Cataloging in Publication Data
Orlans, Harold
The nonprofit research institute.
"Ninth of a series of profiles sponsored by the
Carnegie Commission on Higher Education."
Bibliography: p. 223
1. Research—U.S. I. Carnegie Commission on
Higher Education. II. Title.
Q180.U5Q73   378.1'5'0973   70-37532
ISBN 0-07-010040-3

123456789MAMM798765432

Contents

vii

Foreword

The independent, nonprofit research institute is a phenomenon of the twentieth century. An early one was created in 1913 to serve industry. At the outbreak of World War II, the federal government became the most prominent client of such organizations and launched a few institutes itself. Between 1951 and 1967, the number of federally sponsored nonprofit research centers nearly tripled, increasing from 23 to 67. In 1968, they spent $1,637 million on basic research, applied research, and development—39 percent of all the funds spent by both academic institutions and independent nonprofit research institutes that year. Thus, their expenditures were about two-thirds of those of the universities alone.

These institutions now engage in research not only in industry, but also in national defense programs, public health, space exploration, atomic energy, education, economics, and public policy. Among their impressive technological contributions are development of electrostatic copying, the hypersonic shock tunnel, practical magnetic tape recording, the first deep-diving submarine, and super alloys and other new materials.[1]

The nonprofit research institutes are of particular interest to the Carnegie Commission on Higher Education because they have academic counterparts in organized research units on university campuses, and also because they share one of the university's primary functions. Moreover, several leading universities in the United States have been involved in the cooperative management of independent research and development organizations.

In recent years, independent research institutes have become

[1] Victor J. Danilov, "The Not-for-profit Research Institutes," *Industrial Research,* February 1966.

the subject of new interest as university associations with institutes engaged in classified research have been terminated in some cases, and as these institutes are increasingly proposed as more appropriate agencies than universities as centers for certain types of applied research and technological development. They thus may become a source of greater competition than they have been for research talent and grants. A few of them are even becoming degree-granting institutions.

The fact that some of the independent research institutes — along with the nation's universities — either anticipate or already have been subjected to cuts in research funding makes their operations and experiences particularly instructive for those administering research programs at academic institutions.

This profile by Harold Orlans is, we believe, the first attempt to provide a comprehensive description and analysis of a fascinating scientific and intellectual enterprise that could have increasing impact on the roles of American universities and the progress of our society.

Clark Kerr

Chairman
Carnegie Commission on
Higher Education

January 1972

Introduction

The present study was proposed and financed by the Carnegie Commission on Higher Education. I am grateful to Clark Kerr, chairman of the Commission, for the opportunity to conduct it, and to him and Verne Stadtman of the Commission staff for their administrative and editorial tolerance.

To avoid a conflict of interest during the course of the study, I took leave from the Brookings Institution as a visiting associate at the Program on Technology and Society of Harvard University. I am grateful to Kermit Gordon, president, and Gilbert Steiner, director of governmental studies at Brookings, for facilitating that leave, and to Emmanuel Mesthene, director of the Harvard program, for his hospitality. Jane Draper, administrative officer of the program; Paula Hurd, its librarian; and Susan Goldman, who served as my secretary, were unremittingly helpful.

A study of this kind depends ultimately on the cooperation of many busy people who are willing to devote an hour or more of their time to answering questions and discussing their experience in the hope, but with no assurance, that something of value will emerge. About 90 persons at 30 institutes and a number of government agencies and private institutions served in this way as guiltless collaborators; unidentified quotations are drawn from notes of these interviews, conducted mainly during the second half of 1970. In addition, the following persons kindly offered detailed comments and corrections on the draft or were helpful in other ways beyond the normal bounds of courtesy: Ernest M. Allen, Department of Health, Education and Welfare; Charles A. Anderson, Stanford Research Institute; Kathleen Archibald and Henry S. Rowen, RAND, and Peter Szanton, New York City–RAND Institute; Paul Armer, Stanford University and Harvard Program on Technology and Society; Albert D. Biderman, Bureau of Social

Science Research; Launor F. Carter, System Development Corporation; Victor J. Danilov, *Industrial Research;* Bowen C. Dees and Joseph R. Feldmeier, Franklin Institute; Charles J. DiBona, Center for Naval Analyses; Douglas Dies, American Council of Independent Laboratories; John S. Foster, Jr., and Edward M. Glass, Department of Defense; John C. Honey, Syracuse University; Don E. Kash, University of Oklahoma; Charles V. Kidd, Association of American Universities; Louis Levin, William G. Rosen, and Joseph H. Schuster, National Science Foundation; Robert H. Moulton, Jr., Stanford Linear Accelerator Center; Sidney G. Nelson, National Steel Corporation; Rodney W. Nichols, Rockefeller University; Jesse Orlansky, Institute for Defense Analyses; Archie M. Palmer, Gale Research Center; William Slater, Teachers Insurance and Annuity Association of America; Norman Waks, MITRE; John G. Welles, Denver Research Institute; and Dael Wolfle, University of Washington.

None of the foregoing, nor anyone but myself, should be held responsible for any of the errors which may remain in this report, or for any of the conclusions reached.

Harold Orlans

Part One
The Nonprofit Sector

1. The Nonprofit Sector

Independent nonprofit[1] research institutes are administratively independent, often separately incorporated, non-degree-granting organizations that devote most of their annual expenditures to the development of new technology and to research in the natural and social sciences, engineering, humanities, and professions (though expenditures, especially nonfederal expenditures in the latter two areas, are poorly documented). Institutes differ as to sponsorship, funding, and private or public character.[2] They include:

- *Federal research and development (R&D) centers* such as the Jet Propulsion Laboratory, the Brookhaven National Laboratory, and RAND are owned or predominantly financed by a federal agency and operated under contract by universities or independent organizations.

- *Applied research institutes* such as Battelle, the Stanford Research Institute, and the Midwest Research Institute conduct proprietary work for private industry as well as R&D for the government, the results of which may be either confidential or freely publishable.

- *Operating foundations* such as the Carnegie Institution of Washington, Resources for the Future, and the Institute for Advanced Study devote more than half of the annual yield from their endowment interest and principal to research by their own staff.

- *Endowed institutes* such as the Brookings Institution, Wistar Institute, and Sloan-Kettering Institute derive less than half but more than a tenth of their annual expenditures from their own endowments.

- *Cushioned institutes* receive recurrent income from membership dues; contributions; publication sales; clinical fees from physicians and hospitals; grants from voluntary health agencies, foundations, state and local governments; or other sources. For example, the Jackson Laboratory received $1.7 million or 44 percent of its 1970 $4.0 million revenue from the sale of mice and biologicals; philanthropic grants to the Sloan-Kettering Insti-

3

tute from 1960–68 ranged from $2.1 to $3.0 million a year, or 24 to 32 percent of its operating expenditures of $8.1 to $10.0 million; and the American Institute for Economic Research in 1968 received 77 percent of its $429,000 income from the sale of publications and dues from more than 5,000 "sustaining members."

- A variegated array of *project institutes* subsist on contracts and grants or, to put it more baldly, on their wits and reputation. Among them are the Riverside Research Institute, the Hudson Institute, the Cold Spring Harbor Laboratory of Quantitative Biology, the Institute for Cancer Research, the American Institutes for Research, and the Bureau of Social Science Research.

Some institutes can with equal accuracy be classified two or more ways. Moreover, funding, management, and objectives may change from year to year. Most institutes are relatively small organizations with modest assets and few staff, whose fortunes can alter markedly with a change of director or a major contract. This instability renders it difficult to compile complete, accurate, and timely lists of institutes or reliable and comparable statistics about their activities. The R&D statistics published by the National Science Foundation (NSF) are the best available; yet, having at one time been responsible for gathering them, I believe I may with fairness say that they could and should be improved. We lack even an annual listing of the addresses of the significant 400 independent research institutes, let alone the phone numbers, principal administrators, expenditures, and other information.

The useful but expensive and incomplete *Research Centers Directory* (1968 edition) lists some 300 independent institutes and 4,200 institutes that were integral components of United States and Canadian institutions of higher education.[3] That 1 to 14 ratio of independent to academic institutes is misleading. Many academic institutes are little more than letterheads for the aspirations and putative responsibilities of faculty. NSF statistics suggest that, during the 1950s and 1960s, the ratio of expenditures for R&D in independent institutes to that in academic institutions ranged from 1 to 1.1 to 1 to 1.6; the ratio of professional personnel engaged in R&D ranged from 1 to 1.8 to 1 to 2.4, counting graduate students, and from 1 to 1.3 to 1 to 2.0, excluding them. In other words, independent institutes utilized 39 to 45 percent of the funds and 29 to 43 percent of the professional personnel devoted to R&D at nonprofit organizations. The absolute magnitudes involved are indicated in Table 1.

TABLE 1 *Funds and professional personnel utilized in R&D by academic and other nonprofit institutions, 1954–1968*

	1954	1958	1961	1965	1968
Million dollars					
Academic institutions	$377	$ 592	$ 969	$1,822	$2,600
Other nonprofit organizations	271	515	801	1,349	1,637
TOTAL	$648	$1,107	$1,770	$3,171	$4,237
Percent nonacademic	42%	47%	45%	43%	39%
Professional R&D personnel (thousands)					
Academic institutions	25.0	36.5	42.4	54.9	66.9
Other nonprofit organizations	10.3	16.0	20.2	30.5	37.8
TOTAL	35.3	52.5	62.6	85.4	104.7
Percent nonacademic	29%	30%	33%	36%	36%
Excluding graduate students					
Academic institutions	20.3	29.2	33.6	41.4	48.8
Other nonprofit organizations	10.2	15.8	19.9	30.1	37.4
TOTAL	30.5	45.0	53.5	71.5	86.2
Percent nonacademic	33%	35%	37%	42%	43%

SOURCE: National Science Foundation, 1969c, pp. 26–27 and 11; the data on personnel are expressed as full-time equivalents.

Of the $25.3 billion national expenditures on R&D in 1968, $4.2 billion, or 17 percent, was utilized by nonprofit institutions. However, these institutions accounted for merely 4 percent of national expenditures on development, 20 percent of expenditures on applied research, and fully 68 percent of basic research expenditures. The R&D expenditures of universities have been devoted almost exclusively to R (research); those of independent institutes have been allocated in fairly equal proportions to development, applied research, and basic research (Table 2).

TABLE 2
Expenditures of academic and other nonprofit institutions on basic research, applied research, and development, 1968

	Million dollars			
	Basic research	*Applied research*	*Development*	*Total*
Academic institutions	$1,990	$ 510	$100	$2,600
Other nonprofit institutions	545	589	503	1,637
TOTAL	$2,535	$1,099	$603	$4,237

TABLE 2
(continued)

	Basic research	Applied research	Development	Total
	Percentages			
Academic institutions	77	20	4	100
Other nonprofit institutions	33	36	31	100
TOTAL	60	26	14	100

SOURCE: National Science Foundation, 1969c, pp. 29, 31, 33.

If from NSF's estimate of $1,640 million R&D expenditures by nonacademic, nonprofit organizations in 1968, we subtract $60 million for expenditures by organizations not considered here and add $20 million for expenditures in nonscientific fields excluded from foundation surveys, the following *very* rough table can be prepared (Table 3).

TABLE 3
R&D
expenditures by
different types
of independent
institutes, 1968

		Expenditures (millions)		
Type of institute	*Number*	*Total*	*Average*	*Median*
Federal R&D center	67	$1,180	$17.6	$1.6
Applied research institute	14	230	16.4	6.6
Other institutes	320*	190*	0.6*	
TOTAL	400*	$1,600*	$ 4.0*	

* Estimated.

Part Two

The Origin of Nonprofit Species

2. Federal R&D Centers

The notion of "federal research centers" was introduced by the National Science Foundation in 1953 in its first survey of federal research expenditures at universities and other nonprofit institutions:

One of the significant developments resulting from the growth of Federal scientific activities in recent years has been the "research center" operated for the Government by a nonprofit institution. Although there are numerous variations, the most common characteristic marking these centers is the existence of a continuing collaboration between the Government and the parent institution. As a result of this collaboration, the Government sets the objectives and general work plans of the center and supplies funds to operate it, while the parent institution provides chiefly managerial services. In the nature of the work they do and in their size, organization, and methods of operation, these centers resemble Government laboratories more closely than the usual research and development activities of nonprofit institutions (National Science Foundation, 1953, p. 1).

The closeness of these centers to the government is indicated by their being listed in a recent *Directory of Federal R&D Installations.*[1] Most of their physical plant is owned by, and most of their annual income is derived from, a federal agency which is their principal patron. The critical distinction between intramural federal laboratories and federally sponsored research centers is that the former are staffed by civil servants and the latter by private citizens. That distinction has an historical dimension: Before World War II, intramural laboratories were the accepted site for most federally financed R&D outside of agriculture; after the war, research centers and the entire sector of private industrial, educational, and research institutions became the accepted alternative. The critical distinction between R&D centers and other nonprofit institutes is that the

9

former are designated as such on a master list maintained by the NSF for the interdepartmental Committee on Academic Science and Engineering. They obtain the bulk of their income from a single federal agency (often on a level-of-effort contract), and they can accept additional funds only with that agency's approval, whereas other institutes are free to seek funds as they wish.

The quotation with which this section started exaggerates the current role of the government in setting the objectives of many centers. Especially in the case of basic research centers sponsored by NSF and the Atomic Energy Commission (AEC), these objectives are commonly set by each center and by leading scientists, with the government's concurrence and within governmental budgetary and policy constraints. The independence of centers from the controls imposed on intramural laboratories is attested by their salary schedules and personnel practices, and the effort of many centers to diversify their sources of support and to broaden their work beyond the interests of their sponsoring agency. Some, such as RAND, were established with private funds and regard themselves as independent organizations; upon dissolution, their assets would not revert to the government. A number have broken administrative ties to universities; some have forsaken their center status, with its special relationship to a single federal agency, preferring to compete for governmental and private contracts like other nonprofit organizations; a few, such as the System Development Corporation (formerly RAND's System Development Division), have been transformed into profit-making organizations; and one, the Hudson Laboratories, once administered by Columbia University under Navy contract, has recently been absorbed by the Naval Research Laboratory.

The prototypical center is large, located off-campus, and staffed mainly by a full-time, nonteaching staff whose appointments are not subject to review by university departments. These characteristics are partly attributable to the centers' administrative history; partly to a distinction between sponsored research which is relatively integrated with, and that which is more peripheral to, academic functions which NSF staff wanted to highlight by the original "center" concept[2]; and partly to the definitions and procedures employed in collecting the subsequent statistics. Most centers are large by definition; an organization is not classed as a research center unless its minimum annual budget is $500,000.[3]

In 1951, the 23 centers managed by universities or other nonprofit organizations received $122 million, or an average of $5.3 million each, from the federal government; in 1969, 67 such centers received $1,164 million, or an average of $17.4 million each, from the government. This tripling in the number and more than ninefold rise in the funding of centers was comparable to the tripling (from 203 to 616) in the number of higher educational institutions receiving federal funds and the more than tenfold rise (from $143.5 to $1,521.1 million) in the funds received from the government for on-campus R&D during the same period (National Science Foundation, 1953, pp. 32, 41; and 1970b, p. 34). There was a marked shift in federal funding from centers managed by single universities toward those managed by groups of universities or by independent nonprofit organizations. Thus, in 1951, only 3 of the 23 centers, with 10 percent of the funds, were managed by groups of universities or independent organizations; by 1969, 36 of the 67 centers, with 43 percent of the funds, were so managed.

The recent protests by students and faculty against university involvement in Defense Department projects and the problems which universities have had in managing their normal functions have (as of January 1971) served to remove from the university fold perhaps nine research centers and applied laboratories. From the outset, NSF has contracted with consortia of universities for the management of its national research facilities to obviate the political difficulties of assigning that privilege to a single institution; the AEC, Office of Education, and National Aeronautics and Space Administration (NASA) have adopted a similar course for many of their new basic, and even some applied, research centers. In many situations, the formation of new nonprofit organizations has proved more attractive than contracting with existing institutions which may be either less tractable, less independent in outlook, or less fully devoted to the interests of the sponsoring agency.

WARTIME ORIGINS It is difficult to determine "the" date of origin for a good many centers. Welles and his associates set the date for the formal organization of nine centers 2 to 20 years earlier than most investigators. For example, they give 1933 as the year of origin of what in 1946 became the Naval Biological Laboratory managed by the University of California at Berkeley; the Lawrence Radiation Laboratory at Berkeley can be traced back to the invention of the cyclotron in 1929 by Ernest Lawrence or at least to its designation in 1936 as "The Radiation Laboratory." Similarly, the Jet Propulsion Laboratory, which the California Institute of Technology has operated first for the Army and then for NASA, goes back at least to 1936 when Theodore von Karman, colleagues, and students "had to move their dangerous and noisy experimnetal rocket activities a safe distance away from the campus."[4]

So much for antecedents. The initial thrust for the formation of federal R&D centers came in the World War II involvement of university scientists in defense work. Of the 33 nonprofit centers examined by Welles, eight—the AEC laboratories at Ames, Argonne, Los Alamos, and Hanford; the Navy's Applied Physics Laboratories in Maryland and Washington, its Center for Naval Analyses, and its Ordnance Research Laboratory—were founded in 1941–1943, and three—the AEC's Brookhaven National Laboratory, the Air Force's RAND, and the Army's Operations Research Office—in the immediate postwar years 1946–1948.

The eight wartime centers and those of earlier origin were initially managed by a university or (at the AEC Hanford and Mound Laboratories) an industrial firm. One can only speculate about why no nonprofit institute managed a major government center during this period. The Carnegie Institution of Washington, Woods Hole Oceanographic Institution, Franklin Institute, and Battelle Memorial Institute were among the 25 nonprofit institutions receiving the most funds from the Office of Scientific Research and Development (OSRD) (Baxter, 1946, p. 456). Indeed, a naval antiaircraft proximity fuse was first designed at the Carnegie Institution, of which OSRD director Vannevar Bush was head, but, to complete that development, Bush asked Johns Hopkins University to manage what thus became the Applied Physics Laboratory (Welles et al., 1969, p. 317). Perhaps universities were favored because, being far larger organizations than most institutes, with larger plants and fluid assets and far more professional, administrative, and support personnel, they could more readily undertake a major technical enterprise. As independent research institutes have grown, they have undertaken the management of several federal research centers. Although the centers have been relatively small, there is one outstanding exception: the Battelle-managed AEC laboratory at Hanford, Washington, whose 1969 budget was $56.2 million.[5]

Associated Universities, Inc., and the RAND Corporation were the first significant nonprofit corporations formed specifically to conduct R&D for a federal agency. Each set an administrative pattern that was to be emulated by other organizations.

The status of such nonprofit organizations—are they truly "private" or "public," "independent" or "captive"?—has been the subject of endless debates. However, in a world colored as much by feelings as "facts" and in which perhaps undue feelings can be engendered by seemingly minor facts, it should be noted that both these pioneer organizations were founded with small but symbolically and legally significant amounts of private capital which gave them a sense of independence not shared by all nonprofit organizations sprung from the brow of the government.

For two basic reasons, the AEC has allocated to research centers a far larger proportion of its R&D expenditures than has any other federal agency (Table 4). (1) Like NSF, but unlike the Department of Defense, NASA, and the Public Health Service, the AEC operates no major laboratories of its own; its centers—especially those designated as "multipurpose" or "multiprogram" laboratories[6]—therefore serve many of the functions performed by other agencies' intramural laboratories. (2) The critical role of university scientists in the wartime Manhattan Project led to a continuation of arrangements with universities and university consortia in the postwar period.

TABLE 4 *1969 obligations at nonprofit R&D centers, by agency*

Agency	*All sectors**	*R&D centers* *Total*	*Profit†*	*Nonprofit‡*	*Percent at nonprofit centers*
Atomic Energy Commission	$ 1,435.7	$ 914.3	$404.3	$510.0	35.5
National Science Foundation	264.9	25.1		25.1	9.4
Department of Defense	7,943.8	320.4	9.9	310.5	3.9
Department of Health, Education and Welfare	1,326.5	35.8		35.8	2.7
National Aeronautics and Space Administration	3,815.9	101.9	2.4	99.5	2.6
Department of Transportation	291.3	4.7		4.7	1.6
All other agencies	769.3	1.6		1.6	0.2
TOTAL	$15,847.4	$1,405.3	$418.1	$987.2	6.2

* Including obligations at government laboratories, private industry, universities, and other nonprofit organizations.

† Centers managed by profit-making firms.

‡ Centers managed by universities, university consortia, and other nonprofit institutes.

SOURCE: National Science Foundation, 1969a, vol. 18.

After the end of the war with Japan in August 1945, General Leslie Groves remained as executor of the Manhattan Project's crumbling estate until it was inherited by the AEC on January 1, 1947. In the intervening months, scientists emerged from their secret laboratories to public life. "We were the victors," recalled one physicist in a December 1970 interview—and to the victors belong some spoils. The University of California held sway at Los Alamos and Berkeley in contracts that have remained unbroken since 1943. The University of Chicago had relinquished the distant Oak Ridge laboratory to the Monsanto Corporation but held the management contract at nearby Argonne, though regional groups of universities pressed for influence at both sites.[7]

To complete Army plans for a nuclear laboratory in each major region, a contractor had to be found for the proposed laboratory in the Northeast. Most scientists from that area having worked during the war at Chicago, Oak Ridge, or Los Alamos, no one university seemed, by experience or scientific standing, unquestionably to merit that assignment. When scientists proposed Columbia, Groves reputedly responded, ". . . if you really want a cooperative endeavor, make it a cooperative endeavor."[8] The result was the formation in July 1946 of Associated Universities, Inc. (AUI), by Columbia, Cornell, Harvard, Johns Hopkins, the Massachusetts Institute of Technology, Princeton, Pennsylvania, Rochester, and Yale, each of which pledged $25,000 for initial capital. (No public university in the region, one informant explained, then had a physics department strong enough to stand beside those of these private institutions.) A contract for the management of the Brookhaven National Laboratory at Upton, Long Island, was negotiated by AUI and the Army, and revalidated a few months later by the AEC.

AUI had many teething problems. But by starting fresh it was able to serve the basic research interests of university scientists sooner and more fully than Argonne, Oak Ridge, and Los Alamos, with their heavy responsibilities for classified and applied work on nuclear weapons, reactors, and materials (Hewlett & Duncan, 1969, p. 225). Ameliorating the feuds among rival universities and catering to the interests of academic scientists, AUI thus became an attractive model for the management of government-funded, privately operated basic research facilities.

In 1954, NSF requested AUI to investigate the desirability of, and two years later to establish and operate, NSF's first research facility, the National Radio Astronomy Observatory at Green Bank, West Virginia. Similar organizations manage NSF's three other centers: the Association of Universities for Research in Astronomy (a consortium of four private and six public universities scattered across the country) operates (1) Kitt Peak National Observatory in Tuscon, Arizona, and (2) the Cerro Tololo Inter-American Observatory in Chile; the University Corporation for Atmospheric Research (with 18 public and 9 private universities) operates the (3) National Center for Atmospheric Research at Boulder, Colorado.

When MIT declined to assume sole responsibility, the Department of Defense accepted its suggestion that several universities designate representatives for the governing board of the Institute for Defense Analyses (IDA), established in 1956 at the request of the Secretary of Defense. Initially 5 and later 12 universities (4 public and 8 private, from the four major regions) were represented on the IDA board until 1968 when, following student protests and faculty inquiries, the universities were relieved of responsibility for appointing members. Of the 22 board members in 1969, 13 were designated as "academic," 7 as "public," and 2 as "IDA" trustees; each served as an individual and was elected for a fixed term by the self-perpetuating board. IDA thus affords the first example (or the second, counting Argonne's 1948 reversion) of a research center changing from a consortium to conventional board management.[9]

The AEC attempted to temper the national and regional animosities aroused by President Lyndon Johnson's rejection, in 1963, of the proposal of another consortium, the 15-member Midwest Universities Research Association (MURA), for the construction of a $170 million accelerator[10] by fostering the formation of not one but two new consortia:

1 In 1964, the AEC approved a proposal to establish a new organization of Midwest universities which would superintend the University of Chicago's management of Argonne National Laboratory. The Argonne Universities Association (AUA), an enlarged and broadened rendition of the ill-starred MURA, with 18 public and 11 private university members ranging from the Universities of Texas and Arizona in the West to Pennsylvania State University in the East, was formed in July 1965; and in November 1966, after more than two years of discussions, new contracts were signed,

under which Chicago was to operate the laboratory pursuant to programs, budgets, and policies approved by AUA—and, of course, the AEC.

2   The leviathan of corsortia, the Universities Research Association (URA), was organized in 1965 at the initiative of the AEC and the National Academy of Sciences with a view to operating the National Accelerator Laboratory, presently under construction at Weston, Illinois, near Chicago. At the founding meeting at Academy headquarters in June 1965, 26 universities as well as AUI were represented; three months later, the URA bylaws named 34 institutions whose participation would be invited; by January 1970, there were 51 member institutions, including the University of California campuses at Berkeley, Los Angeles, and San Diego, the State University of New York campuses at Buffalo and Stony Brook, Virginia Polytechnic Institute, and the University of Toronto.

The 20 regional "educational laboratories" established in 1966 by the U.S. Office of Education represent not so much a direct application as a broadening of the consortium principle. The boards of these nonprofit centers are composed of representatives, not only of universities and colleges but also of state departments of education, local school systems, and, in many cases, professional associations, civic and cultural groups, library associations, research organizations, private foundations, industry, and labor. In fact, the governing council of many laboratories is so large that, like that of URA, it must in turn elect a smaller and more manageable group to act on its behalf.

In 1969, consideration was given to URA's managing the Lunar Science Institute, a Houston center of NASA, designed to facilitate the examination of lunar materials by university scientists. However, for reasons yet to be discovered, NASA chose instead to contract for that purpose with yet another, very similar organization which materialized forthwith: the Universities Space Research Association (USRA).[11] Like URA, USRA was formed at the invitation of the National Academy of Sciences; in 1969, it had 48 member institutions, 39 of which also belonged to URA. Both organizations were lodged in the same District of Columbia building which also housed the overflow of Academy headquarters, and "discussions have been held . . . to seek the best means of cooperation between them, of partially combining the meetings of the respective Councils of Presidents, and of securing reduced costs and increased efficiencies" (Ramsey, 1970, p. 4).

All told, in 1969, 31 of the 67 nonprofit R&D centers were managed by consortia representing two or more nonprofit institutions. Such consortia have sought unsuccessfully to promote the establishment of additional facilities. For example, a Northeast Radio Observatory Corporation of 13 Northeast institutions was formed in 1967 to urge construction of a 135-meter $28 million steerable dish antenna; but four all-California members of Associates for Radio Astronomy favored construction of a 100-meter $18 million steerable paraboloid antenna at Owens Valley, California; while the all-Midwest Committee on Institutional Cooperation of the Big Ten and the University of Chicago proposed construction of a 360-foot $20 million instrument—*not* in Massachusetts or California (McElheny, 1967).

The consortium device has proved a convenient way to obviate, or, perhaps more accurately, to screen from public view, the internecine feuds that have periodically divided and weakened scientific forces in Washington. An additional attraction is "the increased number of congressmen" which consortia "can bring into sympathetic acquaintance with the national laboratory in their midst" (Orlans, 1967, p. 60). Overall, consortia appear to be a useful way to set policies for equitable access to national basic research facilites by qualified scientists. However, their success in the management of applied R&D centers is more doubtful:

To ensure equitable access, it should be sufficient to have on the governing board of a laboratory trustees from a number of high quality institutions of different types (including liberal arts colleges and perhaps industrial firms, which are not usually included), regions, scientific approaches, and fields. It should *not* be necessary to put on the board men from so many institutions that it reads like a directory of the region's, or the nation's, graduate schools, of low as well as high quality. Such a board may be useful for public relations purposes and to elicit political support from many universities and congressmen; but it is not an efficient means either of management or representation. It is maintained in bylaws that trustees are not to (and affirmed, at the best laboratories, that they *do not*) act as representatives of their institutions; and that if they *did,* this would open a channel of appeal from management decisions about machine use which would render effective operation of the laboratory very difficult. Why, then, is it necessary to have so many institutions in on the act? In fact, the participation of many institutions appears meaningless (i.e., non-functional), the significant decisions being delegated to smaller committees, or may adversely affect the status of the laboratory and the quality of its work and staff.

Nor does it appear wise to extend multi-institutional management to laboratories with major programs of applied research and development whose effective execution requires a clear concentration of managerial responsibility and the power to act rapidly and flexibly. Earlier experience has also demonstrated the danger that a group of academic institutions may give greater priority to programs of pure, and less to applied, research than the government's interests may dictate (Orlans, 1967, p. 215).

Albert Crewe, former director of the Argonne National Laboratory, which has been afflicted with more than its share of pendant consortia, has asked whether the proliferation of multi-institutional management is not self-defeating, for "we face the ultimate prospect of every university being a part of the management of every laboratory. Such a solution is obviously ludicrous." A better procedure, he suggests, "would be for the laboratories to have simpler management but for all operators of laboratories to be members of a National Convention which could establish and enforce the ethics of such laboratory management" (Crewe, 1966, p. 105).

RAND   Nothing succeeds like success, but publicity and even notoriety can be deceptive facsimiles. The RAND Corporation has had its full measure of all three. The prototype "think tank," it has come to represent not merely an important type of institute but a type of intellectual who may be respected or excoriated more readily than he can be ignored. Over the years, RAND has spawned numerous derivative organizations and many other organizations and individuals have been influenced by its methods and ideas, either by voluntary emulation or in obedience to the authority exercised by the many RAND staff and alumni who have held high administrative and advisory positions in government.

RAND has been criticized as amoral (a stance further criticized as immoral, inhumane, and socially irresponsible) and as a servant of its clients rather than the public; the same has been said of much government-sponsored research. But it has not been charged with stupidity or incompetence.

RAND's rise to prominence was facilitated by a number of circumstances: the absence of rival organizations of its type; the existence of significant problems amenable to operations and systems analyses and the development of these methods for resolving them; and a sympathetic client, the Air Force, which was able to implement advice it wished to take. One circumstance was especially important in defining RAND's character, the kinds of staff it attracted, and its accomplishments: a contract providing a large sum of money under unusually broad terms that afforded much security and intellectual and administrative autonomy.

Late in 1945, General H. H. Arnold, Commanding General of the Army Air Forces (the Department of the Air Force was born in September 1947) proposed a $10 million contract with the Douglas Aircraft Company, confirmed by letter of March 2, 1946, for what became known as Project RAND (for "research and development").[12] "The initiative for the idea came in considerable measure" from Arthur Raymond, the chief engineer of Douglas, and his aide Franklin Collbohm, president of RAND from its inception until 1967.[13] The circumstances under which the project emerged were similar to those that the other Army general, Leslie Groves, confronted at the time:[14] a need to develop new and more permanent arrangements whereby civilian engineers and scientists could continue the critical technical work they had begun during the war.[15] The project would bring together scientists and engineers "for the study of V-1 and V-2 rocket techniques and other intercontinental air techniques of the future."

Bruce Smith writes that among the reasons for selecting Douglas —aside from the fact that the idea had evidently originated there— were the Air Force's "successful working relationships with the company during the war"; also Donald Douglas was a man General Arnold "knew and trusted . . . and who could be relied on in what was after all a rather vague and uncertain venture."[16] It was deemed "impossible" to assemble a high-quality group of scientists within the government because of their aversion to direct military administration and "the poor salaries and inflexible personnel practices that prevailed in the civil service at the time." Also, Smith observes, "the founders thought that a university would not consider having anything to do with highly classified research projects of this kind. That this estimate turned out to be incorrect did not lessen its effect in steering RAND away from direct university ties" (Smith, 1966, p. 42). Why Air Force officials had this puzzling thought about universities, Smith does not explain.

The transformation of Project RAND, two years later, from a small undertaking by a large manufacturing company to an independent nonprofit center is illuminating. Our account is drawn from Bruce Smith's study (1966, pp. 51–74).

Not long after the Douglas contract was signed, both the Air Force and the company began to have reservations about it. The Air Force felt the project was moving slowly, that Douglas was not recruiting enough first-class people to the work, that the company's initial altruism had been replaced by a "strictly business" outlook, and, indeed, that Douglas "was making an excessive profit" from its overhead charges. For its part, Douglas began to fear that the project was a business liability. Smith reports "The award of a large air transport contract in 1947 to the Boeing Company, which the Douglas people had expected would come to them, helped to crystallize the feeling within Douglas that Project RAND was a liability because the Air Force was extremely anxious to avoid the appearance of giving preferential treatment to Douglas."

The conflict of interest was not a fact but an ineliminable suspicion. Who could prove that *some* of the special knowledge without which RAND could not function was *never* used by Douglas? How could competing companies be persuaded that Douglas *always* won its contracts in fair and equal competition? How could these companies talk openly and honestly with the Air Force or RAND, when Douglas engineers might learn what they said?

Project RAND was to have been insulated from Douglas's normal business; some had thought or hoped that Douglas would set up an independent nonprofit foundation to sponsor RAND and ensure that insulation. To convince the other aircraft companies that the project was aboveboard, an advisory council was formed — shades of Argonne! — composed of the presidents of Douglas, Boeing, Northrop, and North American, but the presidents were less than enchanted or dutiful about attending. However, the council's last meeting in February 1948 drew a full turnout, for the subject was RAND's separation from Douglas. A participant recorded: "All members of the Council . . . expressed themselves as being in hearty agreement with the move."

Now, industrial sponsorship was not considered. An independent nonprofit corporation, chartered in California, was decided upon "because it was relatively easy to establish and it would afford maximum flexibility of operation."

A small matter of money arose, which has faced many other institutes at their formation or transformation. While Air Force Chief of Staff General Carl Spaatz welcomed the change and was ready to transfer to the new corporation the funds remaining (something under $5 million) from the original $10 million award, he specified that the corporation must be first created and be demonstrably capable of discharging its contractual obligations — that is, that it not only meet the legal requirements for a nonprofit corporation but have adequate operating capital. This caused a brief delay, but it gave RAND its special feeling of independence.

The critical initial capital of $1 million was pieced together by San Francisco lawyer H. Rowan Gaither, a friend of Collbohm, from two sources: a $600,000 bank credit extended on the condition that RAND first obtain $400,000 from other sources, which it did with a $100,000 loan and a guarantee of $300,000 credit from the emerging Ford Foundation. Gaither himself soon played a key role in the foundation's emergence and became its president as well as chairman of the RAND Board. (The appointment of lawyers and fund raisers to nonprofit boards is a proclivity not only of pro- but antiestablishment organizations, such as the Institute of Policy Studies and the Cambridge Institute.) Thus RAND was chartered in May 1948, "To further and promote scientific, educational, and charitable purposes, all for the public welfare and security of the United States of America"; and that November, it received its first Air Force contract.

To say the Douglas experience explains why no Department of Defense R&D center is today managed by private industry would be to oversimplify things and make too much of what can be transitory statistical artifacts. For example, the Hanford and Savannah laboratories of the AEC were for many years omitted from NSF's accredited list of R&D centers because each was but a part of a larger contract with General Electric and DuPont, respectively, for the production of fissionable materials. After the General Electric contract was segmented and Battelle took over responsibility for the R&D piece in 1965, the Hanford laboratory was entered on the lists as a nonprofit center.[17]

The government does not invariably learn from experience. From 1954–1960, the Air Force retained Ramo-Wooldridge, a scientific-engineering firm, to help it superintend and coordinate the work of industrial contractors in producing intercontinental ballistic missiles. To mitigate the danger of self-dealing, Ramo-Wooldridge was barred "from hardware production of items associated with its technical management function in the ballistic missile program." As a further measure of protection, the contract was handled by a specially organized, separately incorporated subsidiary, the Space Technology Laboratories (STL). Nonetheless, criticism of the arrangement mounted from the aerospace industry and the Congress, on the grounds that STL's special knowledge and responsibilities might prove profitable to Ramo-Wooldridge. Accordingly, the House Committee on Government Operations recommended in September 1959 that STL "be converted into a non-profit institution akin to the Rand Corporation and other private and university-sponsored organizations which serve the military departments and other agencies . . . on a stable and continuing basis." The following year, the nonprofit Aerospace Corporation was established to perform the functions formerly discharged by STL, from which it obtained its core personnel.[18] Evidently, this kind of experience made the Department of Defense increasingly reluctant to contract with profit-making, and especially with manufacturing, companies for the management of R&D centers. In 1960, centers under profit-making management received 62 percent of Defense center funds, but in 1964, only 28 percent and in 1968, but 4 percent.[19]

However, conflict of interest is not necessarily eliminated by nonprofit management. Under any form of management, a conflict may arise between the interests of trustees or staff in the welfare of the organization and in that of another (profit or nonprofit) organization with which they have financial or emotional ties. Aerospace Corporation president Ivan Getting has argued that private universities are not qualified to undertake the kind of systems engineering and technical direction which Aerospace (and the nearby Jet Propulsion Laboratory of California Institute of Technology!) performed "because a university is dependent on its income and endowments; and these endowments come largely from industry. So a university immediately has a conflict of interest in evaluating the work of corporations" (*Systems Development and Management,* part 3, 1962, p. 977).

Nor is elimination of conflicts of interest the only objective sought by the government in its choice of center management. Thus, conflicts probably pose a greater danger in the newer and more highly concentrated nuclear power industry than in many defense industries. Nonetheless, in order to promote the growth of the nuclear industry, the AEC has deemed it desirable to contract with commercial firms for the management of many of its centers.[20] NASA has contracted with the American Telephone and Telegraph Company for the management of Bellcomm, which has been characterized as "a profit RAND for NASA."[21]

Private industry has periodically complained about "unfair competition" from tax-exempt nonprofit organizations; such complaints may one day moderate the flow of Defense dollars toward nonprofit centers. Nonetheless, the independent nonprofit advisory center pioneered by RAND and the Air Force and copied by the Army, Navy, and Secretary of Defense (out of need, envy, or self-protection?) and by other governmental agencies has plainly established itself as a viable and useful institution.

OTHER KINDS OF R&D CENTERS In addition to the consortia-managed basic research facilities and the independent "RAND" type of organization, four other kinds of nonprofit R&D centers can be identified:

1   Basic research centers managed by single universities, such as the Berkeley Radiation Laboratory, the Ames Laboratory, and the Stanford Linear Accelerator Center, managed for the AEC by the University of California, the Iowa State University of Science and Technology, and Stanford University, respectively. The Navy-financed Hudson Laboratories of Columbia University, also of this type, have been closed down; the Army-financed Mathematics Research Center at the University of Wisconsin was reclassified as an on-campus research facility in July 1970, which fact did not, unfortunately, prevent it from being blown up by self-styled revolutionaries a month later. Of course, the gradual removal of such centers from the university arena, by one administrative means or another, has been attributable not only to budgetary considerations but to a less friendly climate of opinion, both on campus and in the Congress, about Defense-sponsored research at universities.

2   "Hardware" laboratories for applied research in, and the development of, military, space, and nuclear technologies, of which (excepting civilian nuclear power reactors) the government is a major or exclusive purchaser. Many such laboratories got their start during World War II; typically they are managed by a single university or independent nonprofit institute. In many ways they are a "contract" version of intramural government laboratories such as the Naval Research Laboratory, the Army's Fort Monmouth Laboratories, or NASA's Space Flight Center at Huntsville, Alabama. Principal examples are the two nuclear weapons laboratories at Livermore and Los Alamos, managed by the University of California; and AEC's Pacific Northwest Laboratory, managed by the Battelle Memorial Institute; the Air Force-funded, MIT-operated Lincoln Laboratory, the Navy-funded, Johns Hopkins-operated Applied Physics Laboratory, and the NASA-funded Jet Propulsion Laboratory operated by the California Institute of Technology.

3 Centers managed by single universities and nonprofit organizations, which engage in systems engineering and in coordinating and giving technical direction to the work of industrial contractors, such as the independent nonprofit Aerospace and MITRE corporations, both Air Force creations. Some of the Jet Propulsion Laboratory's work is also of this character.

4 Centers established by the Office of Education in the 1960s for research in education and the development of educational curricula, materials, and methods. The "R&D centers" (which, despite that *D,* have been engaged predominantly in research) have been managed by single universities. As has already been noted, the "regional

TABLE 5
Relative expenditures for different kinds of work at 33 nonprofit R&D centers, 1967

Agency and center	*Expenditures and type of work (percent)*			
	Basic research	*Applied research*	*Development*	*Systems analysis**
Atomic Energy Commission				
Ames Laboratory	80	5	15	
Argonne National Laboratory	51	23	27	
Brookhaven National Laboratory	80	10	10	
Cambridge Electron Accelerator	100			
Lawrence Radiation Laboratory, Berkeley	95	5		
Lawrence Radiation Laboratory, Livermore	10	20	70	
Los Alamos Scientific Laboratory	10	20	70	
Pacific Northwest Laboratory	10	10	80	
Princeton-Pennsylvania Accelerator	100			
Princeton Plasma Physics Laboratory	51	49		
Stanford Linear Accelerator Laboratory	100			
Secretary of Defense				
Logistics Management Institute		9		91
Institute for Defense Analyses	10			90
Air Force				
Aerospace Corporation		10		20
Analytic Services				100
Electromagnetic Compatability Analysis Center		100		

educational laboratories" (which are more heavily involved in developmental activities) are under the management of independent nonprofit organizations containing on their boards representatives of many public and private, state and local educational and community agencies.

An indication of the highly diverse concerns of R&D centers can be gained from Table 5, which reports estimated expenditures of 33 centers, not only for basic research, applied research, and development, but also for systems analysis and systems engineering.

Systems engineering†	Total	
	Percent	Dollars (millions)
	100	$ 8.3
	100	75.3
	100	68.3
	100	3.6
	100	37.7
	100	106.2
	100	91.6
	100	40.4
	100	5.1
	100	6.3
	100	22.4
	100	1.2
	100	14.9
70	100	74.8
	100	1.3
	100	4.7

TABLE 5
(continued)

Agency and center	Expenditures and type of work (percent)			
	Basic research	Applied research	Devel-opment	Systems analysis*
Francis Bitter National Magnet Laboratory	100			
Lincoln Laboratory		90	10	
MITRE		10		25
RAND	10	20		70
Army				
Center for Research in Social Systems		100		
Human Resources Research Office	6		94	
Research Analysis Corporation				100
Navy				
Applied Physics Laboratory (Johns Hopkins)	10	20	60	
Applied Physics Laboratory (University of Washington)		38	41	
Center for Naval Analyses				100
Hudson Laboratories	100			
Naval Biological Laboratory	100			
Ordnance Research Laboratory	20	20		
NASA				
Jet Propulsion Laboratory		25	60	
National Science Foundation				
Kitt Peak National Observatory	100			
National Center for Atmospheric Research	100			
National Radio Astronomy Observatory	100			

* Systems analysis and planning—"the conduct of strategic, tactical, and logistic studies and the initial design (through problem identification, synthesis of alternative solutions, the establishment of objectives, measures, and criteria) of systems for the solving of complex problems, and the furnishing of assistance with plans or planning" (Welles et al., 1969, p. 238).

† Systems engineering and technical direction—"the engineering and management effort required to design and develop a complex group of related components or subsystems, and the technical direction of their production and integration into a working system" (ibid.).

SOURCE: Welles et al., 1969, p. 344 (recalculated).

Systems engineering†	Total	
	Percent	Dollars (millions)
	100	2.5
	100	74.2
65	100	36.4
	100	22.8
	100	2.1
	100	3.4
	100	11.8
10	100	62.9
21	100	2.9
	100	9.3
	100	4.7
	100	2.0
20	100	8.1
15	100	226.3
		12.4
		14.3
		5.2

3. Applied Research Institutes

The applied research institutes listed in Table 6 are separately incorporated nonprofit organizations which conduct ad hoc project research for industry as well as for federal, state, and local governments. Though the bulk of their income now comes from the federal government, the three pioneer institutes of the genre, Mellon, Battelle, and Armour (now the Illinois Institute of Technology Research Institute), were founded well before World War II, when the government did not fund massive contract research. Originally, these three worked almost exclusively for private industry, which did much to determine their operating practices and policies. All institutes today retain as one central purpose a readiness to conduct applied, developmental, engineering, or technico-economic work for national, regional, or, in many cases, foreign industry. Indeed, despite their nonprofit status, NSF for many years classified them as "industry-oriented" organizations and included their expenditures in the industry sector of the national R&D accounts.[1] Like R&D centers, their work for government agencies is often classified or confidential; but, unlike most centers and many (not all) other nonprofit organizations, they are also prepared to conduct proprietary work—that is, work whose findings (reports, data, and patents) become the exclusive property of the company which contracts for it.

The number and organization of applied research institutes changes periodically; a degree of arbitrariness inevitably enters into their classification. It is particularly difficult to find a meaningful, consistent, and practical test of whether an institute is "independent" of a university. Many classifications are attributable to convention. Thus, the Stanford Research Institute has been regarded as "independent," but only in 1970 did it break free of Stanford University; it was then given five years to shed the name

Institute	Founded
Stanford Research Institute	1946
Battelle Memorial Institute	1929
Cornell Aeronautical Laboratory	1946
Illinois Institute of Technology Research Institute	1936
Southwest Research Institute	1947
Franklin Institute Research Laboratories	1946
Midwest Research Institute	1944
Syracuse University Research Corporation	1957
Southern Research Institute	1945
Research Triangle Institute	1959
University City Science Institute	1964
Gulf South Research Institute	1964
Spindletop Research	1961
North Star Research and Development Institute	1963

* Excluding federal research centers managed by Battelle and Illinois Institute of Technology Research Institute.

SOURCE: Danilov, 1969, and institute reports.

"Stanford." The Mellon Institute was part of the University of Pittsburgh from 1913 to 1927; subsequently, it was independent until 1967, when it merged with the Carnegie Institute of Technology to create the new Carnegie-Mellon University. Victor Danilov has good ground to regard the Denver Research Institute as an applied research institute, but I have excluded it as being more closely tied to the University of Denver than are the four other applied institutes to the institutions whose names they bear — the Illinois Institute of Technology Research Institute,[2] the Stanford Research Institute, the Cornell Aeronautical Laboratory, and the Syracuse University Research Corporation. Though patent-holding, contract-receiving, independently incorporated institutes such as the Purdue Research Foundation, the Wisconsin Alumni Research Foundation, and the Ohio State University Research Foundation[3] resemble applied research institutes, they have commonly been considered part of the institutions with which they are affiliated.

Location	1968 volume (millions)
Menlo Park, California	$ 64.2
Columbus, Ohio	49.8*
Buffalo, New York	32.8
Chicago, Illinois	26.6*
San Antonio, Texas	16.1
Philadelphia, Pennsylvania	7.9
Kansas City, Missouri	7.0
Syracuse, New York	6.2
Birmingham, Alabama	5.7
Research Triangle, North Carolina	5.4
Philadelphia, Pennsylvania	3.0?
Baton Rouge, Louisiana	1.9
Lexington, Kentucky	1.2
Minneapolis, Minnesota	1.0
	$230.8

THE THREE PIONEERS   The Franklin Institute of the State of Pennsylvania for the Promotion of the Mechanic Arts, founded in 1824, is the oldest nonprofit institute conducting applied research, and reputedly the first private body to receive federal research funds—they were given by the Treasury in 1830 to Alexander Bache, great-grandson of Benjamin Franklin, after whom the institute was named, for the purchase of equipment to investigate the cause of steam boiler explosions (Dupree, 1957, p. 50). However, for its first hundred years, the Franklin Institute was essentially a progressive secondary and trade school (offering, at various times, education in a general high school curriculum, stenography, navigation, and design); thereafter, it became a technical library, museum, and the custodian of the Bartol Research Foundation, an institute endowed in 1918 to conduct basic physical research.[4] Its involvement in applied research began during World War II, when its museum staff, augmented by Navy personnel, engaged in weapons and instrumentation R&D for the Office of Scientific Research and Development. The Franklin Institute Research Laboratories, established in 1946 as a division of the Franklin Institute, continues R&D for military and other governmental and industrial sponsors.

If federal R&D centers may be termed quasi-governmental, applied research institutes may be termed quasi-business and not just because they work for industry and charge a fee, but also because of their cost consciousness, their vigorous search for customers, and their solicitousness to clients. Despite its for-profit status, A. D. Little, Inc., is commonly accepted by these "not-for-profit" institutes as a sister organization. Founded in Boston in 1886, A. D. Little is the oldest independent institute with a continuous history of doing research for industry, and its survival is proof that an independent professional service firm can overcome conflict-of-interest problems that may be encountered by a manufacturing company in conducting R&D for the government.

Though the large applied research institutes have developed predominantly national clienteles, regional support was critical in their formative years. The earlier institutes established themselves in the older industrial regions; the newer ones, in adjoining territory. Thus, with A. D. Little established in New England, the next three institutes were founded before World War II—in Pittsburgh, Columbus, and Chicago, sequentially; during the 1940s, a second wave spread to the Midwest, Far West, South, and Southwest; and the smaller and newer institutes have filled in the geographic interstices.

The first two not-for-profit institutes established in this century, Mellon and Battelle, took different administrative courses.

The industrial fellowship idea upon which the Mellon Institute was based was developed in 1906 by Robert Duncan at the University of Kansas. It called for a manufacturer to give a temporary fellowship to the university for the study of a problem, "the solution of which would mutually benefit both the manufacturer and the public."[5] In 1910, the brothers Andrew and Richard Mellon invited Duncan to introduce such industrial fellowships at the University of Pittsburgh. Pleased with the results, they each gave $1 million in 1913 to endow a Mellon Institute for Industrial Research at the university. In one view, the Mellons were acting as public-spirited citizens, because the fellowships strengthened science and the university as well as the quality of industrial products and processes. In another view, this was simply a way to get research done more cheaply than by setting up central laboratories in the Mellon's oil and aluminum companies. Few companies then maintained such laboratories—General Electric and DuPont were exceptions.

Being given to a specific investigator for a fixed term of at least an academic year, the fellowships were better suited to individual than to cooperative research. The fellowship agreement enabled the sponsoring company "to employ or take into its regular service any or all of the incumbents working on this Fellowship," which many companies did as they established their own laboratories. Accordingly, a high rate of turnover developed and the average tenure of Mellon Institute staff in the 1960s was about five years. In 1962, the Mellon family gave an additional $10 million endowment to enlarge the institute's basic research activities, which had previously absorbed perhaps a fifth of the $5 million annual budget. But, in a way, that grant constituted a recognition of the failure of the institute's industrial research to prosper; it had never broadened very much outside of chemistry. As it turned out, the endowment provided the bride with a more attractive dowry for her 1967 marriage. However, the Carnegie Institute of Technology was not a suitor; the reluctant bride was given away by her trustees.

The successful formula of contracts for research on short-term problems by staff teams assembled from requisite disciplines has been credited to Battelle, an institute born under an incredibly lucky star that rose as the unlucky one of its founder set. In 1923, Gordon Battelle, heir to a fortune his father had accumulated as president of the Columbus Iron and Steel Works, died of appendicitis at the age of 40. Battelle had "attended" Yale but did not graduate. He must have been familiar with contract research since he had once commissioned A. D. Little to study the utilization of mining scraps and tailings. In his will, he left $1.5 million "for the foundation of a 'Battelle Memorial Institute.' . . in or near the City of Columbus, Ohio, for the purpose of education in connection with the encouragement of creative and research work and the making of discoveries and inventions in connection with metallurgy of coal, iron, steel, zinc and their allied industries." The sum was augmented by $2.2 million from the estate of Battelle's mother, who died in 1925, just before the institute was incorporated. A few years later, concerned about the institute's steel investments, the trustees converted them to cash, putting Battelle in good shape to weather the 1929 market crash which might otherwise have wiped it out.

The institute's most remarkable good fortune was the work it began in 1944 on an electrostatic printing process it took over from the inventor Chester Carlson and later, in exchange for a major equity, transferred to what is now the Xerox Corporation. In 1968 alone, sale of some Xerox stock gave Battelle a capital gain of $47 million; as of December 1969, its investments had a market value of $211 million. Counting its laboratories in Frankfurt and Geneva, and its contract to manage the AEC laboratory at Hanford, Washington, Battelle's total 1969 revenue from some 3,400 studies for over 1,700 government and private sponsors was $133 million.

The "Xerox" of Chicago's Armour Research Foundation,[6] founded in 1936 by several faculty members of the Armour Institute of Technology, is a magnetic tape recording process that has yielded over 300 patents and some $1 million annual royalties (Reeves, 1967).

From 1944–1947, six new applied research institutes were established and from 1957–1964, after a puzzling 10-year hiatus, six more. The lack of births during the past few years is no doubt attributable to the retrenchment of federal R&D programs. Usually, the new institutes have been formed at the initiative of prominent businessmen, with the help of university faculty and administrators. Particularly in the latter period, institutes also received financial help from state governments, which sought to promote industrial development and to redress what they regarded as the excessive concentration of federal R&D funds on the East and West Coasts.

UNIVERSITY OFFSHOOTS Two of the better-documented cases involving institutes associated with major universities are worth relating.

The Stanford Research Institute (SRI) was formed in 1946 by the Stanford trustees in cooperation with several West Coast industrialists.[7] Henry Heald, president of the Illinois Institute of Technology, acting as a consultant to San Francisco industrialist Atholl McBean, had strongly recommended it; presumably, his advice reflected Illinois Institute's experience with Armour. The university press release of September 1946 announcing formation of the new institute recalls the rationale of the Mellon Institute:

"The institute plans to do the kind of research that industry itself might do if each company could set up its own comprehensive research organization, supported by the resources of a great university."

The SRI articles of incorporation made it plain that service to industry was also designed to serve the university, for among the stated purposes of SRI was:

To promote the educational purposes of the Leland Stanford Junior University by encouraging, fostering and conducting scientific investigations and pure and applied research . . . and to devote its resources to the advancement of scientific investigation and research and to the assistance of the Leland Stanford Junior University in the promotion and extension of learning and knowledge;

To provide, equip and maintain laboratories, experimental and other facilities for general and specific scientific and industrial research and to make such facilities available to the Leland Stanford Junior University and other institutions. . . .

Matters did not, in fact, work out that way. Despite the ultimate control and ownership by the Stanford trustees who elected the SRI board, SRI took an independent course. Though both the university and institute prospered on government research funds, they did so independently rather than jointly. To be sure, professional relationships arose and some professors and graduate students participated —and continue to participate—in SRI projects. But no larger and firmer union developed, and hostility also surfaced—"our people looked down their noses at their people," a university administrator remarked. The divorce of 1970 gave de jure recognition to the de facto separation of many years standing.[8]

SRI was started with a loan of $500,000 from the university, which was later repaid; in addition, SRI made contributions of about $800,000 to the university. That was the total financial return Stanford received from its investment until the settlement in 1970. Why did the university trustees not insist on a larger return, as they were in a position to do? Evidently SRI officers and trustees successfully opposed such payments, which would have reduced the institute's ability to enlarge its facilities and staff.

The Syracuse University Research Corporation (SURC) was established in 1957 in an attempt to increase the volume of research in the university environs. At the time, faculty seemed to be fully occupied with project research, which had reached a $2.6 million plateau. By importing full-time staff to conduct classified and applied R&D that would be inappropriate on campus, it was thought that the university's research facilities would be enlarged, more opportunities would be afforded for graduate student training and faculty recruitment, and "the growth of the University's reputation as a major institution of higher learning would be accelerated."[9] By attracting industry, perhaps to university-owned land which would appreciate, SURC might even make money for the university and contribute funds to student fellowships.

But the new institute was seen mainly as a way to meet the competition of rival universities. Federal R&D was booming and could not be neglected by any institution that wanted a position of leadership in science and education. As Chancellor Tolley told the Syracuse board:

. . . Cornell got ahead of us by establishing the Cornell Aeronautical Laboratory at Buffalo. On their campus the General Electric Company established a center of research very similar to the one Bendix Aviation is establishing at the University of Michigan. Stanford has begun organizing its laboratories. We really have no option. We shall either play a very modest game which will get us nowhere, or we shall compete with the best universities in the country. M.I.T., Cornell, and Harvard are our chief competitors in the East.

The goal of increased government research was realized; by 1969, SURC had an R&D volume of $6.9 million, much of which was classified research for the Department of Defense. Thus, "In the view of the Executive Vice President of SURC [expressed in 1969] it has not yet made as significant a contribution to the University as is desired. This contribution would need to be intellectual and public service related since financially SURC is independent of the University. Its assets are not the University's assets."

Neither the applied institutes which set out to serve local industry nor those which were also to serve a university quite achieved their purposes. To grow and remain solvent, the former had to stake out a national clientele; the latter's applied interests afforded few points of cooperation with faculty engaged in basic research, though greater collaboration has developed with engineering departments. In the 1950s both kinds of institute were engulfed in the tidal wave of government R&D programs which bore them off in unforeseen directions. A. D. Little, the bulk of whose work is still conducted for private industry, has remained more steadfast in its purpose than the not-for-profit institutes.

4. Other Kinds of Research Institutes

If history is an effort to find meaning and art, not to mention brevity, in events which lack them in the measure that the historian provides, then perhaps a good history can be written even of the origin of some 300 other diverse institutes. However, lacking the knowledge necessary to write it, a few remarks about each remaining type of institute must suffice.

OPERATING FOUNDATIONS Operating foundations, as I have defined them, utilize more than half of their endowment income for research by their own staff; NSF uses the same 50 percent line to demarcate operating and granting foundations.

Like the granting foundations, the operating foundations were established by wealthy men whose names they often bear. John D. Rockefeller and Andrew Carnegie established two of the most famous and influential, the Rockefeller Institute for Medical Research in 1901 (it became the Rockefeller University in 1965), and the Carnegie Institution of Washington in 1902. The Carnegie Endowment for International Peace, which is perhaps as much of an educational as a research foundation, was founded in 1910; of more recent vintage are the Kettering Foundation of Ohio (1927), the Institute for Advanced Study in Princeton (1930), and the Noble Foundation of Oklahoma (1945).

A basic idea seems to have underlain the formation of both the Carnegie and Rockefeller institutes: the marshaling and organization of first-class people and technical resources can produce as striking progress in science and medicine as in the great industrial corporations. That organization was subtle, not crude; it did not dragoon, but allowed the fullest freedom to eminent investigators — though not to assistants and technicians. Nonetheless, it was a sophisticated, benevolent organization which adapted to the

39

requirements of science some important principles of industry. As one writer observed in a volume honoring the retirement of John Merriam, president of the Carnegie Institution from 1921–1938:

> Again, as never before, there is team work among investigators who recognize neither national nor group boundaries. Neither are there "trade secrets" in scientific research. . . . An army of investigators . . . trained for the tasks, relieved of economic worry, supplied with every facility required, and working in tacit cooperation, accounts for the epoch-creating achievements now being made in the various fields of scientific research. . . .
>
> Not until the coming of agencies definitely founded and financed for the prosecution of research, with staffs of specialists on full-time salary, and with heavy investments of capital in buildings and equipment, did research take on aspects of a business enterprise, chief feature of which being the adoption of a planned program of work, comprehensive and forward looking in general outline, detailed and definite in respect to daily schedule (Bunker, 1938, pp. 715–716, 730).[1]

If that could be said of such a bastion of pure and unfettered inquiry as the Carnegie Institution, how much more can it not be said of the more applied institutes which have since proliferated? The underlying idea is: In academia there is anarchy, whereas in institutes there is at least order and at best union.

In contrast to other institutes, whose scope of work has tended to expand adventitiously, many operating foundations, restrained to live within income from a relatively fixed endowment,[2] have stayed within narrower fields. Given a relatively stable and aging staff, such narrowness can lead to stultification; this the foundations have sought to avoid with special fellowship programs for graduate students and young investigators. With the security they offer and the freedom from teaching, deadlines, writing proposals, and demanding sponsors, operating foundations have attracted men, and stimulated research, of marked distinction. The Carnegie Institution, the Rockefeller Institute, and the Institute for Advanced Study have acquired reputations in pure science and scholarship rivaled, if at all, only by those of a few universities.

A small but significant group of operating foundations are those which, subsisting on capital, would obviously become extinct if it were not replenished or replaced by another source of income. Several have been established by the Ford Foundation grants: The Center for Advanced Study in the Behavioral Sciences, the Fund for the Republic and the Center for the Study of Democratic Institutions (lineal descendent of the fund), Resources for the Future, the Center for Applied Linguistics, and the Educational Facilities Laboratory. Despite financial difficulties, none has yet expired. The struggle for continued life is as strong among institutes as among people.

ENDOWED AND CUSHIONED INSTITUTES Endowed and cushioned institutes receive at least 10 percent of their income from a recurrent source. At endowed institutes, that source is their own endowment, which gives them a greater degree of independence. Even a relatively small endowment income can significantly strengthen an institute's hand in negotiations with sponsors, as Orville Brim, president of the Russell Sage Foundation, has observed: ". . . it would seem that some ratio of endowment income to external funds, whether it be twice as much, an equal amount, or perhaps one-tenth of the external funding, would permit an organization to pick and choose among the externally funded projects those which are consonant with its own objectives" (Brim, 1967).

Several endowed institutes are also financially cushioned in a second way — for example, the Brookings Institution, by conference fees and publication sales; the Wistar Institute, by journal sales; and the National Bureau of Economic Research, by some 300 annual "contributing subscribers."

For both kinds of institute the secret of financial security is not to expand far beyond their reliable income. Such restraint has been difficult during the research boom of the 1950s and early 1960s. The temptation is strong to take on a temporary project and add staff which cannot be supported from endowment income. By doing so, an operating foundation can evolve into an endowed institute, and an endowed institute into a project institute. The temptation to expand is extraordinarily hard to resist, especially in an inflationary era when additional income is needed merely to meet the rising costs of a stable staff.

The tendency to expand has been offset to some extent by the tendency to divide. Rising national R&D expenditures induce staff defection and fission among institutes. However, the late 1960s have *not* been such a period. Institutes, like universities, have recently been in a state of financial stringency; budgets have at best held stable, forcing them to reduce staff by attrition or dismissals.

Two groups of cushioned institutes are notable: trade institutes (which are not discussed further in this study) supported by firms in a particular industry, business, or craft to conduct research of commercial usefulness; and biomedical research institutes which may specialize on one particular organ or disease. Many arose as adjuncts to the work of prominent physicians and surgeons at hospitals, clinics, or health agencies, since patients' gratitude or hope for effective treatment can provide a source of income as bountiful as an oil well.

Some 60 biomedical research institutes were in 1970 members of the Association of Independent Research Institutes, formed in 1962 to arrange annual meetings and to represent common interests in dealing with agencies such as the Internal Revenue Service (IRS) and the Public Health Service (PHS), on which they are heavily dependent. Recognizing the important role of nonprofit institutes in medical research, PHS has paid special attention to their problems. PHS has also included them in its formula grants[3] (unlike NSF, which confines such grants to degree-granting institutions). In 1966, PHS made a pioneering block grant, to be renewed annually for five years, which covered almost half of the operating expenses of the Sloan-Kettering Institute for Cancer Research. Had all gone well and had appropriations continued to rise, such grants were to have been extended to the M. D. Anderson Hospital in Houston, the Roswell Park Memorial Institute in Buffalo, and perhaps other institutes. However, the House Government Operations Committee criticized the grant on the grounds that it could support some poor quality work, because proposed research would not, like other PHS awards, be subject to approval by a national panel of scientists.[4]

Should the National Cancer Institute receive a large infusion of funds, as seems likely (February 1971), it may devise a way acceptable to the Congress to give major institutional awards for directed research on cancer. PHS has not, like the Department of Defense and the Office of Education, established new R&D centers, as there are enough biomedical institutes to meet its needs. However, many PHS officials—as well as physicians and medical research entrepreneurs—believe that a massive and concerted attack on special biomedical problems should now be mounted with the help of research institutes.

PROJECT INSTITUTES The project institute, the most motley and volatile type of institute, subsists on contracts and grants, with little other recurrent income.

Such institutes have been born in many ways, but perhaps most frequently as ventures of faculty who, dissatisfied with the constraints of projects administered by their institutions, may be adventurous in their spare time while retaining the security of tenure. The university may deem a proposed project commercial or mundane; it usually sets limits to the salaries of project staff; it may prohibit or limit consulting fees to fellow faculty and the augmentation of an investigator's academic year salary from project funds. Often, faculty resent the amount of overhead taken by the university from "their" funds. Such restraints can be overcome by setting up an independent institute near the university and using its facilities (library, laboratory, faculty club, etc.) as needed. A professor who spends too much time at his own institute may fall from grace, but if he has tenure, what can the university do?

Many outside institutes choose near-campus locations: The cheap labor of graduate students and their wives; ready access to the library, bookstores, consultants, visiting scholars, and government officials; the general ambience of scholarship; and perhaps also the lower rent all render that area attractive, especially for budding institutes with small budgets. Thus, the Center for Policy Studies, started by Columbia University sociologist Amitai Etzioni; the Cambridge Institute, started by Harvard professors Christopher Jencks and Gar Alperovitz; and the nonprofit National Opinion Research Center, directed, successively, by a number of University of Chicago sociologists, are all located near campuses. The 1968 report of the nonprofit Marketing Science Institute explained that it moved from Philadelphia to Cambridge because of an arrangement with the Harvard Business School, whereby "members of the . . . faculty and graduate students will become involved in the Institute's research program," while "MSI staff will have access to HBS and Harvard University facilities such as the libraries, computation center, etc."

Other institutes have sprung from research which could no longer be happily accommodated at their former institution. Thus, in 1967, the staff of Columbia University's Electronics Research Laboratories left Columbia, where classified military research was no longer welcome, and incorporated themselves as the independent nonprofit Riverside Research Institute; MIT's Instrumentation Laboratory may soon be similarly separated. RAND has fathered a host of independent institutes. Its System Development Division was set up as the independent nonprofit System Development Corporation in 1957, because it had grown so large and its work —

preparing computer programs and training staff for the Air Defense Direction Centers — had become so different that it threatened to upset RAND's central policy purposes. ANSER (Analytic Services, Inc.), the Air Force's "'short-order' think tank" (Leavitt, 1967)[6] was incorporated in 1958 with officers, capital, and management services drawn from RAND (Smith, 1966, p. 123). The Hudson Institute was founded by Herman Kahn, and the Institute for the Future, by other RAND staff, when RAND proved unenthusiastic about their interests and methods. Not long after the Urban Institute was established in 1968, at President Johnson's request, to serve as a high-level, urban-policy "RAND" for the government, especially for the Department of Housing and Urban Development, a change of the national administration and of sources of funding (the Ford Foundation and the Department of Transportation proved more friendly than HUD's Secretary George Romney) transformed it from an R&D center to a project institute. Indeed, by 1970 the activities of RAND itself had become so diversified that it should no longer be classified as an R&D center and, in all probability, would not be were that center concept not identified so much with RAND in the mind of the Congress.

Part Three

Institute Personnel
and Operations

5. Tax Status

Some persons believe that it would not be the end of either the world or of research institutes if their tax exemption were eliminated. One official of an applied research institute ventured this opinion in an interview; and, of course, the imposition of a 4 percent tax on net investment income by the 1969 Tax Reform Act has not meant the end of private foundations. However, the tax loss to the Treasury and gain to an organization are not the only consequences of exemption. Exemption has come to signify that an organization serves the public interest; its financial importance can lie less in the taxes saved than in the contributions received by exempt organizations, which taxpayers can deduct from their taxable income.

The deduction for contributions is perhaps the most significant of the preferential provisions (of federal income tax law and regulations) benefitting science. Its principal advantage is in providing a subsidy free of governmental red tape and restraint. Its chief disadvantages lie in the unevenness and relative arbitrariness of the subsidy and in the fact that the amount of the subsidy is greater for the high-income taxpayer than for the low. Affluence more than interest, ingenuity, or worthiness determines the extent of federal support (Wolfman, 1966, p. 30).

IS PROPRIETARY RESEARCH TAXABLE? The profit derived by any exempt organization from research for a government agency is not taxable, nor is the profit derived by a college, university, or hospital from research for any sponsor. But the taxability of a nonprofit institute's profit from proprietary research for profit-making companies has been in dispute. One IRS definition of "scientific research in the public interest," that "the results of such research (including any patents, copyrights, processes, or formulae resulting from such research) are made

47

available to the public on a nondiscriminatory basis," would seem explicitly to deny exemption for proprietary research. However, a few paragraphs along, scientific research is in the public interest if

> . . . carried on for the purpose of aiding a community or geographical area by attracting new industry to the community or area or by encouraging the development of, or retention of, an industry in the community or area. Scientific research described in this subdivision . . . will be regarded as carried on in the public interest even though such research is performed pursuant to a contract or agreement under which the sponsor or sponsors of the research have the right to obtain ownership or control of any patents, copyrights, processes, or formulae resulting from such research [Internal Revenue Service Code 501(*c*) (3), 1967].

My efforts to clarify this question at several applied research institutes and the IRS left me more confused than I had been before. According to one informant, IRS has recently set up a special unit to study the question, which is investigating Battelle afresh as if it were an unexplored island in the Antarctic.

Like IRS, applied research institutes have interpreted the law variously. Battelle and the Franklin Institute, among others, have not paid taxes on profits from proprietary work but some institutes have done so since the issuance of 1961 IRS regulations on the taxability of income from activities unrelated to those for which their exempt status was granted.

> The new regulations clearly exempt from taxes the income that not-for-profit institutes derive from work done for the government and for certain other clients. But they are less clear about income derived from proprietary research—that is, from research done confidentially for a corporation hoping to profit by the results. A number of institutes, including Battelle, take the position that because such research speeds up the introduction of new products and processes it is in the public interest, and thus meets one of the criteria for exemption included in the new regulations. As a consequence, they do not pay taxes on earnings from proprietary research. S.R.I., however, believes such earnings are taxable, and will therefore pay some $600,000 in taxes to the government this year (Klaw, 1966, p. 214).

According to various sources (Smith, 1966, pp. 192–193; "Report of Stanford," 1969, pp. 9–11; and Stanford Research Institute), SRI paid no income taxes from 1946 through 1960. In 1961, it paid $40,000 in taxes on income from proprietary work; in 1965, $563,000; in 1967, an estimated $385,000; and in 1968, $273,000. But in 1969, SRI was in an anomalous situation. It had made a profit on its proprietary work, a loss on its governmental work, and a net loss on its total operations (due, in part, to a decline in the volume of research and its disruption by student protests). In such a situation, a profit-making company would pay no tax: why should a nonprofit organization? Accordingly, SRI paid no tax and asked IRS to clarify its legal position, which that inscrutable agency is still apparently doing. In December 1970, SRI counsel G. A. Steel summarized the situation as follows:

For the years 1961 through 1968 SRI paid Federal Income Tax on its net income from certain categories of proprietary research based on SRI's interpretation of the applicable tax regulations.

In 1969, when SRI experienced a net operating loss from its total operations, but not from its proprietary research, SRI determined it had no taxable income.

SRI feels that tax regulations dealing with nonprofit scientific organizations are ambiguous and have not been consistently applied by the taxing authorities.[1]

With that last statement I heartily concur. Officials of nonprofit institutes attest that IRS's operations resemble those of a court of law. IRS confines itself mainly to the facts and circumstances of a case. Unlike other executive agencies, it is reluctant to enunciate general policies—and perhaps with good cause, if such policies would open up gaps in the government's fortifications against tax avoidance.

The Southwest Research Institute, Illinois Institute of Technology Research Institute, and the Research Triangle Institute have also paid income taxes. Research Triangle president George Herbert has said: "I personally do not feel that the nonprofits, taken as a group, should necessarily be wholly exempt from taxation. . . . There is justification for paying taxes on that portion of income derived from research which is held in confidence and the results of which become the exclusive property of the industrial sponsor" (Danilov, 1966, p. 5).

Many institutes pay certain state and local taxes. For example, in 1968 Battelle paid $712,000 in county property tax and $254,-000 in state sales tax; the Franklin Institute pays local property taxes on a new research facility; and RAND pays state and county property taxes. Nonprofit institutes also pay taxes on profits of separately incorporated for-profit affiliates—e.g., Illinois Institute of Technology Research Institute's Corplan Associates, which engages in management consulting, and Battelle's Scientific Advances, Inc., which develops and manufactures new products by acquiring or establishing new companies and selling them off when they become commercially viable.

ACTIVITIES ENDANGERING EXEMPTION The designation of an organization as nonprofit, and thereby eligible for deductible contributions, is dependent upon its submission of an application and evidence of its purposes, including articles of incorporation,[2] bylaws, and a statement of receipts, expenditures, and assets. When an application is approved, the organization will be entered in a list published by the Treasury for the information of potential contributors (*Cumulative List,* 1969). The nonprofit status may be terminated any time IRS determines that an organization has violated its definitions and regulations. "The status of the following as exempt organizations . . . has been terminated and contributions to them are not deductible" prefaces a list IRS publishes periodically. The following were on recent lists.[3]

- The Center for Latin American Studies, Inc., Ormond Beach, Florida
- Colorado Institute for Research, Denver, Colorado
- Council on Research in Economic History, Cambridge, Massachusetts
- Cystic Fibrosis Research Institute of Pennsylvania, Inc., Philadelphia, Pennsylvania
- The John Slade Ely Center for Health Education Research, Inc., New Haven, Connecticut
- Foundation for International Research and Development, Lubbock, Texas
- Gerontological Research Foundation, St. Louis, Missouri
- The Grassland Research Foundation, Chickasha, Oklahoma
- Health Research Foundation, Inc., Boston, Massachusetts
- Housing Research and Development Co., Inc., Rapid City, South Dakota
- Institute of International Labor Research, Inc., New York, New York

- Marine and Fisheries Engineering Research Institute, Inc., Woods Hole, Massachusetts
- National Research Foundation, Chicago, Illinois
- Tree Research Institute, Ankeny, Iowa

No public explanation is given for the removal of exemption, which may be the result of a change of name, a merger, or financial collapse as well as prohibited commercial or political activities.

An example of the termination of exemption because of commercial activities is the case of the American Institute for Economic Research, of Great Barrington, Massachusetts. In March 1957, after almost 20 years of exemption, IRS determined that, as its economic bulletins were not primarily research reports but rather a form of investment counseling, it was "primarily engaged in a business for profit. . . ." After protracted levies, appeals, and negotiations, the institute paid some $70,000 in taxes. Subsequently a new corporation, American Institute Counselors, Incorporated, was established to conduct the activities which had led to the revocation of exempt status, and the institute recovered its exemption as of August 1963 (American Institute, 1968).

The line between "research" and more routine testing can be difficult to draw, and the American Council of Independent Laboratories contends that applied research institutes are often engaged in the latter. However, were they to do too much openly commercial work, they would endanger their tax exemption. This restraint on the character of the work that nonprofit institutes can legally undertake is dutifully incorporated in the charter or bylaws of many institutes. Thus, the Institute for Policy Studies Certificate of Incorporation states that "The Corporation may not exercise any power . . . which would disqualify it from exemption from income tax under the provisions of the Internal Revenue Code of 1954, as it may be amended from time to time. . . ." The exemption application of the Urban Institute states that "No part of the receipts of the Institute will represent payment for business or commercial services to any private sponsor. . . . If privately sponsored, such research will be carried on in the public interest . . . within the meaning of [IRS] Regs. 501 (c) (3)–1(d) (5)."

For institutes engaged in social science and policy research, the proscription of "political" activity can pose special problems. The IRS regulations have stated that an organization is not exempt

. . . if its articles expressly empower it —

(i) To devote more than an insubstantial part of its activities to attempting to influence legislation by propaganda or otherwise; or

(ii) Directly or indirectly to participate in, or intervene in (including the publishing or distributing of statements), any political campaign on behalf of or in opposition to any candidate for public office; or

(iii) To have objectives and to engage in activities which characterize it as an "action" organization . . . (IRS Code, Reg. 1.501(c) (3)–1(b), 1967, p. 33,030).

The regulations go on to define an "action" organization as one which devotes "a substantial part of its activities" to attempts "to influence legislation" by any national or local governmental body, which participates "directly or indirectly, in any political campaign on behalf of or in opposition to any candidate," or which "advocates, or campaigns" for or against any legislation "as distinguished from engaging in nonpartisan analysis, study, or research and making the results thereof available to the public." Nonetheless, a nonprofit organization may engage in certain charitable and communal activities detailed in another regulation:

Relief of the poor and distressed or of the underprivileged; advancement of religion; advancement of education or science; erection or maintenance of public buildings . . . ; lessening of the burdens of Government; and promotion of social welfare by organizations designed . . . (i) to lessen neighborhood tensions; (ii) to eliminate prejudice and discrimination; (iii) to defend human and civil rights secured by law; or (iv) to combat community deterioration and juvenile delinquency. . . . The fact that an organization, in carrying out its primary purpose, advocates social or civic changes or presents opinion on controversial issues with the intention of molding public opinion or creating public sentiment to an acceptance of its views does not preclude such organization from qualifying [as exempt, so long as it does not engage in action defined as "political"] (IRS Code, Reg. 1.501 (c) (3)–1(d), 1967, p. 33,033).

The distinctions between "political," "research," "educational," "propagandistic," and "charitable" actions are not always clear and can be subject to different interpretations. As Internal Revenue commissioner Randolph Thrower has remarked, distinguishing "education" from "propaganda" presents special "difficulties with respect to ideological groups, and particularly those having a predetermined, rather narrow, socio-political program. . . . Solomon had no greater problems and under existing law a tax exemption is no more divisible than a baby."[4] Accordingly, the wisdom and legitimacy of borderline activities causes recurrent uncertainty that is not relieved by the common proscription of "political" activities in the institute charter.[5]

Institutes on the right, center, and left are equally vulnerable to the charge of "propagandistic" or "political" activity. In 1965, Democratic Representative Wright Patman questioned whether the American Enterprise Institute for Public Policy Research "was being used as a cover for political activities" on behalf of 1964 Republican presidential candidate Barry Goldwater. "Several of the Institute's advisers were principal members of Barry M. Goldwater's campaign brain trust . . . ," a *Washington Post* reporter wrote. "Its president, William J. Baroody, was widely regarded in Republican circles as a key adviser to Goldwater during the campaign" (Stern, 1965, p. A9).

Five years later, Senator Goldwater questioned whether Brookings Institution (and the Ford Foundation) was not engaged in political lobbying:

With a degree of arrogance astounding even in Washington's liberal circles, the Brookings Institute is planning a defense budget of its own. . . .

I believe a valid question can be raised over whether it is a legitimate activity for an organization which is supported in large part by funds from tax-exempt foundations.

It raises in my mind the question of whether special tax advantages should be accorded for purposes such as the preparation of an outside defense budget and its attendant effort to influence members of Congress who are charged with voting on estimates presented by legitimate offices of the government.

. . . can such activity be regarded as lobbying for a special point of view. . . ?

After some 100 congressmen advanced a reduced defense budget based upon material in a book Brookings had published, Senator Goldwater asked the Department of Justice to investigate the propriety of this work by an exempt institution.[6]

A Washington *Evening Star* reporter stated that advisors of President Nixon believed that "Democratic castouts from the Kennedy-Johnson era have found haven" in nonprofit institutions.

Brookings, the Ford Foundation, and the Kennedy Institute of Politics at Harvard were cited:

> . . . they have launched a tax-exempt assault on the political, economic and social structure of the country.
>
> They are accused of clandestine political activities, and writing books and articles and turning out speeches for their allies on Capitol Hill in a concerted attempt to blacken the administration and promote a series of liberal causes ranging from unilateral disarmament to the advancement of educational television and dissolution of the military-industrial complex.
>
> A good deal of research data has been drawn together to show that such accusations are well supported. This should be useful to the Treasury Department in drawing up regulations to implement the new limitations voted by Congress on foundation financing of politically related causes and institutions . . . (Wilson, 1970, p. E3825).

"By giving a tax exemption to an organization like the Institute for Policy Studies, our government is allowing tax exemption to support revolution," Senator Strom Thurmond has charged. ". . . The Institute . . . is concerned with developing broad changes in our social structure without reference to the political structure upon which our Nation is based. Its members seek to override the republican form of government. . . . They are studying ways of promoting widespread disruptions in our social fabric" ("Institute for Policy Studies," 1969, p. S128130). That institute has been repeatedly subjected to such charges, and it has been audited repeatedly by the IRS.

The Center for the Study of Public Policy, a Cambridge Institute whose leaders have had some ties to the Institute for Policy Studies, has distributed to employees a four-page statement explaining why they should abide by the legal prohibition of partisan political activity: "The financial survival of the Center depends on each employee's following the above guidelines, since violations can lead to a loss of tax-exempt status." Each employee must sign the following:

> I have read the guidelines of the Center for the Study of Public Policy with respect to political and other activities. I agree not to involve the Center in any partisan political activity. In the event that I cannot continue to abide by this agreement, for whatever reasons, I will resign as an employee of the Center.

Not all IRS regulations implementing the 1969 Tax Reform Act had been issued in latter 1970 when this study was being conducted; hence institute officials could not assess what the full effect of the law would be.

Plainly, it would tighten the proscriptions on political activity and lead to increased IRS scrutiny, which had in any event gradually been growing. In 1961, IRS examined the returns of only 1,913 exempt organizations; by 1969, 11,845 returns were examined and a special branch had been formed to superintend this auditing. From 1964–69, almost 1,200 revocations were recommended. IRS agents have focused on the nature of organization activities rather than on financial matters (Wolfe, 1970; Bacon, 1970).

The new law prohibits not merely "substantial," but *any* political activity by "private foundations," which include a large, but still indeterminate, number of nonprofit research institutes. Fines are imposed on such foundations as well as their officers for spending money "to carry on propaganda, or otherwise attempt to influence legislation." Staffs may not express views on the policy aspects of any legislation, unless the views represent nonpartisan analysis; they may present their views on pending legislation to a governmental body only on written request; and they may not help in the preparation of partisan speeches or try to influence legislation.

Since the new law prohibits political activity by exempt organizations but not by their staffs as citizens acting on their own behalf and on their own time, one effect should be to sharpen administrative measures to distinguish "institute" and "staff" time, and to disassociate institutes from responsibility for the work and opinions of their staffs. For example, Brookings' staff writing for the *Washington Post,* presumably on their own time, no longer identify themselves with Brookings. The Center for the Study of Public Policy cautions its staff:

The Center places no restrictions whatever on the individual activities of its employees. There are, however, certain kinds of activities which may appear at first glance to be "individual" but which actually involve the institution as well. . . . They include the following:

1. *Use of Center stationery. All* political activity, including fundraising, should be conducted on personal stationery.

2. *Use of the Center's address and telephone number.* All political

activity, including fund-raising, should use the employee's home address for return mail and should use his home telephone as a call-back. . . . The quickest way to identify the Center with one or another "cause" is to have people who think they are calling that cause find that the phone is answered "Cambridge Institute.". . .

3. *Use of Center titles.* . . . Employees should . . . ask themselves whether Center identification is (a) in the best interests of the Center, or (b) likely to be resented by colleagues. Having asked these questions, they are free to act as they see fit.

4. *Center office supplies.* If mimeograph paper, copiers, etc., are used for any unofficial business, whether political or personal, the Center must be compensated.

5. *Center clerical services.* Center clerical employees on regular duty must not be asked to do typing, mailings, filing, or the like for any partisan political cause. Employees are free to engage in such activities on an uncompensated basis. Since the Center does not keep regular business hours, this distinction cannot be interpreted as a rigid prohibition against typing a letter to a Congressman between nine and five. It does, however, mean that Center employees are all expected to put in 35 hours per week on Center business, and not to reduce their Center activities simply because they are also engaged in some individual political activity which takes substantial time.

6. *Public statements.* No Center employees should make any public statement, verbally or in writing, implying that the Center has a corporate position on *any* subject, political or otherwise, without first obtaining a vote to that effect from the Board of Trustees. In general, the Center does not take positions on matters not directly related to its institutional objectives or internal organization.

The 1969 tax law also requires that "substantially all" (a phrase many legal counsel have taken to mean at least 85 percent) of the income of "private foundations" be distributed for exempt functions. This will make it more difficult for R&D centers and the institutes now classified as "private foundations" to accumulate assets from fees, operating profits, or investment income.

To escape being classed as a "private foundation," a research institute must qualify as an *educational* organization or a *public* organization. The latter requires that more than one-third of the institute's income come from at least 33 sources; no source may count as more than 1 percent of that third, and each government agency is counted as a separate source. A "public organization" may not receive more than a third of its support from investment income. Although the National Bureau of Economic Research and some applied research institutes have qualified as "public" organizations[7] and the Institute for Advanced Study has qualified as an "educational" organization, it appears that the majority of institutes will be unable to meet either test and will fall under the severer restraints imposed on the activities and finances of "private foundations."

6. Personnel

Trustees are theoretically and legally responsible for hiring the director, approving operating policies and programs, and overseeing the institute's financial health and public reputation, but they generally do somewhat less than that.

The larger the board and the less frequently it meets, the less influence is any one trustee likely to have. Boards of 50 (National Bureau of Economic Research), 51 (Universities Research Association), or 208 (Committee for Economic Development) must function differently than the smaller boards of the Battelle Memorial Institute (6), the American Institutes for Research (9), or the Russell Sage Foundation (12). Of the Office of Education's regional educational laboratories, Stephen K. Bailey remarks, "Some boards became so large as to be completely unwieldy and Executive Committees were established to function for most purposes as the whole. . . . As in so many other organizations, the director or manager and the chairman of the board became the most forceful determinants of policy and planning" (Bailey, 1970, p. 15).

Most trustees serve without pay; a few receive honoraria of $100 to $200 per day for a few days each year; still fewer have annual retainers of several thousand dollars—for example, in 1965 the board chairman of RAND received $6,000, as did the Ford Foundation board chairman. While the service of a man of means is unlikely to be affected by a modest fee, a substantial fee can betoken a degree of genuine responsibility (which is not to suggest that unpaid trustees work less hard).

As a businessman, Gordon Battelle seems to have assumed that the board of his institute would not be honorific but had serious work to do and members should be compensated accordingly. His will specified "a salary of three thousand dollars . . . per annum and expenses" for each trustee; in 1968, Battelle trustees received

$10,000 a year, $4,000 more than directors of Xerox. In contrast, the articles of incorporation of the Carnegie Institution of Washington state that "the services of the trustees as such shall be gratuitous." Yet neither institute has lacked for eminent trustees.

When Andrew Carnegie met in 1902 with the first board he remarked, "The President of the United States writes me . . . , 'I congratulate you especially upon the character, the extraordinarily high character, of the trustees'" (Haskins, 1967, p. ix). Battelle's first board was more insular, though it included Warren Harding, "my friend and President-elect of the United States."[1] In 1969, the six Battelle trustees were John A. Wheeler, physicist; John R. Pierce, electrical engineer; B. D. Thomas, past president of Battelle; Sherwood L. Fawcett, the present president; Gerald Battelle Fenton, a Columbus businessman (a trustee since 1925); and chairman Clair E. Fultz, a Columbus banker. The 24 trustees of the Carnegie Institution are men of standing in industry (Greenewalt, Trippe), finance (McChesney Martin), science (Bush, Townes), and education (Ashby).

The traditional board has been criticized for not representing the public. Thus, to Philip Green, the RAND board

. . . reads like a burlesque of [C. Wright] Mills' notions of the "power elite," not merely in who is included—great universities and scientific research centers, public utilities and the monopolistic mass media, big oil, defense industry—but in who is excluded—labor unions or federations, the small liberal arts colleges, public power and rural electrification associations, independent small business or media operators, independent organizations of scientists and scholars (Green, 1968, pp. 317–318).

Boards might well diversify their compositions: at the worst, this should add intellectual excitement to tediously sober discussions and at the best, impart a broader conception of public responsibility. But it probably makes more sense to set up new institutes to pursue neglected public purposes than to expect existing ones to serve *every* public interest. Absolute pacifists have little place on the RAND board; on the board of the former Peace Research Institute, they have a more, and aggressive generals a less, evident function. Yet Edward Teller and the radical pacifist A. J. Muste were both "advisory members" of the Hudson Institute. When a body is as diverse as that of the boards of many educational laboratories, it may serve as a source of intellectual stimulation but hardly as an efficient instrument for policy formulation. Indeed, a project institute like Hudson may not require the kind of policy guidance and program restraints that are important for most R&D centers. The "purpose" of Hudson, one reader remarks, "is so intellectually eclectic . . . that defining a mission in any serious sense is simply inappropriate."

The conflict-of-interest dangers posed by the interlocking membership of some trustees on the boards of other institutes and private industry were discussed in the Bell report:

. . . there is a significant tendency to have on the boards of trustees and directors of the major universities, not-for-profit and profit establishments engaged in Federal research and development work, representatives of other institutions involved in such work. . . . we see the clear possibility of conflict-of-interest situations developing through such common directorships that might be harmful to the public interest (*Report to the President,* 1962, p. 13).

Scientists and scholars are wont to suggest that more of them should be on institute boards. But the function of most boards is not to prepare a detailed program of work or to sit in professional judgment on staff reports. Rather, it is to establish, review, and legitimate broad institutional policies and objectives and, in general, to act as an intermediary and a buffer between an institute, sponsors, and the public. Though the many scholars on the board of the National Bureau of Economic Research or the Twentieth Century Fund have helped to maintain the scholarly standards of publications (have they more control over fund allocations or do they review manuscripts?), they appear to have had less effect on the product of such project institutes as the National Opinion Research Center or the Bureau of Social Science Research (have they less control over funds and working conditions?). On the other hand, RAND, Brookings, and the Institute of Advanced Study, on whose boards fewer ranking scholars sit, have many other ways to maintain the quality of their work.

The functions of a board will be viewed differently by trustees, officers, staff, sponsors, and the public: the ideal trustee should be a wealthy, influential, informed, tactful diplomat or tightrope walker. Above all, a good board should contribute to an institute equipoise and a sense of purpose as well as one of self-limitation.

A weakness of federal R&D centers managed by single universities is their lack of an independent board. To be sure, university trustees—at the University of California, the regents—serve as a board, but they are so preoccupied with the university's problems that they can give little time to the center. As a consequence, the directors of their centers, especially those engaged in classified and developmental activities, may operate with less restraint than is the rule at independent centers. One reason for the misfortune of Project Camelot, some have argued, was the lack of effective review of the Special Operations Research Office by the American University board.[2] The point has some validity. However, a university can appoint a special committee or administrator to supervise the center.

The weak control exercised over R&D centers by many universities and some independent boards has been recognized by the Defense Department. That could be tolerated, perhaps even encouraged, when things went well, but when they went badly, something had to be done. "We had been catching hell for the FCRC's [R&D centers] for many years," remarked a Defense official, referring mainly to the congressional hearings during the 1960s on salaries, expense accounts, peripheral benefits, and freewheeling ways of the Defense Department think tanks. "To get things set right, we felt it was necessary that we be able to say that these were organizations with dedicated trustees who were looking over the management and giving direction." Accordingly, in 1967, John Foster, Jr., Director of Defense Research and Engineering, called the assistant secretaries for R&D of the three services together and asked them to see that their centers had genuine, active boards.

What in fact ensued (what could be done about university-managed centers) I do not know. ". . . nothing very much happened," a former Defense official observed, "with two exceptions: first, much more penetrating and comprehensive reviews of salaries were made; and second, the top management of each service took a more analytical approach to the kinds of problems they were assigning" to centers. Some universities evidently appointed an advisory committee for their center or informed an existent committee about the Defense Department's concern.

Diligent trustees can do much to ensure that centers are administered efficiently. But Defense center boards, as well as the boards of other institutes heavily dependent upon federal funds, have an inherent weakness: they must operate within the regulations, budgets, interests, and responsibilities of their federal sponsors. This point is often neglected by faculty and student committees seeking to redirect the military R&D of university-managed centers and institutes. Alan Pifer has rightly characterized it as a generic weakness of the government-sponsored nonprofit organization:

> . . . the paths of these organizations become characterized by frequent changes of direction induced by Washington's concerns of the day, rather than deliberate courses set by the organizations' own boards of trustees. This process in turn can diminish the interest of the trustees, and hence their sense of responsibility—which is the very heart of effective voluntary private service in the public interest. . . .

> . . . power and responsibility are shared uneasily between a board of trustees and government. While in a showdown the trustees, it is true, could threaten to dissolve the corporation, government on its side has the power at any time to starve it to death financially, or use its financial power to shape the organization's program. And since financial power of this kind implies the acceptance of responsibility, a measure of the final responsibility for these organizations must inevitably remain in Washington, in a federal agency in the first instance but ultimately with the Congress (Pifer, 1966, p. 9; 1967, p. 10).

THE DIRECTOR Without getting into personalities, it is difficult to say much about the director other than that he is undoubtedly the man most responsible for shaping the character of an institute. The senior full-time officer, often the only officer who is a member of the governing board,[3] he is usually a man with both professional and administrative experience, with some recognized standing among both the patrons and the producers of research.

An institute has no alumni, citizenry, state legislature, students, or tenured faculty to anchor it to the past and limit its freedom of action. Therefore, in large matters as well as small, a director can impose his judgment, interests, and taste upon an institute to a degree that a president cannot do upon his university. The tidiness or sloppiness of an institute's offices and staff; the efficiency of phones, mails, and purchasing; the helpfulness of administrators, librarians, and editors; staff cameraderie and the sense of shared or separate professional purpose can be attributed more to the character of the director than to any other single factor.

Again and again, officials of the AEC have stressed that the quality of their R&D centers was influenced more by the director than by the organization responsible for the contract. Thus the character of Argonne changed more with several directors under the same contractor than did Oak Ridge with the same director under two contractors. The troubles and amorphousness of the Office of Education's R&D centers may be partly attributable to the brief tenure of their directors: at least half of the centers changed directors during the first four years (Bloom, 1968, p. 182).

At all R&D centers, both the sponsoring agency and the contractor must normally approve the choice of a director. His control over salaries, management practices, program, and budgets, being subject to review and approval by the sponsoring agency, is more limited than at other institutes.

If a center director must be something of a politician to mediate successfully between his board and the government and gain as much freedom as he can by maneuvering among the levels and factions of government, the institute director may perhaps be called a benevolent despot. To be sure, he is a manager of professional men, not slaves, and his authority will be tempered, not only by mercy and the job market but by simple intelligence. Staff have more power over the outcome of a program than the director, who can only pray that all will turn out well. But, at few institutes do the staff members have job security. The power to hire and fire, to reward with a large raise, to approve a professional trip or the retention of an honorarium, to give or withhold the small but vital signs of esteem, is held by the director and his principal officers.

Unlike a university, where each professor is an independent principality, there is little politics at the average institute, because politics is meaningless without power, and power rests with the board and the director. From the standpoint of institutional democracy, this may be regrettable but from the standpoint of administrative responsibility and the ability to act quickly, it represents a principal strength.

PROFESSIONAL APPOINT-MENTS In principle, institutes should be more able than universities to assemble quickly new mixes of professional talent for special projects because they can hire and fire without the restraints of tenure, teaching obligations, departmental deliberations, and faculty politics. In fact, the flexibility of institute staffing is limited by the charity of the director, prior commitments, budgets, and staff turnover.

The formal commitment to professional staff, expressed in an appointment letter or contract, is geared to the stability of institute financing. Some operating foundations offer all senior staff security comparable to tenure. For example, at the Rockefeller Institute, senior staff once received five-year appointments subject to renewal; subsequently, "only . . . the most distinguished professional staff had permanent tenure. Men who did not seem likely to reach full membership . . . were permitted or advised to accept posts proferred by other institutions . . ." (Corner, 1964, pp. 64, 157). At the Carnegie Institution of Washington, the assumption is that senior appointments carry life tenure, although that is not spelled out in the letter of appointment. In December 1970, the Institute for Advanced Study had 26 permanent tenured faculty and a few five- to ten-year visiting appointments.

At an endowed institute such as Brookings, a few staff members hold tenured appointments. "Regular" professional appointments are made for a year and renewed each spring by a letter from the president which also designates the new salary level for the forthcoming year. "Special" appointments are limited to the period for which their project is financed. At the more thinly endowed Wistar Institute, six persons hold tenure; other staff members are appointed for no stated period. The Sloan-Kettering Institute once offered three-year appointments to staff members who held joint appointments at Cornell, but, with increased financial stringency, appointments are now limited to one year.

At most applied and project institutes, appointments are for no specified term. Within the hazards of the appropriations process, R&D centers have the certitude of a firm annual budget, but that does not ensure a year's security to everyone, since particular tasks may require that some be dismissed while others are hired. At the Stanford Research Institute, the employment agreement states ". . . that my employment is not for any particular term and therefore this agreement is terminable, with immediate effect, at the will of either party." Though it may not be set forth so explicitly, the situation is the same at most institutes.

Despite a budget of less than $600,000 in 1971, the Institute for Policy Studies has tried to foster a sense of security among its staff. According to its bylaws, full-time resident fellows "shall be assured a minimum term of three years, which term shall automatically be renewed for successive three-year periods, without limitation as to the number of terms, unless notice is given . . . at least one year prior to the end of any given three-year term. Notwithstanding the aforementioned termination provision, the appointment of resident fellows shall customarily be regarded as permanent." This institute is noteworthy also for the degree of self-governance and collegiality among its staff members, many of whom are also members of the board. The greater formal insecurity of staff members at most institutes presumably reflects their more pyramidal and authoritarian mode of governance.

When firing takes place, the most that can often be done is to give a staff member the value of accumulated leave. If they are lucky, staff at R&D centers may receive more notice than at project institutes. Thus, the Office of Education's R&D centers try to gear their hiring to the academic year and to terminate no one at midyear (i.e., in February).

Some longer-established centers and applied research institutes relate termination allowance to service. At one institute, the maximum allowance is 12 weeks salary for 15 years of service. "This is the best we can do," the president remarked. RAND tries to give at least a one-month notice (but no additional severance pay) to staff with less than a year's service and at most six months to long-service staff. In 1970, Aerospace Corporation policy called for severance pay ranging from four weeks for under three years' service to nineteen weeks for twenty or more years. The Stanford Research Institute provides professional staff with the alternative of severance pay or notice based on one month for one year's service to a maximum of three months after five years' service.

Institute staff benefit and retirement systems merit a study in their own right, whereas I will here offer only a single observation. William Slater, Research Director of the Teachers Insurance and Annuity Association of America-College Retirement Equities Fund (TIAA–CREF), to which a goodly number of institutes belong, states that their benefit programs, especially retirement plans, are in general slightly superior to the average college faculty plans. This is partly because institutes have been competing with large universities for personnel, and partly because their personnel needs have been more selective than those of colleges and universities. As a rule, large institutes have better benefits and retirement schemes than small institutes.[4]

STAFF DEGREES AND DISCIPLINES Comprehensive data on degrees are not available for all nonprofit institutes but they could not in any event reflect the variations in staff composition among institutes.

About two-fifths of the staffs of R&D centers and other nonprofit institutes are professional personnel, with bachelor or higher degrees; perhaps 10 percent have Ph.D.'s (Table 7). AEC and DOD centers and the applied research institutes employ many engineers. However, at the end of 1967 some 450 biomedical scientists were employed at AEC centers not included in Table 7, principally at Argonne, Brookhaven, and the Berkeley Radiation Laboratory; an additional 350 were employed at the industry-operated Oak Ridge National Laboratory.

Aside from the Office of Education centers, the social scientists employed by R&D centers were located mainly at the Department of Defense "think tanks." In 1967, 129 were at RAND, 97 at the Human Resources Research Office, 81 at the Institute for Defense Analyses, 73 at the Research Analysis Corporation, 48 at the Center for Research in Social Systems, and 41 at the Center for Naval Analyses (Welles, et al., 1969, p. 349). Virtually none were at AEC centers, which, unlike the Defense Department centers, have given little attention to the strategic, operational, social, or economic implications of their technology. (Such implications have, of course, concerned politically minded organizations such as the Atomic Industrial Forum, the Congress of Industrial Organizations, the Joint Committee on Atomic Energy, and the AEC itself. The AEC has also contracted with RAND for certain studies largely confined to physical and mathematical analyses of nuclear explosions.) Of late, some AEC centers have sought to broaden their

TABLE 7
Total and professional personnel at selected nonprofit institutes, January 1967

Personnel	Number and type of institute			
	24 R&D centers		233 other institutes	
	Number	*Percent*	*Number*	*Percent*
Total	13,200	100	30,580	100
Professional degrees	5,495	42	12,730	41
Ph.D. or M.D.	1,160	9	4,010	13
Master's	1,880	14	2,980	10
Bachelor's	2,460	19	5,740	19
Professional fields	5,495	100	12,730	100
Engineers	2,710	49	2,735	21
Physical scientists	1,730	32	4,410	35
Life scientists	85	2	3,360	26
Social scientists	970	18	2,225	18

SOURCE: National Science Foundation, 1969*d*.

competence in the social sciences, but they have been explicitly cautioned about this by the Joint Committee on Atomic Energy.

Many R&D centers and institutes function as do universities, with an "up or out" policy, which leads to a higher turnover among young staff and greater stability at more senior levels. At one large applied institute, the average professional service may be 8½ to 9 years, but 15 to 20 years among management employees. During "normal" times, the turnover was 7 to 8 percent a year; forced terminations raised it to 10 to 12 percent in 1970. At other applied research institutes, the normal turnover has been from 12 to 15 percent. This rate is high compared to industry and universities, says Richard Lesher, who attributes it to the pressures of meeting report deadlines within budget ceilings (Lesher, 1963, p. 117). Traditionally, R&D centers have been more stable, although the peremptory fiats of congressional committee chairmen may undo all their planning.[5] The turnover at RAND was 6 percent in 1960, 8 percent in 1961, but 19 percent in 1970.[6] Of the 1,073 scientists and engineers at the Johns Hopkins Applied Physics Laboratory in January 1968, 70 percent had been with the laboratory more than 10 years and 11 percent, more than 20 years. However, the curtailment of Defense Department center budgets by the Congress, together with the inflation of salaries, has forced many centers to dismiss staff or not to replace those who leave.

SALARIES Information on salaries is closely guarded, although exchanged in confidence so that rough comparability can be maintained by groups of institutes which regard themselves as operating in the same league. More information should become available under new IRS reporting requirements. As a rule, job security and publication freedom are offset against salary; the same man can expect a lower salary at an operating foundation or endowed institute than at a project institute.

During the 1950s and early 1960s, government and university salaries were lower than those at R&D centers; center salaries were lower than those in industry. Government and university salaries have since become more competitive. Even so, meaningful comparisons are best confined to specific organizations or types of organizations.

One careful study by Edward M. Glass of the Department of Defense, based upon 1967 data, showed that staff and executive salaries at Defense centers such as Aerospace, RAND, and MITRE approached those in the aerospace industry and were somewhat higher than those of government laboratory staff, year for year after the receipt of the highest degree. Salaries were lower at centers under university management and at small social science centers like the Human Resources Research Office and the Center for Research in Social Systems. Though university engineering faculty had, on average, lower salaries than engineers at R&D centers, their annual income (including consulting income and summer research salaries) was higher.[7] The higher salaries prevailing at independent centers can be seen in Table 8.

As the table also shows, salaries at Air Force centers were higher than at Army and Navy centers. Because the Army and Navy spend proportionately more of their R&D funds intramurally, they may be less tolerant of contractor salaries that are decidedly higher than civil service scales.[8] However, this principle (if it is one!) does not

TABLE 8 *Top executive salary at 13 defense department centers, March 1970*

Center	Agency	Executive	Salary
Independent nonprofit			
Aerospace	Air Force	I. A. Getting	$97,500
RAND	Air Force	H. S. Rowen	70,000
MITRE	Air Force	R. R. Everett	60,000
Institute for Defense Analyses	DOD	M. D. Taylor	60,000
Research Analysis Corporation	Army	F. A. Parker	46,000
Analytical Services, Inc.	Air Force	S. J. Lawwill	42,500
University-managed			
Lincoln Laboratory (MIT)	Air Force	M. V. Clauser	48,000
Center for Naval Analyses (Rochester)	Navy	C. DiBona	42,000
Applied Physics Laboratory (Hopkins)	Navy	R. E. Gibson	40,000
Mathematics Research Center (Wisconsin)	Army	J. B. Rosser	37,500
Ordnance Research Laboratory (Pennsylvania State)	Navy	J. C. Johnson	33,000
Applied Physics Laboratory (University of Washington)	Navy	J. E. Henderson	32,000
Human Resources Research Office (George Washington)	Army	M. P. Crawford	30,000

SOURCE: Letter from John S. Foster, Jr., director of Defense Research and Engineering, to Senator John Williams, *Congressional Record—Senate,* April 13, 1970, p. S 5594.

apply to the AEC which has kept tighter rein on contractor salaries than the Air Force, although it contracts for *all* its research and development. The explanation once given by Harold Brown, then director of R&D for the Defense Department and former head of AEC's Livermore laboratory, was that, as the government had a monopoly on atomic energy, it had less need to maintain comparability between the salaries at its nuclear R&D centers and in private industry (*Systems Development and Management,* 1962, part 2, pp. 487–488).

Congressmen, whose pay was decidedly lower (in 1962, $22,500 a year), were unenthusiastic about the salaries and corporate comforts enjoyed by the officers of some Defense centers, notably the Aerospace Corporation. For many years, department heads at RAND received salaries higher than that of the Secretary of Defense. This situation has gradually been rectified: in 1961, salaries for GS 18s, the top level of the civil service, were $18,500; in 1970, $36,000. Staff who left one Defense center for government service in 1970 received, on average, raises of 17 percent.

Under Public Law 91-121, enacted in November 1969, no Defense Department funds could be used to pay any salary over $45,000 (the salary of the Defense Secretary) at an R&D center, except with the approval of the President, and such salaries were to be reported to the Congress. In February 1970, President Nixon delegated that authority to the Secretary of Defense, with the following instructions (which were drafted by the secretary's office):

The Secretary of Defense will approve the payment of compensation . . . to an officer or employee of a Federal Contract Research Center whose annual compensation paid out of any Federal funds exceeds $45,000 only when it can clearly be demonstrated that such compensation is needed to employ individuals with the qualifications necessary to the accomplishment of the Center's mission, and taking into consideration the following additional factors: (1) the nature and scope of the work performed by the Center and its significance to the national defense; (2) the nature and scope of the duties performed by the officer or employee, and the importance of such duties to the accomplishment of the Center's work; (3) compensation generally paid to officers or employees of the Government engaged in similar work; and (4) compensation generally paid to officers or employees of private nonprofit organizations other than the Federal Contract Research Centers and engaged in similar work (Nixon, 1970, p. 2951).

Center salary scales and salaries above a certain level have always been subject to approval by government contract officers. Approval applies only to the portion of a salary reimbursed by federal funds; if a contractor wishes to exceed the level set by the government, it may be able to do so from its own funds or the contract fee. The significant departure in Nixon's instruction was the reference to other nonprofit organizations. This reflected the view of key Congressmen that, since R&D centers were noncompetitive and incurred no business risks, their salaries should not (as the Air Force had held in the era of expanding budgets) be comparable to those of private business.

Table 9 reports recent salary data for the highest-paid officer of eight applied research institutes and twenty other institutes of

TABLE 9
Top executive salary at selected nonprofit institutes, 1966–1969

Institute	Executive	Salary*
Applied research institutes		
Battelle Memorial Institute	S. L. Fawcett	$61,250
Midwest Research Institute	Charles N. Kimball	60,000
Illinois Institute of Technology Research Institute	E. H. Schulz	50,000
Stanford Research Institute	W. B. Gibson	46,750
Franklin Institute	Athelstan Spilhaus	45,000
	Joseph Feldmeier	35,460
Southern Research Institute	Howard Skipper	40,000
Gulf South Research Institute	Bruce Graham	39,580(a)
Cornell Aeronautical Laboratory	Henry K. Moffitt	38,400
Other institutes		
Urban Institute	William Gorham	55,000
Universities Research Association	Norman Ramsey	48,000
Carnegie Institution of Washington	Caryl Haskins	45,000
Salk Institute	Jonas Salk	45,000
National Bureau of Economic Research	John Meyer	40,160
Twentieth Century Fund	Murray Rossant	40,000(b)
Center for Advanced Study in the Behavioral Sciences	O. Meredith Wilson	40,000
American Enterprise Institute	W. J. Baroody	40,000(a)
Institute for Public Administration	Lyle Fitch	36,000(a)
Resources for the Future	Joseph Fisher	36,000(a)
Russell Sage Foundation	Orville Brim	35,000(b)

	Institute	Executive	Salary*
TABLE 9 *(continued)*	*Other institutes cont.:*		
	Hudson Institute	Herman Kahn	35,000
	Woods Hole Oceanographic Institution	Paul Fye	35,000(a)
	Carnegie Endowment for International Peace	Joseph Johnson	29,940
	Agricultural Development Council	Clifton Wharton	29,820(c)
	Center for Urban Education	Robert Dentler	25,660(a)
	Washington Center for Metropolitan Studies	Royce Hanson	25,000
	National Opinion Research Center	Norman Bradburn	24,040(a)
	Bureau of Social Science Research	Robert Bower	22,150
	Institute for Policy Studies	Marcus Raskin	19,000
		Richard Barnet	19,000

* See explanation of source, below.

SOURCE: Income tax returns for the latest available year: a = 1969; b = 1967; c = 1966; all others, 1968. "Top" means the highest salary reported, not necessarily the highest executive: thus, during 1968, the vice president of the Southern Research Institute, Howard Skipper, received $2,000 more than the president, W. M. Murray, Jr., and Stanford Research Institute executive vice president W. B. Gibson received a higher salary than incoming president C. A. Anderson. Salaries are reported at an annual rate though in two cases the executive noted did not work full time: Norman Ramsey, professor of physics at Harvard, received $24,000 for his half-time work as President of the Universities Research Association, and Norman Bradburn received $15,646 for 65 percent of his time as secretary of the National Opinion Research Center. Two executives are reported for the Franklin Institute because Spilhaus was president of the entire institute and Feldmeier was director of the Franklin Institute Research Laboratories, the institute's research component. At the Institute for Policy Studies, Raskin and Barnet served as codirectors.

varied character. The salaries of the heads of applied research institutes may convey a misleading impression about staff salaries. While I have no hard data, it is my impression that the salaries at most institutes are not especially high. At one large applied institute, an informant stated that base salaries were higher, in 1970, than those at unspecified universities, but that consulting fees raised the income of many professors above that of the staff.

During the last few years, an unusual situation has developed. As the demand for scientists and engineers has slackened, and increasing numbers of faculty would be glad to leave their institution for good jobs sans students and demonstrations, institutes could hire exceptionally well-qualified staff. However, few have been able to do so, for the R&D income of most institutes appears to have followed the same trends as that of universities. One would expect salaries and salary offers to stabilize or even to decline. Nonetheless, in 1969 and 1970 institutes raised salaries by about 6 percent a year to meet the rising cost of living, preferring, if necessary, to economize by reducing staff.

ADDITIONAL INCOME

At few institutes do staff members enjoy the academic man's freedom to earn and keep additional income; these few tend to be places like the Institute for Advanced Study, which functions like a university.

At most leading universities, the prevailing assumption is that a man is paid to teach two or three classes for two terms, and to set aside additional hours for committee work and student consultation. Beyond that, his time is his own. He may not be free to augment his salary from sponsored research funds during the academic year but he can receive fees from consulting, writing, and lecturing during the school term, copyright work and receive royalties from its sale, and accept additional salary for research or other work during the summer. No professor fills out a time sheet. Faculty were once obliged to report the proportion of "effort" (for example, one-third or one-half) that they had actually devoted to a government research project, but they complained so much that this requirement was dropped. Time clocks are not in fashion on campus.

At most institutes, salaries are computed on a twelve-, not nine-, month basis. Staff are expected to devote full time to research projects, and, for purposes of internal budgeting and external accounting, they normally fill out sheets which indicate how their full time was allocated each month, week, and day. Regardless of the fictions this may entail, it is necessary to provide a precise definition of "full time" that will satisfy government and institute accountants (e.g., at Brookings, this is five working days of eight hours each). Since the product of work done during this full-time week — inventions, designs, books, or reports — normally belongs either to the research sponsor or the institute, so does any income it may yield.

Permission must be obtained from institute and even government administrators for devoting any substantial amount of time to any activities that might interrupt or delay the completion of scheduled projects. Permission must also be obtained for work conducted after hours that might pose a conflict of interest.

The Battelle employment contract provides that staff are "not to engage in the performance of consultant or any other outside employment activities without the express prior written consent of the Director. . . ." A Research Triangle Institute publication states that "the staff member offers his services—his skills, abilities, and professional efforts—'exclusively' to RTI, and that 'all cases of outside interests' require approval by the Institute's president. In practice, however, there is a good deal more discretion built into the policy than is suggested by a strict reading of 'exclusively' or 'all.'"

Small, new, and financially insecure institutes may have fewer and less firm policies. If a director wants to render the institute more attractive to staff, compensate them for low salaries, and make the institute more widely known to prospective sponsors, he may encourage publication and lecturing and permit staff to keep the honoraria and royalties. At one institute with a budget of about $1 million and fairly low salaries, staff members keep most fees; if a great deal of office time has been spent writing a book, royalties are split evenly between the institute and the author. At the Institute for Policy Studies, salaries are so low that it is assumed staff will supplement their income; book royalties go to the Institute only in the case of a few projects fully financed by it. At Battelle, in contrast, honoraria for speeches or articles normally go into a staff education fund. At RAND,

Employees may retain honoraria paid for speaking engagements subject to the following exceptions:

No honorarium will be retained by an employee if it originates either directly or indirectly from a Government source. Honoraria which may be received from such sources should be endorsed over to RAND; however, honoraria should not be accepted from RAND's clients.

No honoraria will be accepted by an employee for speaking before an organization where a conflict of interest may exist or appear to exist by reason of the acceptance of a fee ("Honoraria," 1967).

In sum, institute staff receive little income other than salaries.[9] At any rate, that is the rule. A man whose work is in good shape may be permitted more latitude than one whose work is lagging. And a way can be found around any rule. An institute which frowns on commercial consulting may nevertheless permit a prized staff member to engage in it by giving him a four-day or a half-time appointment. The director is the final arbiter, and there are some things a wise director does not want to know.

7. On Institute Research

INTERDIS-
CIPLINARY
RESEARCH One advantage of an institute, it is said, is its ability to conduct interdisciplinary research unhampered by the university's departmental mode of organization, appointment, promotion, and instruction. Universities have had great difficulty in conducting successful interdisciplinary research, it is generally conceded, and their attempts are often administered by intramural units .which resemble independent institutes but lack their freedom of action. ". . . [T]he present compartmentalization of knowledge in universities in the form of academic disciplines is not coincident with social need. However useful this compartmentalization may be for the inner development of knowledge, it is only marginally useful for the resolution of social questions," writes James Carroll, whose view is widespread among government research administrators. "For this reason urban R&D may ultimately be centered in think tanks and similar organizations rather than in the academic departments of universities . . . " (Carroll, 1969, p. 909).

While institutes have been more (they could not have been less) successful than universities in organizing interdisciplinary teams, the frequency with which such teams are utilized and the extent of their success is commonly exaggerated. Spencer Klaw reports that "To date, fruitful interdisciplinary work has not been so common at S.R.I. [the Stanford Research Institute] as its literature might suggest. 'We must improve the mechanisms by which people can be brought in from other divisions to work on a problem,' [SRI board chairman] Arbuckle says" (Klaw, 1966, p. 222). Richard Lesher writes that at all the applied research institutes he visited, ". . . there was the frank admission by the individual institute administrators that their institute was not conducting enough research of this type." The administrative expense is high and as an institute grows, its internal departments "take on a degree of autonomy" that militates against the free assignment of staff to new projects. "In effect, profit centers evolve within the institute" (Lesher, 1963, pp. 143–147). According to Bruce Smith, "Interdisciplinary research at RAND, far from becoming steadily easier and more effective, has actually grown more difficult in recent years. The individual departments in some respects seem to have grown more self-contained, inward-looking, and conscious of their own prerogatives, and less interested in working on inter-disciplinary projects" (Smith, 1966, p. 144). However, a RAND reader rejoined:

Whether or not this was an adequate description when Smith wrote it in 1966, it does not describe present-day Rand with its organization by programs (communications policy, education, health and biosciences, systems acquisition, etc.) that cut across departmental lines. It does not describe the work in New York City, where Rand staff members attack problems, singly and in groups, without regard to departmental lines or the boundaries of academic disciplines. . . . It does not describe recent work in the biosciences, in health care, on the Philippines, on racial disparities in income, on accountability in education . . . and so on.

Many large institutes are not unlike universities in their disciplinary-departmental organization. Though interdepartmental project teams are often assembled, Roger Levien of RAND observes that it is the permanent departments, not the temporary teams, which "are the means of recruiting, evaluating, encouraging, and rewarding" staff and of helping to maintain their professional status and job mobility. "The alternative organization into problem-oriented departments . . . is not so successful in attracting first-class specialists, who are best recognized and rewarded by their peers and who ordinarily crave their colleagues' company . . ." (Levien, 1969). Alvin Weinberg describes the organization of R&D centers in almost identical terms:

This criss-cross organization—with each scientist having a permanent home in a division but being lent out temporarily to an interdisciplinary project—is the usual organization in applied laboratories. The project leaders generally control the funds; the division leaders, the people. The projects maintain pressure on the division managers to keep their outlook and activities relevant as judged by the projects; the disciplinary divisions maintain pressure on the project managers to keep their activities up to the standards of sophistication imposed by the divisions (Weinberg, 1970, p. 1061).

Levien (1969) suggests that institutes are credited with an undue amount of interdisciplinary research because three other kinds of research, which he calls *multidisciplinary, adisciplinary,* and *cross-disciplinary,* are confused with it. *Multidisciplinary* research is the assembled but discrete work on a problem by men from different disciplines; *adisciplinary* research is the collective study by specialists who employ simple intelligence and experience rather than the techniques of their disciplines; *crossdisciplinary* research is work in an emerging field such as biophysics, which lies at the juncture of two established fields and develops into a discipline of its own. "True interdisciplinary studies," he asserts (and I agree), "are rare, for they demand the intricate merging of insights into a study that responds directly and thoroughly to the policy issue under examination. The threads of the several disciplines should be so tightly meshed and interwoven that they form a smooth and continuous fabric of argument. What generally passes for interdisciplinary research more nearly resembles a patchwork quilt, often with gaping holes."

QUALITY CONTROL AND INSTITUTE QUALITY
The measures an institute can take to control the quality of its work are governed by time and the other resource which sometimes buys time, money.

Only so much can be done to monitor the progress of a study by checking to see that appointed data are collected at the appointed time. All studies cannot be scheduled with equal reliability, nor is it always possible to pause in mid-course and determine how good the data are and to collect better data if they are poor; it is even less possible to start off in a fresh direction. When time is limited, the initial project design sets in process a chain of work that cannot be significantly altered.

When the deadline approaches, a project budget is nearly exhausted, and a director or department head receives a pitifully poor draft report, his alternatives are determined by his sense of professional workmanship, the institute's bank balance, and the sponsor's requirements. If there is money in the bank and the sponsor extends the deadline, the draft can be redone or reassigned (forcing another man to delay other work). If a deadline is firm and funds are exhausted, the draft must be patched up by working overtime or by stealing time from other projects.

This characteristic situation obtains especially at applied research and project institutes, but also, to varying degrees, at any institute that must complete work at a set time within a fixed budget. Quality control is necessarily limited; it is usually conducted by the institute's own staff, and the time invested in it must be withdrawn from other projects. The editorial staff at most institutes of any size can improve the readability and organization of a report, eliminate what is redundant or foolish, and clarify what is unclear; but it cannot add missing data, ideas, and conclusions.

An inquest may be held to determine what went wrong and how that error might be avoided in the future. But research administration is not, like manufacturing, a process that can be broken down into parts and assembled reliably. It is an art whose essence is the understanding and perceptive management of men.

At one applied research institute, a technical council of four senior staff reviews each project to assess the quality of the report and the degree to which the project met its objectives. The magnitude and scope of the work is such that the council cannot serve as a primary agent of quality control; that must be done mainly by the heads of departments and divisions. The council determines whether the departments are doing their jobs satisfactorily and meeting project specifications. In the opinion of council members, weakness in performance is seldom attributable to ignorance or errors in chemistry, metallurgy, or other disciplines. Poor writing is often responsible. Frequently staff did not look at a problem from the sponsor's standpoint. This "reverting to the norms of the academic community" was more common in the pure sciences than in engineering, and most common in the social sciences. Members of one department often were ignorant of what was going on elsewhere. Council members believed their major contribution was to put people from different departments in touch with each other. The council was therefore well placed to do its second job, which was to advise management on who should respond to an RFP (a government *request for a proposal*) — a critical decision, because those who did were likely, later, to do the work.

In contrast to the hectic pace of such applied research institutes, let us consider the relaxed Brookings, an institute which, with a senior staff of some 35, an endowment of some $40 million, and a good standing with foundations and the government, enjoys an enviable financial security. At Brookings, the civil servant's refuge from government and the academician's refuge from classes, time stands still. Though its scenery and dress are doubtless more attractive, Tahiti could not be more serene. Staff members on leave for a year return to find things much as they left them — manuscripts waiting to be cleared or read or rewritten or edited or manufactured, each stage in the tedious process of scholarship requiring infinite patience.

Whereas most institutes produce reports, Brookings produces books. When a manuscript is prepared, the director of one of the three research programs (in economics, government, or foreign affairs) may suggest some changes. When he deems it ready, he will recommend to the president the appointment of three to five outside readers. Normally, these are leading scholars and administrators. In recent years, to promote candor, their names have not been revealed. Their comments may be brief or lengthy and highly detailed. After the author does what he can, within his conscience and ability, to meet their criticisms, the revised manuscript is submitted to the president, who may request more changes before approving it for publication. On one estimate, half the manuscripts in economics go through this scrutiny with minor changes, 5 percent are rejected, and the remainder are substantially reworked. In other programs, the proportion of rejections is probably higher.

Most of the products of Brookings, the National Bureau of Economic Research, the Carnegie Institution of Washington, the Russell Sage Foundation, the Boyce Thompson Institute, the Sloan-Kettering Institute, the Berkeley Radiation Laboratory, and the National Radio Astronomy Observatory are published in books and journals readily accessible in most libraries. Any reader can judge their quality for himself. The assessment of institutes whose work is classified or not readily accessible is more difficult.[1]

The widespread assumption that many institutes provide sponsors with the facts and conclusions they want cannot be dispelled unless that work is open to public scrutiny. Certain opinions about the quality of institute work abound — such as that the AEC laboratories are, as a group, better than those of the Department of Defense;[2] that RAND is very good; that much of the work of applied research institutes is pedestrian; and the same is said of the Office of Education's R&D centers. Contrariwise, Benjamin Bloom writes: "What I have been able to read of the published as well as unpublished reports of research by the [Office of Education] centers, strikes me as being of first order quality. . . . There is little doubt in my mind that the reports (published or not) by the centers have been and are likely to be among the best in education from the viewpoint of care and scholarship" (Bloom, 1968, pp. 186–187).

For the enlightenment of sponsors and the public, who ultimately pay for most research, it would be useful to conduct periodic studies of institute quality (or rather, since quality is multifaceted, qualities). For instance, take the 130 or so centers and institutes for which information on annual federal expenditures is now available. What are the names, degrees, fields, and publications of the officers and department heads? How many are members of the National Academy of Sciences or the American Academy of Arts and Sciences?[3] What is the number of their staff in various salary brackets? The overhead rate? The capital assets? The volume of government work obtained through bids? By sole-source negotiation? What is the volume of work for private sponsors? What proportion of the work is made public?

Quality ratings of university graduate departments by department chairmen and scholars have been conducted at intervals.[4] Would it be feasible to extend this procedure to research institutes? One study (the results are a closely guarded secret)[5] has already been made of the quality of Defense Department centers and intramural laboratories. Such studies could yield a picture of institutes' comparative administrative efficiency, scholarly reputation, originality, independence of outlook, and so forth.

The government must often evaluate the performance of a center or institute to decide about contract awards and to monitor center programs and management. However, these judgments are normally confidential. One can infer something of their character from budgetary actions, as, for example, the recent termination of support by the Office of Education of several regional educational laboratories. President Johnson's science adviser, Donald Hornig, has stated:

Procedures in use in the Government for both in-house and contractor R&D appraisal involve such techniques as visits to the laboratory by teams of agency management representatives; evaluation of results by agency management and—especially where more basic research is involved —by outside advisory groups; and continuing reviews of laboratory operations through reports, audits, conferences, day-to-day contacts, and so on (*Utilization of Federal Laboratories,* 1968, p. 22).

In 1964, a subcommittee of the President's Science Advisory Committee chaired by Emmanuel Piore was appointed to conduct an inquiry about federal laboratories. "Reflecting a concern that some Government laboratories are scientifically unproductive, the study. . . hopefully will establish some guidelines to what makes a creative Government laboratory." It was "almost inevitable," *New York Times* reporter John Finney wrote, that government R&D centers would also be included in the study (Finney, 1964).

The results have not been published.[6] And in 1970, a presidential task force called for a virtually identical inquiry, and William McElroy, director of the NSF, asked that a "periodic review for quality control" be established "in a routine fashion," to "facilitate the disbanding or reorientation of these centers. . . ."[7] Since such a review would be of evident interest to an economy-minded Administration and to private research institutions eager to receive any R&D funds that might be saved from government laboratories, conceivably it will eventually be conducted.

STAFF INDEPENDENCE AND RESPONSIBILITY At a university, a tenured professor may be fired for not meeting classes, but not for not publishing; the university has no responsibility for his talks, papers, and books nor any procedure for reviewing them. (An interesting, little-known exception occurs at medical schools, where department chairmen often review papers prior to their submission for publication.) It does assume responsibility for harboring a project, by the signature of a senior administrator on the research proposal. That signature may be routine or forthcoming only after diligent inquiry. But there, the university's responsibility ends. If an investigator submits a poor report or no report at all, that is his problem; the university has no legal or moral obligation to return the sponsor's money or to appoint a second investigator to discharge the obligation properly.

At a research institute, however, a staff member is hired to do research and his other activities are ancillary. The institute's reputation and (except for operating foundations) financial security rest solely on its research. A staff member who fails to deliver a report will normally be dismissed.

An endowed or cushioned institute or R&D center may be more relaxed about deadlines than an applied or project institute, emphasizing the quality, rather than the volume, of work; but sooner or later a report must be submitted. The reporting of basic research and of research sponsored by foundations, government grants, and "Project RAND"–type contracts tends to be more flexible than that of applied research conducted under more minutely detailed contracts.

Applied research and project institutes subsisting largely on the latter type of contracts must complete their reports or go out of business; and the final contract payment may be withheld until receipt of a "satisfactory" report. It is this combined financial and political pressure to meet deadlines and satisfy clients that gives these institutes their special character and reputation. The reputation is for reliability—and for a degree of pedestrianness, for only pedestrian work can be reliably delivered.

If a man labors under such constraints of time and cost and a need to please a client that he must produce work which he feels is *not* his best, can he be held solely responsible for the content and quality of that work?

True, no intellectual can operate without some constraints imposed by his fellow men, publishers, editors, colleagues, and family; hence all can rightfully disclaim some responsibility for their work.[8] But insofar as a staff member of an institute works under greater constraints than a professor, he bears correspondingly less, and his institution more, responsibility for the work. "Less" is not "none" and "more" is not "all." The apportionment of responsibility will vary with the institute, project, and individual. But the contrast between the professional independence (or institutional irresponsibility) of university professors and the dependence (or institutional responsibility) of institute staff remains.

The situation is sufficiently ambiguous, and the advantages to all parties—sponsor, institute, and investigator—of claiming or disclaiming responsibility are sufficiently uncertain, so that every type of disavowal and avowal of responsibility will be found at some time in the work of some institute.

The typical applied research institute contract gives the sponsor full "ownership" of the results insofar as they can be assigned in the form of patents, copyrights, blueprints, and data. Thereby, once a report is transmitted to the client, the institute relinquishes a degree of control which professors normally retain; in that sense, an institute investigator cannot be held as responsible for the uses to which it is put as a professor may be. However, contracts usually prohibit a sponsor from using the name of the institute in advertising or legal actions without express permission.

Government officials are, likewise, ambiguous about their responsibility for the result of research expenditures. Long hectoring about scientific and academic freedom has sunk in; and, in any event, officials know that they cannot guarantee the outcome of work that is inherently unpredictable. So, like investigators and institutes, they want credit only for success and not for failure. The NSF does not require technical reports in its normal research grants, but does ask to be informed of any unusual findings—that is, of those which will impress the public and the Congress with the value of foundation-sponsored work. When it serves their purpose, officials may use the findings of contract research with or without attribution; at one applied research institute, I was shown a report that a federal agency had published verbatim without indicating the source, as if it had been written by agency staff. But they do not want to be held responsible for—the only accurate way to put it is circularly—work that they do not want to be held responsible for. Thus, a report on the AEC's Weston accelerator begins:

This report was prepared as an account of Government sponsored work. Neither the United States, nor the Commission, nor any person acting on behalf of the Commission:

A. Makes any warranty or representation, expressed or implied, with respect to the accuracy, completeness, or usefulness of the information contained in this report, or that the use of any information, apparatus, methods, or process disclosed in this report may not infringe privately owned rights; or

B. Assumes any liability with respect to the use of, or for damages resulting from the use of any information, apparatus, method, or process disclosed in this report ("Notice," 1967).

A less legalistic disclaimer by the Labor Department reads:

The material in this project was prepared under a Grant from the . . . Department of Labor. . . . Researchers undertaking such projects under Government sponsorship are encouraged to express freely their professional judgment. Therefore, points of view or opinions stated in this document do not necessarily represent the official position or policy of the Department of Labor.

Unlike universities and professors, institutes and their staffs feel constantly obliged to make disclaimers; and yet no end of disclaimers seems sufficient to cleanse the investigator, institute, or sponsor of an element of shared responsibility.

From the standpoint of a staff member, disclaimers enhance his freedom to express views with which institute officers and board members may disagree. But regardless of the wish of enlightened sponsors and directors to promote such freedom, the public can at any time call them to account for it. No number of disclaimers can keep the press, public, or government from labeling work as a "RAND" or "Brookings" study, as an exchange between two senators and the vice-president of the Brookings Institution illustrates:

Senator Bennett. . . . When the newspapers report that this particular point of view is supported by the Brookings Institution do you disavow it?

Mr. Hartley. Well, sir, we try to disavow it in the beginning when a publication is issued, but it is almost impossible to keep up with all the places where the Brookings Institution is quoted as saying such and such is true. The best we can try to do is to protect ourselves in the very beginning, and we always try to make clear in every press release we issue announcing a publication that the material which is issued is the result of a study made by an individual, and does not represent the view of the institution.

Senator Curtis. . . . I take issue with the idea that the proper role of an institution such as yours is to disavow what your scholars write. I think you should take responsibility for it and make it available to everybody in return for the tax-exempt privilege. Your research should be of the type and of the quality that you would not have to disavow (*Tax Reform Act,* 1969, p. 5563).

The normal Brookings disclaimer states that "In publishing a study, the Institution presents it as a competent treatment of a subject worthy of public consideration. The interpretations and conclusions in such publications are those of the author or authors and do not purport to represent the views of the other staff members, officers, or trustees of the Brookings Institution." According to the bylaws of the Institute for Policy Studies, "All studies will reflect solely on the views of the individuals participating in them, and the Institute will not itself sponsor any given viewpoint." Max Singer, president of the Hudson Institute, states ". . . our principle is that the views of individual members of the staff on substantive issues are not subject to direction or control by anyone: management, Trustees, Members, or outsiders . . ." (Singer, 1969, p. 2).

Such disclaimers are honest and true. Yet if they represent all that is true about these institutes, how does it come about that the collective product of each institute, while not uniform and unvarying, has a distinctive character: The Brookings Institution operating within the "establishment," the Institute of Policy Studies, outside, and the Hudson Institute specializing in free-ranging ideas and speculations and in countering liberal dogma?

The answer, I believe, lies not alone in staff selection and the processing of manuscripts—tedious at Brookings and perfunctory at many other institutes—but in an institute's professional standards,[9] which each staff member in good standing tries to understand and to meet as best he can. That is perhaps the most fundamental and inescapable responsibility which each institute bears for the work of its staff: the stamp of its professional self-image.

Some institutes acknowledge the responsibility they can in no event escape by submitting reports with no individual's name attached, in the corporate manner of government agencies. The personal pronoun is unbecoming to a government official who is supposed to act in accordance with general policies, not personal preferences; and government publications are supposed to convey facts, not opinions. The dispassionate approach of science and engineering can induce a similar impersonality. Indeed, when scientific and engineering work is done by large teams, how can any one person take credit for the results? Even if he has directed the team, he can at most bear such responsibility as a captain bears for his troops.

Some institutes are flexible, adding or removing a caveat of individual responsibility as the sponsor wishes. According to one informant, Battelle reports normally carry the name of the author (every page bears the "B.M.I." label) but no special disclaimer. However, a disclaimer is added if requested—for example, if a government official anticipates with more anxiety than pleasure that he may be held responsible for a study. Although RAND is most careful in defining the degree of responsibility for a report, one RAND official made light of much of the disclaimer routine. "There are people in the Air Force who want a RAND label on their position papers and try to bend our efforts in their direction. . . . We don't have a 'RAND' position . . . except that some customers don't want that [disclaimer] on and . . . so it goes on and off all the time. The Secretary of the Air Force says, 'Here's a report which RAND doesn't believe, as *we* [the Air Force] don't, and it cost us

$500,000.' We've had endless discussions of the exact wording of the disclaimer but it's not worth the paper it's written on."

As of August 1970, RAND nevertheless had five separate reports series: *internal notes,* for distribution solely within RAND; *papers,* reproduced solely as a courtesy to staff, which "cannot be used . . . to convey the results of research done under a contract . . . unless the research has previously been reported to the client . . ."; *working notes,* which transmit unedited results to a client rapidly and without editing; *reports,* which receive "careful editing, technical review, and printing"; and *administrative reports,* "contract-required, periodic reports to the client on the status of work. . . ."

Formerly, (the practice has been dropped) RAND associated itself with the conclusions of a few reports by means of a formal recommendation:

The formal recommendation is a special communications device that is used on rare occasions when RAND management wishes to bring some important matter to a client's attention. The formal recommendation consists of a letter from RAND's President . . . to a representative of the sponsoring agency recommending a specific course of action. The batting average for getting some sort of client action in response to a formal recommendation has been quite high (Smith, 1966, p. 202, footnote 6).

Plainly, a formal recommendation, to which board members and officers subscribed, carried weight. The Air Force could not disregard it as readily as a staff report. A formal response was made which, according to one ancient statistic, was usually favorable.[10] Nevertheless, for the staff member, such intervention has two drawbacks: delay, since it can be time-consuming to have a report reviewed; and the substantive changes that may be required in order to secure concurrences.

At few institutes—a notable example is the Committee on Economic Development—do officers and/or board members formally concur with the conclusions of staff work. The procedure requires a subservience of staff to a higher authority which is more characteristic of political and operational than of research organizations.

ON AN INSTITUTE'S "INDEPENDENCE" Universities and nonprofit institutes claim to examine intellectual and technical questions with a degree of independence which government and industry lack because of their political and commercial interests. Government officials, however, can yield to no private citizens their responsibility to serve and, indeed, to define the public interest. Industrial spokesmen protest the arrogation by nonprofit institutions of a degree of objectivity which transcends the human lot: nonprofits, they are wont to say, have interests of their own. Radicals charge that "think tanks," professors, and endowed institutes all serve their federal and foundation sponsors or, more broadly, an elite "establishment" dedicated to the preservation of established economic and social institutions rather than to their radical transformation. Let us examine these terms, *independence* and *the public interest,* a little more closely.

Independence is like virtue or integrity, something which no self-respecting institution can admit to lack. Every institution can find some ground for uniqueness and some basis to challenge the uniqueness of other institutions. The university scientists on the President's Science Advisory Committee (PSAC) and other governmental committees are chosen, not only for distinction, but because of their independence; yet, a former PSAC member asserts, "It would not be a great exaggeration" to characterize them "as a lobby for the scientific university" (Weinberg, 1963, p. 11). Academic men who publish in the open literature claim greater intellectual freedom than the staffs of institutes which restrict publication, but the Franklin Institute Research Laboratories, which conducts classified and proprietary work, avers that it "can undertake research, development, and engineering projects for both government agencies and private industry . . . with an objectivity and lack of bias inherent in complete separation from both commercial and academic interests."[11] Richard Barnet, codirector of the Institute for Policy Studies, which accepts no government money, declares, "It is our independence that distinguishes us from the think-tanks. . . . The universities and think-tanks are working on problems *for* somebody . . ." (Clapp, 1969, p. 76). The Planning Research Corporation, a for-profit operations research company founded by Robert Krueger of RAND, stoutly denies that nonprofit institutes have any special objectivity:

The objectivity argument was correctly given at a time shortly after World War II when no professional service, for-profit organizations existed, and the objectivity of these nonprofits was being compared primarily to the large aerospace companies who appeared to have a hardware bias. However, for at least 15 years now, for-profit professional service organizations have existed and this argument doesn't hold since for-profit professional service organizations have absolutely no motive not to be objective. (Indeed, FCRC's [federal R&D centers like RAND] are in some degree possibly less objective because of close ties to a particular sponsoring government element (Planning Research Corporation, 1970).

Thus, all kinds of institutions can legitimately claim some kind of independence and none can escape some kind of self-interest. Surely the simple truth is that each is *relatively* independent of the special interests of others. Professors (without stock holdings and consultantships) may be able to assess a technology with greater independence than engineers of the affected industry; industrial engineers have no evident interest in the allocation of government funds among universities; a for-profit research company has less interest in the outcome of a study of medical costs than a nonprofit hospital, surgeon's association, medical insurance company, or union health service; and so forth.

Several factors contribute to an institute's independence.

"Get capital" was John D. Rockefeller's advice to the ambitious. Capital is to an institute what land is to a farmer: a source of independence from the changing fortunes of the marketplace. Operating foundations, which need please no sponsor, are, in principle, the most independent of institutes, though the staff must still please the director; he, the trustees; and they, one another. The president and board, in turn, must satisfy the state attorney, Congress, the IRS, and, in varying degrees, the public at large. The liberal Center for the Study of Democratic Institutions and the conservative American Institute for Economic Research have reasoned they can achieve greater independence from public contributions than from endowments. (Political candidates seek, but do not always find, independence in the same way.) The bylaws of the American Institute for Economic Research state:

In order to avoid any possibility of bias resulting either from an attempt to satisfy wealthy donors or to protect substantial invested funds, the Institute shall seek to derive its support primarily from many small contributions by the general public and the distribution of publications and reports presenting the results of the scientific reasearch undertaken. No attempt shall be made to seek an endowment fund from wealthy interests ("First Thirty-Five Years," 1968, p. 4).

Institutes not blessed with endowment have found two diametrically opposed routes toward financial security: a large level-of-effort contract or a multiplicity of small contracts. The level-of-effort contract, often for five years with a budget set by annual negotiation, has given many but not all R&D centers greater financial stability than nonendowed institutes. But this financial stability cannot be equated with intellectual independence without a separate examination of the terms of the center contract and the actual working relationship between center and government staff. The Air Force has given RAND a degree of independence in determining its own work matched by few other centers involved in policy or applied research. Even greater freedom may be delegated by the tolerant leaders of the NSF and the AEC to centers engaged solely in basic scientific research. Applied research centers and institutes which work in large measure on problems assigned by their sponsors can be said to forgo only their programmatic, not their intellectual, independence, so long as they retain their freedom to think as they please about the problems; we will return to this point shortly. Since it makes no sense to thrust a technical problem upon staff who are incompetent to deal with it, the loss of professional independence entailed in being "given" a sponsor's problem can be less than is imagined by academic men (who do not lack professional constraints of their own).

It is hard to believe that some institutes prefer innumerable small projects to a few large ones, but that appears to be the philosophy of the gargantuan Battelle, where it is reasoned that a great many sponsors provide more security than a few; plainly, applied institutes are more independent of any one sponsor than an R&D center can be of its sponsoring agency. Whether a center is better off—that is, more secure financially and more free programmatically—with one or with several major federal sponsors is much debated today. Formerly, when rising federal expenditures enabled centers to expand budgets and staffs yearly, most were content to hold to a single agency; now, many are cultivating additional agencies.

A second factor upon which the idea of institutional independence can rest is freedom of operation: an institute's ability to set its own administrative regulations, salaries, and personnel benefits; the freedom of staff to talk to anyone they wish and to report the results of their work to whomsoever they please. On these tests, again, endowed institutes and basic research centers are usually the most independent, but no type of institute is free to operate exactly as it pleases in every respect. Administrative and salary restrictions have been imposed on most R&D centers; few applied research centers and institutes allow staff to publish without prior approval; and all institutes must refrain from partisan political activity.

There is a natural tendency for an institute to make much of the particular freedom it enjoys. For example, those whose staffs are free to publish demean the value of privileged information; staffs engaged in classified research speak of the excitement and importance of their work—one staff member argued half seriously that those who publish freely can hardly be doing anything *very* important. RAND staff pride themselves on the freedom to determine the work they do for the Air Force. However, staff of other Defense centers do not act or speak like meek, docile, and servile men; they hold that their freedom is greater than supposed, since they, in fact, initiate much of their work, if only through the persuasion of government officials.

Radical critics charge that he who pays the piper calls the tune by putting the questions to be answered, and that institutes therefore serve the interests of sponsors rather than of "the public." "RAND has been intellectually independent to the extent of strenuously questioning its employer's concrete policies," Philip Green allows, but "it has *not* been 'independent' to the extent of questioning either the nature of the jobs they are performing or their basic values. . . ."

It is no secret, for instance, that some present RAND personnel disagree with American policy toward China and have produced work that can be read as calling into question certain basic American values in this area, rather than mere policy preferences. At the same time, it is impossible to believe that those agencies that fund RAND's work—especially the Air Force—will continue to support research that does not give them any payoff and is not likely to do so in the future. . . . were RAND to become known as a prominent lobbyist *against* the administration's Asian policy, as it was *for* deterrence policy, it would surely lose its favored position. Be that as it may, my proposition is certainly not put to the test by the mere fact of RAND's being hospitable to diverse viewpoints. Research embarrassing to the client can, after all, be ignored (as, there is every evidence, work emanating from RAND which is critical of our China policy is being ignored). On the other hand, research deemed helpful by the client has a special chance to be influential . . . (Green, 1968, pp. 314–317).

John Foster, Jr., Director of Defense Research and Engineering, also asks, "Can 'independent consultation' occur in a meaningful way when DoD is the principal employer of so many leading scientists? Putting this more crudely, hasn't DoD bribed the academic research community?" His answer is a plain "no." Research money does not make honest men dishonest:

No matter what side of an issue they are on, and no matter whose payroll they are on, most American scientists concerned with defense are not shy! The nation, the research community, and the academic community, thrive on debate. I support it. I get in and enjoy it. . . . If university scientists and engineers were entirely out of Defense work, they simply could not participate as technically informed individuals in debates on critical defense issues. They could not contribute as effectively to the public understanding essential for our system of government (Foster, 1969).

I do not think these two positions are far apart. As Winston Churchill did not become His Majesty's First Minister to preside over the dissolution of the British Empire, so no agency deliberately fosters its own destruction. Self-preservation will inevitably limit the research it sponsors and the advice it pays for (though it receives gratuitously much advice that falls outside that limit).[12] A sophisticated agency will solicit a wide range of advice, for the wider the range, the greater will be its alternatives for action and its readiness to anticipate and rebut public criticism.

Though all nonprofit institutes must refrain from partisan political activity in the narrow sense of supporting one political party or candidate, in a broader sense all must have a definable political and ideological character. Staff, officers, and trustees, being human, have identifiable political convictions and tolerances; indeed, institutions may be categorized as "left," "right," or "center" according to the general disposition of staff and trustees (which need not be identical, but must overlap). Thus, the Institute for Policy Studies is "left"; the Brookings Institution, predominantly "centrist" or "liberal" today, as it was "conservative" in the 1930s; the American Institute for Public Policy Research is "conservative." Granted, ideological outlook may assume more significance in social, economic, and policy studies than in the sciences and engineering.

If particular institutes have an identifiable political outlook, then none is absolutely "independent" in the sense of having no ideological commitment. A significant capacity for independent judgment remains, within the institute's ideological horizon.

THE "PUBLIC INTEREST" What nonprofit institute dares state that it does not serve the "public interest"? Charity and wisdom may incline a profit-making organization to do so, but that is ancillary to avowedly private purposes. Nonprofit institutes, however, assume special statutory obligations to serve the public in exchange for their special tax status. According to a plaque in the Brookings entryway, Robert Somers Brookings was a "believer in the power of knowledge to serve the public interest"; RAND provides scientific analyses "for governments and for other human institutions that serve the public interest" and "research at Rand pursues problems wherever they may lead, without concern for special interests or bureaucratic positions on policy and technical issues"; the Institute for Public Administration conducts only research "clearly in the public interest"; the "primary objective" of Battelle, president S. L. Fawcett writes, "is the advancement and utilization of science for the benefit of mankind"; "The ultimate client of the Center [for Policy Research] . . . is Society; its needs guide the Center's work . . ."; "The [Hudson] Institute is . . . committed only to intellectual quality and to the national and world interest."[13] And so it goes. There is no reason to question the sincerity of these statements—only the operational procedures by which they are defined, and the peculiar circumstances that enable so many institutes to serve so many sponsors and, simultaneously, the public.

Of course, the "public" is another form of virtue, a projection of one's larger and kinder inclinations (which are yet, on any saintly scale, appallingly narrow) upon the body politic.

"Public" is often, probably too often, equated with "government." As has been noted, the taxability of institute profits from proprietary research has not been resolved, but profits from research for any governmental unit—federal, state, or local—are unquestionably exempt. Were there no other reason, that alone would render most institutes hospitable to government agencies. The larger reason is a lack of choice. Government has grown so dominant in so many fields that few institutes can subsist without its funds. Applied research institutes set up to serve industry now derive the bulk of their income from the government and it is likely that only a small fraction of institutes—operating foundations, some endowed institutes, and a few others (mainly cushioned institutes pursuing doctrinal interests)—today operate mostly on private funds.

As the executive agencies of government represent special constituencies—in defense, agriculture, labor, commerce, health, education, and so forth—they often reflect the parochial interests of these constituencies rather than the broader public interest. Insofar as our federal government of limited powers does define and represent that broader public interest, it does so through the overarching policies of the Congress and the White House. However, neither of these bodies has the funds, the staff, or the time to administer or monitor major R&D programs. Except for the small but important contracts occasionally let by a few congressional committees, presidential commissions, the National Security Council, and other units in the Executive Office of the President, these high policy-making bodies normally rely on research commissioned by executive agencies and, of course, on the free information, advice, and pleading of every vocal national interest group and individual.

For all the defects and parochialism of federal executive agencies, institute administrators affirm that they are far more experienced, tolerant, and broad-gauged contractors than are state and local government agencies and private industry. Only private foundations are ranked with, or ahead of, federal agencies in the breadth and importance of questions posed and the professional and administrative freedom permitted. But foundations can provide financial support to few institutes and they have come under attack from both the left and the right as representing another form of self-interest—presumably that of enlightened or unenlightened capitalism—rather than the divergent "public" interests which their critics divine.

While executive agencies may be criticized on many grounds—parochialism, political timidity, and their controls over the release of reports—as spokesmen for the public interest they have assets that other community groups lack in equal measure: their resources, their legal legitimacy, and their administrative responsibility. Businessmen and radicals, farmers and professors, criminals, students, white racists, black militants, revolutionists and reactionaries who challenge the legitimacy of government agencies have no more legitimate, representative, and responsible agencies to substitute for them.

"Who is the client?" in government-sponsored domestic research, asked the provost of a great university. "The executive? The community? But it is very hard to interact with 'the community.'" The identical question was asked by a committee of the New York City Council which had protested the volume of confidential research and consulting contracts let by the mayor's office to the New York City–RAND Institute, McKinsey & Co., and other groups:

Who is the Client?
When a consultant works for government, who is the client? Is it the executive branch which engages him, or the legislative body which raises the funds to pay him, or the citizen whose stake in his work may be far more vital than a stockholder's interest in a private corporation?

The consultants presently employed by the city and the agencies which retain them believe beyond any question that the client is the executive branch of government.

We conclude, however, that the client is not solely the executive branch, but the legislature as well and ultimately the city's citizens. It cannot be otherwise in a free society ("Excerpts," 1970, p. 25).

Unfortunately, the "city's citizens" cannot speak with one voice to a consultant; and legislatures have not normally been equipped to administer a substantial research program, though some interesting proposals have been advanced to enable them to do so.

The doctrine of full disclosure to the public of the findings of publicly financed research is, like the Wilsonian doctrine of open diplomacy, a utopian goal. It can counteract inclinations toward excessive secrecy, but taken too seriously it can only attenuate the quality of research by limiting its objectives, data, conclusions, and recommendations to those which can be freely revealed. A degree of confidentiality is as necessary to good government as to good diplomacy, good journalism, good social research, and good human relations.

In conclusion, it may be said that "the public interest," like beauty, lies in good measure in the eye of the beholder. For most practical purposes, most research institutes have equated it with the interests of executive governmental agencies. That equation contains manifest deficiencies but it is difficult to find—and to finance—a better one. Two limited alternatives are the interests represented by legislatures and by private foundations; and, of course, any private group or individual is free to advance his own.

Since the agencies which fund research play such an important part in defining the public interest, those citizens and scholars who are dissatisfied with prevailing definitions can only seek to establish new agencies which promulgate better definitions; and, to a modest extent, this has been done. Senators who criticized the role of the Department of Defense in financing foreign area research sought to establish a National Social Science Foundation to sponsor such research; the scholars connected with the Institute for Policy Studies, the Cambridge Institute, and the Bay Area Institute, who criticize all governmental financing, obtain funds solely from private sources; and it is not recorded that Karl Marx applied to any government agency for assistance in studying his conception of the public interest.

Part Four

Some Trends and Problems

8. Proliferating Institutes

Sometimes it seems to me that institutes are looked to for the salvation of humanity and certainly of the nation and most certainly for the solution of every national problem. What is more singular, it is often a *new* institute that is called for to deal with each new problem, which occasions the gloomy thought: Why will a new institute succeed if old ones have failed? And how long does it take a new institute to grow old?

A National Science Board commission recently called for the creation of 25 interdisciplinary institutes to conduct research on, and in direct ways alleviate, major social problems. Though the number of institutes was specified, the problems were not (*Knowledge into Action,* 1969, pp. 87–95). However, a fat folder I have kept for several years contains requests and proposals for the creation (usually by the federal government) of the following institutes:

A National Back Institute proposed by Senator Joseph Clark as a new part of the National Institutes of Health. "Why not an institute to coordinate our efforts to unravel the mysteries of the ailment of the back?" (*Congressional Record—Senate,* November 20, 1967, p. S 16782.)[1]

"Senator Ralph Yarborough, the new chairman of the powerful Labor and Public Welfare Committee, is sponsoring a bill for a lung institute; other proposals call for a kidney institute, a gastrointestinal institute, an institute for marine pharmacology, and a biomedical engineering institute. . . . Late last year a new Eye Institute and Institute for Environmental Health Sciences were set up" ("Washington Science Outlook," 1969, p. 19).

A National Institute of Building Sciences proposed by Senator Jacob Javits and eight other senators as a government-funded, independent nonprofit organization "to develop and publish standards affecting all building

99

materials; to develop and publish standards for use in local building codes; to promote and coordinate tests and studies of new building products and construction techniques"; . . . (*Congressional Record—Senate,* June 19, 1969, p. S6769).

An Institute for Environmental Studies proposed by the Environmental Study Group of the National Academy of Sciences as a nonprofit organization financed partly by government and mainly by private sources to "1) do long-range planning for the enhancement of the environment; 2) provide early warning on potential threats to the environment; 3) conduct rapid analytical studies in response to emergencies; 4) carry out rapid field analysis; and 5) systematically study and analyze the social, political, economic, administrative, legislative, and other factors that influence environmental decisions and the management of the environment" (*Institutions for Effective Management,* part I, January 1970, pp. 8, 17–18).

A National Laboratory for Environmental Science proposed by the same environmental study group as a government-funded, private organization operated "perhaps by a consortium of universities . . . to carry out research in environmental science, and . . . be responsible for the quick-reaction field function . . ." (Ibid., p. 44).

An Institute on Retirement Income proposed by Senator Harrison Williams as "a think tank agency" like the Urban Institute to "conduct studies and make recommendations designed to enable retired individuals to enjoy an adequate retirement income" (*Congressional Record—Senate,* October 1, 1968, p. S 11815).

A National Institute of Crime Prevention and Detection proposed by Representative James Scheuer, of uncertain structure but seemingly akin to one of the National Institutes of Health, to bring interdisciplinary talents to bear on "developing the knowledge we need to devise new tools, new methods and procedures, and new laws to bring tranquillity and security to every American street and every American home" (*Congressional Record—House,* July 14, 1966, p. 14993).

Six Federal Regional Maximum Security Research Centers for the Criminally Insane proposed by Representative Roman Pucinski, "for housing prisoners convicted either under Federal laws or State laws for the purpose of intensive research into their past behavior patterns . . . from such research we can devise techniques for early detection of the potential criminal . . . [and] develop standards and guidelines for police enforcement officials" (*Congressional Record—House,* July 20, 1966, pp. 15604–5).

An Institute for R&D on Crime and Criminal Justice proposed by the Institute for Defense Analyses as a major, private, federally financed organization for scientific and technological research by interdisciplinary teams on "basic studies on crime . . . operation [and management] of the total criminal justice system . . . information systems . . . means for preventing and deterring crime . . . police apprehension . . . criminalistics . . . and offender rehabilitation . . ." (*Task Force Report,* 1967, p. 82).

An Institute for Continuing Studies of Juvenile Justice proposed by Senator Charles Percy and Representatives Abner Mikva and Edward Biester as a federal organization "to devise better ways for dealing with juvenile offenders" ("Juvenile Institute," 1969).

A Suburban Institute proposed by Maryland State Senator Fred Wineland as a privately financed organization located in his county to study "serious sociological problems" in the suburbs. The institute would "ascertain the causes and extent of each problem and then design and recommend relevant action programs to alleviate and prevent them" ("Sickles, Wineland," 1968).

A National Institute of Education proposed by President Nixon as an educational counterpart to the National Institutes of Health "to begin the serious, systematic search for new knowledge needed to make educational opportunity truly equal . . . to develop broader and more sensitive measurements of learning. . . . In doing so, it should pay as much heed to what are called the 'immeasurables' of schooling . . . such as responsibility, wit, and humanity as it does to verbal and mathematical achievement" (*New York Times,* March 4, 1970, p. 28).

An Institute of Urban Communication proposed by the National Advisory Commission on Civil Disorders (the Kerner Commission) as a private nonprofit organization to "review press and television coverage of riot and racial news and publicly award praise and blame."

An Institute for Scientific Judgment proposed by Arthur Kantrowitz as a federally created organization of uncertain character to hear opposing advocates on important issues with technical elements and then publish "a statement of scientific facts as currently seen by unbiased judges" together with their opinions (*Science,* May 12, 1967, pp. 763–764).

A National Goals Institute proposed by Arjay Miller as a federally created and financed interdisciplinary organization "to develop an overview of America's needs and resources. . . . The mission . . . would be limited to setting forth those quantifiable needs that are basic to social progress and on which there is general agreement. . . . Something of this kind is needed if we as a nation are to see our problems whole and learn to deal with them effectively. Unless we adopt a total view, we must resign ourselves to patchwork progress" (*Journal of Finance,* May 1969, pp. 177–179).

A number of *National Socio-Technical Institutes* proposed by Alvin Weinberg as modified R&D centers with both "software" and "hardware" skills—"mission-oriented institutes that combine the characteristics of

RAND or the Brookings Institution and those of Los Alamos"—to mount a concerted attack on major social problems with a technical component (Weinberg, 1967, 1970).

A number of *"social problem research groups or institutes"* proposed by the President's Task Force on Science Policy and supported by "sufficient Federal funds"; apparently they would be private organizations of not merely an interdisciplinary but an interoccupational character—"wide participation by industry, labor, and the professions generally" (*Science and Technology,* 1970, pp. 18–19).

A *National Institute for the Social Sciences* proposed by Senator George McGovern as a quasi-independent federal agency. "I am convinced that if an appropriate viable Federal structure is created it will make a significant contribution toward solution of the multiple social problems of today and tomorrow. This Institute will provide a practical blueprint for action by relating multifarious national priorities to fiscal reality. It will provide members of Congress with a unified body of data . . ." (*Congressional Record—Senate,* November 11, 1969, p. S 14085).

A *National Institute for Advanced Research and Public Policy* proposed by a National Research Council Committee as a federally financed research center "to strengthen the capacity of the federal government to use the knowledge and methods of the behavioral sciences effectively," to "provide a setting for . . . future-oriented studies," and to "facilitate the recruitment of behavioral scientists into the government by providing grants for innovative research throughout the country" (*The Behavioral Sciences,* 1968, p. 105).

The list could be extended *ad infinitum,* and warrants a few observations.

The word *institute* may be used not only to designate operating organizations such as those discussed in this monograph, but also agencies which fund research. Perhaps the best-known example of both usages is the National Institutes of Health (NIH),[2] which operates its own laboratories and also administers extensive research grants.

Since the objectives of both types of "institute" are also extraordinarily diverse, ranging from scholarly contemplation to mass engineering—everything from the contemplation of navels to the development of naval reactors—plainly one must know precisely what kind of organization and activity is being proposed before its merits can be assessed. Yet many proposals are so painfully vague that this can be quite impossible. A choice example is the National Institute of Education, whose nature and objectives remained obscure a year after it was proposed by President Nixon in March 1970. Indeed, the Administration thereupon contracted with RAND to tell it what it was asking for.[3] Such vagueness may represent a calculated strategy to enlist broad political support by postponing battles over budgetary allocations until after an institute has been established; or, as is often the case with the proposals of scholars, it may simply reflect ignorance of administrative realities.

To call for a new operating institute is not merely a way to focus resources on a problem; it is a statement that the normal mode of academic organization is inadequate for that purpose. It expresses a wish to establish an organization which will give central, and not peripheral, attention to a problem; to assemble a "critical mass" of talent and equipment for a coordinated assault; to break free of established institutions and make a fresh start; and, no doubt, to exploit prevailing interests and opportunities, and to capture available funds, in the manner of any other entrepreneurial enterprise.

Empty entrepreneurship has been criticized by Dael Wolfle and Paul Dressel as serving pointlessly to disperse and weaken existing institutions. In a 1963 editorial in *Science,* Wolfle wrote:

There is one kind of independent research institution that we wish to challenge: the small, inadequately financed one that is formed to secure government grants and contracts and to live on the proceeds of such support. . . . These are institutions established for the pleasure, the profit, or the aggrandizement of their organizers. . . . They are financially dependent upon agencies that support them, but since they are not really needed by those agencies, the support is likely to be on a short-term or individual-grant basis . . . in terms of the total scientific effort, all they accomplish is to move a few men from university laboratories and contact with students to enable them to carry out pretty much the same kind of work they could have done at their universities, often with better resources of colleagues, library, and equipment. Neither in terms of economics nor the advancement of science does it seem desirable to support such institutions (Wolfle, 1963).

Addressing themselves to needless institutes within universities, Dressel and his coauthors (1969) observe that some institutes "have obviously been formed by faculty and administration agreement in the hope . . . of attracting foundation or federal funds. Some have been introduced simply to provide title and status to attract or keep a widely recognized scholar. . . . Other institutes have resulted from the entrepreneurial efforts of individuals. . . . What is clear is that the development of institutes is often opportunistic, expedient, and competitive. . . . The basic difficulty is that universities have come to be dominated by their professors rather than by their purposes."

Universities are now paying more attention to their purposes than they did a decade ago. Many have adopted stricter criteria and review procedures for the admissibility of sponsored research and for the formation of new institutes. The slackened demand for Ph.D.'s and the abatement of federal expenditures will enable university administrators to exercise tighter control over faculty research. It remains to be seen whether this will reduce the number of new academic institutes or merely change their objectives, in keeping with new national needs and intellectual fashions.

The birth of institutions, as of babies, is more a natural than a rational process. All that can normally be asked is that sponsors make an open-minded inquiry as to the need for a proposed institute, and be governed accordingly. A fundamental consideration in assessing that need is the value of the proposed work. But there are innumerable, incommensurable measures of value. Thus medical research has a singular human value. Without good health, John D. Rockefeller, Sr., thought, little can be accomplished, and surely his institute has been one of the best and most valuable of private, as NIH has been one of the most valuable of governmental, institutes.

Value per dollar or program poses a sterner test—for example, the philosophy and physics programs of the Rockefeller Institute and the cancer chemotherapy program of NIH have been criticized by qualified scientists. RAND has been more valuable to the Air Force than to the Army, and each year's budget tests its continuing value. The work of the Stanford Research Institute and Battelle has been of greater value to government and industry than to pure scientists. Before announcing late in 1970 the forthcoming elimination of several regional laboratories, the Office of Education had presumably concluded that they were of less value to the nation than the remaining laboratories. Were we to accept the similar bureaucratic and sociological assumptions that all institutions fulfill essential social functions, the value of an institution could almost be equated with its income and longevity.

Of course, the value of proposed work must be judged not only by its significance but by its practicability. Neither in pure nor in applied research is success certain, unless the work is too routine to merit the term "research." A problem may be extraordinarily difficult and yet so important that we should try to solve it: for example, the problem of developing a breeder reactor, fusion power, or a cure for cancer or the common cold. However, the importance of a problem is not sufficient cause for the government to spend large sums of money on it. There must be some expectation of progress or the work should not be undertaken (or, subsequently, continued). It may be highly desirable to eliminate old age and death, blindness and sickness, anguish, fear, anxiety, loneliness, hatred, madness, and murder: but what are the prospects that research will do so?[4]

What private citizens do with their money is more their own affair; all the public need ask is: Does an institute injure anyone, and does its work warrant tax exemption? Private citizens, therefore, may establish institutes to study ways of eliminating gravity, developing extrasensory powers, or promoting peace, altruism, astrology, and modern art.

In applied research and engineering, success means a new and better product or process. It may even be possible to estimate its economic value. In the pure sciences, the most common tests of success are intellectual judgments made within each profession. The proposed pure scientific installations which have been the subject of most widespread debate, because they are among the most expensive, have been the large high-energy accelerators. There is no evident point at which physicists would themselves halt their inquiries, and the construction of increasingly expensive accelerators, if Congress and the taxpayers did not intervene.

Whereas in high-energy physics the public faces the issue of cost, in social science it faces the issue of knowledge itself: of the fruitfulness of different approaches and the degree to which meaningful and useful knowledge can be obtained about designated behavior. As our social problems have become exacerbated, more and more calls have been made upon the social science disciplines which seem best able to understand and, hopefully, to solve them. Many of the institutes listed at the beginning of this chapter are of that type. Their prospect of success in understanding social problems and in devising effective courses of action for dealing with them rests heavily on the present state of the art in these disciplines and the possibilities of improving it. It serves only the short-term interest of some social scientists to pretend that they can now answer adequately many of the questions they are asked; and, in my opinion, the likelihood of markedly improving their capacity to do so is less than is commonly admitted. If that is true, proposals to establish social problem institutes should be examined with special care to ensure that their tasks are realistic and demonstrably performable. Institutes that are financed with public funds should serve a function that is demonstrable not only to their staff, but to the public at large. Research should be a tool, not a religion.[5]

9. Diversification

In recent years, many institutes—especially those working predominantly for the Department of Defense, AEC, and NASA—have attempted to diversify their sponsors and activities. The main reasons are a tightening of R&D expenditures, a congressional ceiling on Department of Defense center budgets, and a sense that the nation faces critical problems which are not the responsibility of these three agencies. An additional reason is a growing fatigue with, and/or aversion to, military, nuclear, and aerospace technology, which is viewed as wasteful, destructive, or simply irrelevant to deeper national and human needs.

It should be stressed that antimilitary (still less, antitechnological or scientific) sentiment is not so potent at institutes as it is on campuses, where the issue has been aggravated by the vulnerability of students to the draft and the vulnerability of faculty to students. In response to "confrontations," applied research institutes have reaffirmed their readiness to conduct Department of Defense R&D. At Department of Defense centers, open staff opposition to defense work simply would not be tolerated; however, that position is entirely compatible with efforts to secure nondefense funding. As we shall see, the Department of Defense itself has endorsed such efforts.

So, each in its own way, institutes have attempted to undertake work which is socially "relevant." On one coast, RAND has moved into studies of domestic problems; on the other, the Institute for Advanced Study is establishing a program in the social sciences. (About the same time, each institute got a new director who was an economist; each director accepted his post with the understanding that he might try to broaden the institute's activities.) Similarly, the Brookings Institution inaugurated studies of social and welfare economics and politics; the National Bureau of Economic Research began studies of the economics of health, crime, the courts, cities, and the problems of social measurement; the Riverside Research Institute, heavily involved in radar research for the Department of Defense, started to work on education, police communications, and biomedical engineering; Herman Kahn's Hudson Institute, long dependent primarily upon Department of Defense financing, now receives a substantial portion of its income from private industry. Its January 1970 newsletter states that "for the first time in Hudson's history, defense-related studies will be less than 50 percent of Hudson's total effort." The proportion of applied research institutes' income from private industry has been rising, whereas that from the Department of Defense has been falling. If the remainder of this chapter is devoted to the diversification efforts of R&D centers and especially of Department of Defense centers, it is simply because these are particularly well documented.[1]

The poorly funded Office of Education centers have always been free to seek funds from other sources (and also to compete for additional Education Office funds). As the funding of Department of Defense and AEC centers slackened, their centers displayed greater interest in, and these two agencies exhibited greater tolerance of, diversification. However, to date, success has been limited; much effort has been extended to little avail.

PERVERSE STATISTICS The relationship between government statistics and government policy can be perverse. When meaningful policy hinges on meaningful statistics, policy makers grasp at statistics as a drowning man grasps at a log—or stick. But social statistics are not instrumented stellar observations; they represent the fallible observations of many men about other equally fallible men.

These reflections are prompted by the recent case of Department of Defense R&D centers. "I've got a little list," said the Mikado's Lord High Executioner. It seems that a fallible little list of the department's centers which NSF had maintained for statistical purposes since 1951 or 1952 and began to publish annually in 1962—perhaps they were not published earlier to hide defects in the list that then became plain—was soon seized upon by the Congress as the basis of budgetary restrictions.

In 1965, following congressional inquiries into salaries and perquisites at Department of Defense centers, the House Committee on Appropriations initiated restrictions on Department of Defense center budgets which were renewed for four succeeding years.[2] They have loosely been called budget "cuts," but in the Washington idiom, that can mean cuts in administration requests— which is not necessarily a cut in appropriations. If an organization escapes from the iron financial curtain of Defense centers for the free world outside (as most would like, but few have been able, to do), is its budget available for distribution to remaining centers or is it (as I imagine) subtracted from the total pool?[3] The Director of Defense Research and Engineering has usually been free to make allocations within the budgetary pool, so that the budget of a center may rise or fall more than that of the pool. However, though the formal congressional ceiling on the center appropriations was relaxed in fiscal 1970,[4] the pressure on their budgets did not ease.

After a sharp rise in fiscal 1966 and a modest rise in 1967, Department of Defense obligations to nonprofit centers have remained stable; AEC obligations rose modestly for a few years longer before leveling off (Table 10). The obligation of "other agencies" during this period consisted, in fact, of NASA obligations to the Jet Propulsion Laboratory, which have dropped, and of NSF and Office of Education obligations to their centers, which have risen moderately.

Department of Defense obligations to 16 individual centers are reported in Table 11. For most centers, 1967 was an equivocal year, 1968 a decidedly bad one, and 1969, somewhat better. After the financial havoc of 1968, 13 centers received small increases, but, allowing for inflation, most were worse off in 1969 than they had been in 1966.

What is missing from Table 11 is any indication of the funding

TABLE 10
Agency obligations at nonprofit R&D centers, 1965–1971

	Agency obligations (millions)			
Fiscal year	*Total*	*DOD*	*AEC*	*Other*
1965	$430.3	$148.9	$190.4	$ 91.0
1966	810.5	261.0	427.5	122.0
1967	890.0	294.1	445.0	150.9
1968	948.3	295.8	481.2	171.3
1969	963.9	299.7	495.5	168.7
1970*	969.3	290.1	504.5	174.7
1971*	969.8	291.3	492.5	186.0

*Estimated.
SOURCE: National Science Foundation, 1966–1970.

TABLE 11 *Defense Department obligations to R&D centers, 1966–1969 (millions of dollars)*

Center	Fiscal year			
	1966	*1967*	*1968*	*1969†*
Aerospace	$ 66.2	$ 74.9	$ 72.0	$ 74.3
Lincoln Laboratory*	40.4	59.5	39.1	40.0
Applied Physics Laboratory (Hopkins)*	37.4	48.7	32.8	37.5
MITRE	27.9	33.2	32.6	34.1
RAND	19.6	20.8	20.4	21.2
Institute for Defense Analyses	13.3	11.2	10.5	10.9
Research Analysis Corporation	11.2	9.8	9.6	10.0
Ordnance Research Laboratory*	9.5	8.1	7.2	7.4
Center for Naval Analyses*	7.0	9.1	8.8	9.2
Applied Physics Laboratory (University of Washington)*	6.0	2.8	3.2	3.0
Electromagnetic Compatability Analysis Center	4.9	4.8	4.7	4.5
Hudson Laboratory*	4.8	4.7	4.8	3.4
Human Resources Research Office*	2.8	3.4	3.4	4.0
Center for Research in Social Systems*	2.3	1.9	1.6	2.0
Analytical Services	1.3	1.3	1.5	1.6
Army Mathematics Center*	1.3	1.3	1.3	1.4
Hudson Institute¶	.8			
Subtotal	256.7	295.7	253.6	264.4
Subcontracts over $1 million				
Lincoln Laboratory*	23.0	18.2	24.1	27.5
Applied Physics Laboratory (Hopkins)*	18.5	12.2	9.4	12.1
Ordnance Research Laboratory*		1.4	2.2	1.1
Subtotal	41.5	31.8	35.7	40.8
TOTAL	$298.2	$327.5	$289.3	$305.1
Total RDT&E‡	$253.8	$291.6	$252.3	$270.5
Index: 1966 = 100				
Total	100	109.8	97.0	102.3
Adjusted for inflation§	100	104.6	88.0	88.4

* University-managed.
† Estimated.
‡ Research, development, testing, and evaluation.
§ Allowing 5 percent yearly increases in the cost of living.
¶ Not classified as a center after 1966.
SOURCE: *Congressional Record — Senate,* July 9, 1969, p. S 7766.

these centers have obtained from non-Defense sources as well as from Defense agencies other than their primary sponsors. Table 12 gives some data on the degree of financial diversification in 1967 not only at centers of the Department of Defense but also at those of AEC, NASA, and NSF.

Evidently there has been little change in the last four years, for in October 1970 the Office of the Director of Defense Research and Engineering reported the proportion of non-Defense funding at its centers as follows: RAND, 25 percent; MITRE, 20 percent; the Johns Hopkins Applied Physics Laboratory, 10 percent; the Research Analyses Corporation, Institute for Defense Analyses, Center for Naval Analyses, and Lincoln Laboratory, less than 5 percent each; and remaining centers, 0 percent.[5] (These figures refer to all non-Department of Defense sources; those in Table 12, to all sources other than the center's primary sponsor.)

On March 4, 1969, Defense Secretary Melvin Laird sent a letter to cabinet secretaries and agency heads expressing the hope that the Department of Defense centers "may be of assistance to your department in its efforts to overcome our domestic problems." He invited them to deal directly with the centers and offered to assist "in assessing various technical and administrative alternatives." This represented a change in formal Defense policy (though such a change can arise from the official recognition of previously un-acknowledged facts). As Laird stated:

In the past these organizations generally have not participated in non-Defense activities largely because the Department of Defense felt that such "diversification" might dilute the effort assigned to critical national security work. A careful examination of this position determined that in many cases the . . . [centers] have skills which might be used quite fruit-fully by other departments of the Federal Government, as well as state and city governments. . . . We do not expect that the total annual non-DoD activity at any one . . . [center] would exceed more than approximately one-fifth of their total annual effort.

In a covering memorandum, Director of Defense Research and Engineering John Foster, Jr., advised center presidents that "this letter is intended to serve as official approval and stimulus for you to review your opportunities to help with domestic needs such as transportation, urban development, housing, pollution control, medical services and other fields." The 20 percent ceiling was not

TABLE 12
Percent of
nonprofit R&D
center funds
from secondary
sources, 1967

Agency and center	R&D funding (millions), 1967	Percent from secondary sources,* 1967
Department of Defense		
RAND	$ 22.8	35
Research Analysis Corporation	11.8	22
MITRE	36.4	21
Applied Physics Laboratory (Hopkins)	62.9	20
Naval Biological Laboratory	2.0	20
Hudson Laboratory	4.7	14
Center for Naval Analyses	9.3	9
Francis Bitter National Magnet Laboratory	2.5	7
Institute for Defense Analyses	14.9	5
Nine Others	172.7	1 or less
Atomic Energy Commission		
Oak Ridge National Laboratory†	79.2	11
Pacific Northwest Laboratory	40.4	5
Livermore Radiation Laboratory	106.2	3
Brookhaven National Laboratory	48.3	2
Berkeley Radiation Laboratory	37.7	2
Seven Others	212.6	0
National Aeronautics and Space Administration		
Jet Propulsion Laboratory	226.3	0.5
National Science Foundation		
National Center for Atmospheric Research	14.3	16
Two Others	17.6	0

* Including all other government and nongovernment sources but its primary sponsor (for example, at RAND, the percentage includes funds from Defense agencies other than the Air Force).

† Managed by a profit-making company, Union Carbide.

SOURCE: Welles et al., 1969, p. 345. (The Department of Defense entries do not always coincide with those reported in Table 11.)

absolute; but "we would not expect" a center to exceed it "without the general concurrence" of its principal sponsor, who should be informed "about your plans and activities."[6]

According to Defense officials, at a 1968 cabinet meeting President Lyndon Johnson had asked what the departments could do to help solve domestic problems. Defense Secretary Clark Clifford thereupon appointed a committee to suggest concrete steps, and this was one of its recommendations. Thus, as they saw it, the initiative for the diversification policy had come from the Secretary's office. Yet that office could hardly have been unaware of the efforts of many centers, especially RAND and MITRE, to find a way around budgetary ceilings. Subsequently, Daniel Moynihan and some other members of President Nixon's White House staff also pushed the policy in the hope that the Defense centers might improve the research and planning of the newer domestic agencies.

The choice of a 20 percent figure is of some interest. Only RAND exceeded it in 1970; and, whatever anyone else might think, RAND officers have not felt bound by that figure, since they regard RAND not as a "captive" center in bondage to the government, but as an independent, private organization conceived in inalienable freedom. In any event, the problem of most centers has not been to exceed the 20 percent, but to reach it.

In 1962, when Harold Brown held John Foster's post, he had suggested a lower level for, and taken a dimmer view of, diversification:

I have felt . . . [that for a center to take] support from other agencies on something that is related to your main line of endeavor but which your parent agency feels they can't support is justified up to some small fraction of the laboratory's endeavor, maybe 5 or 10 percent. If it gets to be more than that, then you start being a job shop, that is, dependent upon specific projects. Then you get into all the problems that go with that; scrambling for projects rather than taking up an overall mission and feeling enough confidence in its support so that you can keep working on it. . . . (*Systems Development and Management*, 1962, part 2, p. 482).

"Job shop" is an unkind expression for an organization which seems to have no purpose of its own but takes whatever work is available, as a laundry takes any bundle of wash. In the course of my interviewing, it was applied frequently to applied research institutes.

In the past, this expression would simply have been inapplicable to R&D centers; but for some it is now becoming plausible. "Scrambling for projects" is painfully prophetic of the prospect that faces a center which carries diversification so far that it begins to resemble a project institute.

". . . [T]he character of a great research laboratory is determined by its sense of positive purpose," John Foster, Jr., has said. "If a laboratory becomes entangled in a negative purpose—for example, to move away from work on national defense—it may be lame and weak. The challenge to those who wish to move into new areas is to create a new purpose, to chart a new and broad and positive course. When this is done, all else is likely to fall into place."[7] This reads very much like a friendly warning to the Department of Defense centers. But if "a new and broad and positive course" could be created by will and intelligence alone, RAND would be experiencing no difficulties. A matching will and intelligence, not to mention money, must also be provided by research sponsors. And, perhaps most important, the political and social circumstances must be favorable.

To put it another way: a problem must be solvable if research is to solve it, but "domestic social problems" are not solvable in the same sense as mathematical, engineering, and scientific problems. Of course, sensible solutions—5, 10, or 20 solutions—for each problem can readily be designed. But in what sense can an intellectually sensible design that is not implemented yet be called a "solution"? And what credit can be assigned to intellectuals for a solution which the entire nation must adopt? Plainly, the role of intelligence in grappling with human problems is far more complex and far more interlinked with historical events than is its role in dealing with the problems of nature.

Have Defense systems analysts not, then, been working on human problems? To be sure, though of a different order; and they have had notable failures too, such as Secretary of Defense McNamara's ill-fated TFX plane and the Vietnam War. But the Department of Defense can administer its "solutions" more easily than can our cities. Its decisions are more likely to be implemented down the line than is the case in the more democratic and cantankerous domestic arena. Despite interservice rivalries and student revolutionaries, the main enemies of the military are overseas, whereas in domestic affairs our political wars are fought at home.

As the foregoing discussion should indicate, the problems that RAND has encountered in the process of diversification are generic and not peculiar problems.

THE CASE OF RAND RAND's gradual evolution from an organization dealing exclusively with the Air Force to one working with many agencies—its 1969 annual report lists 20 other sponsors of contracts and grants over $50,000[8]—long antedated any congressional ceiling on center budgets. That evolution mirrored the rise of additional powers within the national security establishment. Often RAND did not seek other sponsors: they came to it. Since the Air Force had to sanction, or tolerate, any new venture (for it could always have retaliated by cutting its sustaining contract), it must be held jointly responsible with RAND management for what ensued. If some Air Force officials feared a weakening of their special relationship with RAND, others must have anticipated gains from the growth of their protegé's contacts and knowledge.[9] The subtle and difficult conflicts of political interest and intellectual conscience entailed in serving several masters contesting for power in Washington became evident especially as RAND undertook an increasing amount of work for the Office of the Secretary of Defense.

Since 1949, RAND had worked with AEC laboratories on the physical effects of nuclear explosions and the political and military implications of nuclear and thermonuclear weapons.[10] In 1958, RAND started to work for NASA, at that agency's initiative. That same year, the Advanced Research Projects Agency was set up and turned to RAND for help in the ballistic missiles program. The relationships with the Advanced Research Projects Agency, the Director of Defense Research and Engineering, and the Assistant Secretary for International Security Affairs—all elements of the Office of the Secretary of Defense—became continuing. More recently, at the request of Henry Kissinger, President Nixon's assistant for national security affairs, RAND has undertaken work for the National Security Council.

The foregoing work was considered a normal extension of RAND's involvement in national security affairs, critical responsibilities for which lay outside the Air Force. And this work was not necessarily against Air Force interests, for the new sponsors opened up data that would otherwise have been inaccessible to RAND. By the end of 1970, RAND's Air Force work had sunk to 40 percent of its volume of $27 to $28 million; 35 percent came from other elements of the Department of Defense; and the rest from other federal agencies, the City of New York, state governments, private foundations, and other sponsors.

Bruce Smith suggests that "the really significant steps toward diversification of sponsorship began [in 1959] after the Air Force announced its intention of freezing the Project RAND support at its then current dollar level . . . financial considerations rather than doctrine played the major role, initially at least . . ." (Smith, 1966, p. 126). According to some sources, the special charm of the Air Force–RAND relationship began to fade in the early 1960s after General Thomas White's departure as Chief of Staff. As one informant saw it, "an anti-intellectual clique at the Strategic Air Command" then put the Air Force into opposition to Defense Secretary McNamara,[11] with whom many RAND staff and alumni were closely allied. Charles Hitch, Henry Rowen, Alain Enthoven, Fred S. Hoffman, and William Gorham, among others, joined McNamara's staff and "Albert [Wohlstetter] and Bill Kaufman began floating out of Nitze's office [Paul Nitze, Assistant Secretary of Defense for International Security Affairs]. . . . The people who seemed to understand us turned up in the Defense Department, where sometimes they opposed Air Force policy."

Adding insult to injury, RAND could hardly refuse to transmit to the Secretary of Defense the results of its Air Force work — though "we were always careful to brief the Air Force people first." RAND would try to be tactful about transmitting such information — for example, it would not brief the Office of the Defense Secretary directly after the Air Force had made a diametrically opposite case. And the Secretary did not get all of RAND's Air Force work. When McNamara demanded a copy of every report, "our letters [to the Air Force] got longer — you've got to maintain a client relation."

In contrast to its national security work, RAND's venture into the domestic arena was more deliberate. In the late 1950s, RAND mathematicians and physical scientists received modest grants from NIH to investigate biomedical applications of computers. One of RAND's basic operating principles, and a source of its distinctive style and strength, has been the marked freedom it granted its best people. That included freedom *not* to work for the Air Force. "If some good researchers want to do something and you don't want to lose them," one officer remarked, "you have to let them get their own support." In 1962, a staffer recalled, he took a sabbatical (at RAND) from military work. "At the end of the year, I said I'd like to continue that arrangement and thereafter, to a large extent, I divorced myself from anything to do with the military." Other staff grew interested in pollution, population control, and the future of technology and society (some of the latter would later secede to form the Institute for the Future at Middletown, Connecticut).

In 1962, President Frank Collbohm told a congressional committee that RAND was *not* interested in diversifying its sponsors.[12] Nonetheless, in 1966, the last year of his reign, he appointed a staff committee that recommended that RAND move into areas of social concern. "We gave a half day's presentation to the board, which accepted the recommendation," said a committee member.

When Henry Rowen returned to RAND as president in 1967, it was with the understanding that RAND would enter the domestic arena. (Yes, he had a mandate, an informant agreed, but the board wanted it done gently—"not flying off in all directions.") Rowen shared the conviction of other social scientists that the innumerable social programs launched by President Johnson had been "poorly researched," and, like other economists who, during this period, moved into civilian agencies to help implement the "planning-programming-budgeting" system, he believed that the analytical methods developed for Department of Defense purposes could also help the nation to cope with its abundant domestic difficulties.

By now, RAND had studied urban transportation, water supply, mental health, and local government data needs. Late in 1967, Mayor John Lindsay asked if RAND would come to New York. "The Mayor called and said, 'Boy, do I have problems. Are you crazy enough to help?'" Work began in January 1968, and in July 1969 the New York City–RAND Institute was established, funded by the city at about $2 million a year, staffed and administered by RAND, and governed by a board appointed jointly by the City and RAND. The independent institute was established to indicate that RAND was in New York to stay, to give it some political insulation, and to encourage foundation and other private grants. (The institute received $900,000 from the Ford Foundation on its creation in 1969 and another $340,000 in January 1971.)

Starting with police, fire, housing, and health services, the New York staff then undertook inquiries into water pollution, welfare, drug abuse, budgeting, the courts, correctional systems, neighborhoods, economic development, migration, employment, income differentials, welfare rights organizations, discrimination in employment, and social indicators for the city.

In 1969, the Santa Monica board approved the goal of a fifty-fifty division of military-nonmilitary funding by 1974.[13] Initial diversification had been fragmented—"like a touch-football game, everyone was out for a pass." Now, it was asked, What do the staff want to do? What are they qualified to do? It was agreed that RAND would concentrate on five major areas (plus New York): state and local issues in California; health services and biomedical sciences; the environment; communications policy; and education.

So much for efforts and plans. How have they gone?

One program leader was optimistic. "If we go on for many more years we will be difficult to compete with, primarily because we have sunk our roots in so many arenas and have had no major disasters" (unlike, he noted, the System Development Corporation). (But a senior officer of a large institute considered RAND's work with the New York police department a "disaster," one that *his* institute would never tolerate. To paraphrase him: "We would *see* that our client was satisfied, no matter what.")[14] A moment later, the program leader speculated that RAND might end up as three institutes in New York, Washington, and Santa Monica. "Some people feel it's touch and go if RAND is still in existence in two or three years," one staff member mused. Morale was, he said, low; engineers were being let go and other people were insecure. What would happen when the physics department broke away (as it did in May 1971)?

An aggressive group, the physicists were chafing under the Air Force budgetary cuts. They believed they could do better by setting themselves up independently as a for-profit firm, which could deal directly with the Department of Defense and other clients. Doubtless the break also signified discontent with RAND leadership; it even rekindled memories of the Teller-Oppenheimer, big bomb–arms control debates. The physics department was a $1.75 million a year operation. How much of that money would be lost to RAND? What happened to the Project RAND contract, which had been dwindling for some years, would indicate RAND's present standing with a less than elated Air Force. The case of the "Pentagon Papers" was not likely to enhance that standing.[15]

At the end of 1970, it was moot if the New York City–RAND Institute would survive. "The New York Institute is five years ahead of RAND-California in evolving a viable style of operation," observed one informant—but that meant, also, five years ahead in the new-style difficulties. The difficulties were no secret, being aired periodically in the *New York Times.* Comptroller Abraham Beame stopped payment on RAND's contract and a lawsuit was begun to force payment;[16] Council president Sanford Garelik called RAND's $500,000 study of the police department a "failure" —which Peter Szanton, director of RAND's New York operations, acknowledged it was;[17] key city councilmen criticized the confidentiality of RAND's reports and proposed that the city contract instead with the City University, which they asserted could do the same work more economically. RAND got most applause for its work for the fire department, which stated that "Rand Institute studies that cost the city $600,000 a year had saved the city $7-million a year," and the city housing administrator testified that RAND's work "has been of immeasurable aid, and its future programming is critical if the city is to solve the present housing crisis." Critics challenged both claims.[18]

In diversifying, RAND is moving from the relatively—or should the word be "formerly"?—sheltered world of defense technology, strategy, politics, and finance to the wilderness of urban life. To thrive in the new environment, RAND needs new intellectual equipment, personnel, professional standards, administrative procedures, reflexes, philosophy, sponsors, and a new run of luck. It is most unlikely to get all of that instantaneously. Comparing RAND's performance with that of the Urban Institute, which transformed its sponsors in two years, one RAND official remarked, "They didn't have 25 years behind them." To turn RAND around, he said, was like trying to turn an ocean liner at full steam: "swing the wheel hard round and hold it, and the ship only changes course a few degrees." However, it is equally true that RAND's experience has been neither as dramatic nor as traumatic as that of the Urban Institute, and RAND has the greater stability of a tenfold larger scale of operations.

Under the Air Force contract, the staff had the freedom and leisure to think and converse about long-term problems. "RAND was a continuous conversation in those days." Every hour of every day did not have to be reckoned against a project budget and report deadline, nor did failures have to be reported: they could be written off against the successes, so long as the Air Force was satisfied with the net product. The result was quite academic—too academic, and too remote from immediate Department of Defense problems, a good many people felt. Today, things are different. "We're now up to 75 contracts at any one time and 100 or so in the course of the year."

X stopped in the hall to talk with Y, a staff member said, and his project was charged for a day of Y's time. It hardly matters if that story was a joke, for the days of long conversations are ending and the pace of work is picking up as RAND comes increasingly to resemble other project institutes. (And indeed, its officials have consulted such institutes to learn from them; one institute officer was puzzled why RAND should have trouble doing what his institute had always done.) "We try to avoid small contracts which take a helluva lot of work and represent a greater financial risk"—i.e., yield less return for the staff time invested in proposal preparation. "We're clearly selling. You use your stars all the time—if all the proposals came through, they'd be selling 500 percent of their time." Such is the life of a project institute.

Some put RAND's troubles down to the vanity and naïveté of engineers and economists moving from their orderly computers into the disorderly world. That, no doubt, is part of the problem; and another part is the resentment that well-paid young men may naturally encounter when they study less well-paid older men for the benefit of their superiors. The first problem RAND can do something about; the second is more intractable.

Will RAND pull it off? I certainly hope so, for if RAND fails, what can lesser institutes anticipate? But to succeed, RAND will have to become a very different organization; and if it is to remain a first-class organization, it may have to become a smaller one. Other R&D centers might reflect upon RAND's experience before hastening along the path it has trod.

In a rejoinder to this cautionary tale, a RAND reader states:

My view of RAND is quite different from that presented by you. . . . It is that RAND must continue to work at the cutting edge of some of the most important problems the country faces, that the only way to do this is to tackle the problems in the best way one knows how, and that one shouldn't expect quick results. Adhering to this rule means change and change is often painful, but often necessary as well . . . while I cannot be certain that the course that we have been following will be successful or that it is the best one that might have been chosen, I do feel that not to have struck out on a new course would have been fatal to RAND. There was a widespread view inside and outside of RAND, one which grew during the course of the

1960s, that RAND was digging deeper and deeper ruts and had become less innovative and productive. Whatever might be said of our present uncertainties there are some new paths being carried out. When they get to be ruts we will have to strike out again in new directions.

That is a brave and commendable position. Unfortunately, the man who wrote it in April 1971 was no longer at his job in November 1971. The same month, RAND president Henry Rowen either "resigned" *(New York Times)* or "was fired" *(Washington Post)* in response to cumulative internal problems and deteriorating relations with the Defense Department and the Congress. These had been exacerbated in June by RAND alumnus Daniel Ellsberg's release to the press of the massive classified Defense Department study of "U.S.-Vietnam Relations, 1945–1967." Also in November, the House Committee on Appropriations recommended a $3 million reduction in the Defense Department's $11 million fiscal year 1972 request for RAND, stating in its report:

. . . the Committee directs that no funds from other categories or appropriations be applied to Rand in fiscal year 1972 in such a way as to offset the indicated reduction. . . . [T]he Committee feels strongly that the time has come for the military services to begin phasing out the "think tank" operations which have been supported for more than two decades. The level of proficiency and pay in the Government service is such that the Government should be able to move these efforts in-house. The Committee feels that the Government officials responsible for national defense should be more closely involved in these efforts than they are under the present procedures. The Committee further believes that in matters of security better control can be maintained within governmental organizations than outside the government. The reductions in this area approximate 25% and are based on giving the Department an opportunity for an orderly phase-down.

It was small consolation to RAND that the Center for Naval Analyses, Research Analysis Corporation, and other Defense "think tanks" were subjected to similar treatment by the committee.

Defense officials have stood their ground against this congressional assault and through a combination of hectic conferences and maneuvers appear likely to gain for their centers (as of December 1971) a longer life than might be anticipated from the House Committee report. The wisest course for all parties would be to rethink the function of the centers and find for them a new administrative format, one that would free them from invidious special attention but at the same time subject their government work to the standards of public accountability that all nonprofit organizations should uphold.

10. *Intersectoral Competition*

Professional courtesies notwithstanding, it does not take great insight to perceive the undercurrent of competition between non-profit organizations, between the nonprofit and profit-making sectors, and (though we will give it little attention here) between the entire private sector of nonprofit and profit-making organizations and the governmental sector. When research organizations prosper, as they did after World War II, they can be indulgent about competition, whereas financial pressure heightens rivalries. By all accounts, there has been, in the last several years, a decided increase in the competition for federal R&D dollars, especially in programs concerned with domestic problems. The amount of competitive bidding has evidently risen while that of directed awards made without the formal public solicitation of proposals has declined.[1]

The Rockefeller University, which once disdained government funds (the Carnegie Institution of Washington still does), is increasingly drawing upon them; at RAND, as we have seen, proposal writing is the new way of life, though these are proposals for negotiated or sole-source discussions since, like Brookings and other institutes with a strong academic or public-service tradition, RAND does not respond to RFP's — requests for proposals. That is, it does not bid in open formal competition with other organizations. Other R & D centers have also entered the very real, if informal, competition for negotiated awards. In 1969, the System Development Corporation forsook its nonprofit status to compete openly as a for-profit organization, and it is bruited that the Research Analysis Corporation will soon follow suit. At most research institutes visited during the second half of 1970, the story was similar: increased efforts were being made to sustain the staff.

Most research funds which universities obtain from the government are awarded by sole-source negotiation or by the selection of the most worthy among a number of unsolicited proposals. At many universities, bidding is deemed commercial and incompatible with the principle of self-directed academic research. However, schools of engineering and special research divisions (such as the Denver Research Institute or the Engineering Experiment Station of the Georgia Institute of Technology) may bid competitively for government applied research contracts. Some even maintain offices in Washington to facilitate this bidding.[2] Their competitive outlook is illustrated by the remarks some years ago of the acting director of the Engineering Research Institute of the University of Michigan:

> The type of work engaged upon through the Institute runs the whole gamut from problems which are very fundamental in nature to those which are purely testing in character. . . . We avoid routine testing, but do some special testing. . . . We are, however, in direct competition with research agencies, such as Mellon, Battelle, and Armour Institutes. . . .
>
> In general, the Institute relies on the facilities of the various instructional laboratories for sponsored research. . . .
>
> The solicitation or procurement of research involves advertising. Some of my colleagues shudder when I come right out and call it that. Over the years, we have put out a considerable amount of descriptive material. . . . We have never put paid advertising in any publication . . . the two assistants to the director are expected to get out and contact, in one case, the industries, and, in the other, the Government agencies, so as to bring our service continuously to their attention (Good, 1950, pp. 11–12, 14).

Applied research institutes and project institutes bid vigorously and frequently; most operating foundations and endowed institutes, not at all; the practice of other institutes varies. Here, "bid" is used in the strict sense of responding to a government RFP. Some of the most important competition for the government dollar occurs informally and without public notice. For example, the Harvard-MIT Joint Center for Urban Studies and RAND privately sought the funds that the Department of Housing and Urban Development eventually gave to establish the Urban Institute. The competition among R & D centers, institutes, and universities in NSF's new program of Research Applied to National Needs (RANN) is no less strong for being conducted informally and by unsolicited proposals.

to the manufacture of goods and products, there might be less competition with nonprofit institutions. But today, for-profit companies compete with nonprofit institutes and university research divisions in many government programs, especially for those in the applied natural and social sciences and engineering, operations and policy research, and management consulting. Indeed, in setting up a new research organization, the decision whether to go "nonprofit" or "profit" can be a close one. As their budgets have grown and as they move into applied and directed research, agencies like the National Institutes of Health, NSF, and the Office of Education no longer deal almost exclusively with universities. Ever sensitive to changes in the wind, institutes and companies, in turn, seek to stock and supply the government with whatever research goods are in demand.

In 1970, competitors of the nonprofit Bureau of Social Science Research included the for-profit Greenleigh Associates, the Chilton Co., and A. D. Little, as well as other nonprofit organizations. Battelle's Columbus laboratories compete for government research against its Pacific Northwest Laboratory as well as other applied research institutes, engineering schools such as MIT, industrial research laboratories, and for-profit firms such as A. D. Little, Booz Allen and Hamilton, and the Planning Research Corporation. Important competitors of the former nonprofit and now for-profit computer software System Development Corporation include major universities; the information divisions of such aerospace firms as Lockheed, North American, and McDonnell-Douglas; applied research institutes like Battelle, Southwest Research Institute, Midwest Research Institute, and the Stanford Research Institute; for-profit consulting firms such as Booz Allen, McKinsey, Price Waterhouse, and A. D. Little; and many smaller companies specializing in particular fields of education, documentation, librarianship, transportation, or health. When the Office of Education invited proposals to establish educational policy research centers, it received them from:

American Institutes for Research; Dade County Public Schools with the University of Miami; University of Oregon; Syracuse University with the General Learning Corporation; Boston University with Raytheon and A. D. Little; the University of California at Irvine; Management Technology, Inc.; System Development Corporation; Stanford Research Institute; George Washington University; Western Behavioral Sciences Institute;

Hudson Institute; Brooks Foundation; National Planning Association with Catholic University; Educational Testing Service; Clark Abt Associates; California State College; New York University; Temple University; Academy of Educational Development with McGraw-Hill; University of Florida; University of Wisconsin; and RCA Service Company.[3]

Stanford University and Stanford Research Institute were involved in recurrent competition for funds:

In 1961, when the university launched a $100-million fund drive, the institute undertook not only to make a sizable contribution, but also to refrain from putting the bite on potential donors from whom Stanford hoped to get contributions. However, to the annoyance of President Sterling and of the Stanford trustees, after [Stanford Research Institute president] Folkers took office he persuaded the S. R. I. Board to discontinue the annual gifts the institute had been making to Stanford. He also began talking with [Atholl] McBean, and with other businessmen interested in the institute, about raising an endowment that would enable S. R. I. to do more self-sponsored research. That annoyed Sterling and the trustees even more, and precipitated the decision by the S. R. I. board that installed Arbuckle at the institute as a kind of viceroy (Klaw, 1966, p. 212).

Ernest Arbuckle, Dean of the Stanford Business School, became Stanford Research Institute board chairman in 1966, but thereafter (in keeping with Rufus Miles's law that where you stand depends on where you sit), some informants stated, his sympathy for Stanford Research Institute fund drives grew. Stanford and Stanford Research Institute also competed for federal funds, as did Cornell and the Cornell Aeronautical Laboratory and Syracuse and the Syracuse University Research Corporation.

Though nine presidents of higher educational institutions sit on the Board of the Washington Center for Metropolitan Studies, the center's relations with the institutions have been less than satisfactory. According to one informant, the center's first president "found the local universities either indifferent or hostile, and he in turn became hostile to them. . . . He felt that the universities would talk cooperation but wouldn't give any." In 1965, when the center approached the Ford Foundation for more money, its initial 1959 grant having been exhausted, cooperation was made a condition for the second award; as evidence that that condition would be met, the president departed soon after. However, despite renewed efforts, the center has not had an easy time with the universities. "You can't have relations with 'the' university," the informant explained. "The university is ill-equipped to speak with one voice." A report of the center president points up the difficulties:

> The Center's relationship to the universities is the most critical and the most difficult issue to resolve. . . . As individual institutions become more able to think about urbanism, and as their staffs grow, so seem institutional jealousies to flourish. The new possibilities for federal funding often only arouses such feelings and nurtures them, sometimes making cooperation more difficult . . . the university presidents, harrassed by their own abundant difficulties, think we are sometimes nice, occasionally a bother, and always an uncertain element in their own financial and program planning.
>
> . . . There is every possibility that in five years there could be as many as 4 or 5 separate interuniversity research or community service programs in urban affairs. . . . Given the scarcity of resources when measured against the magnitude of the problems of both the metropolis and of higher education, this is not only unfortunate, but unforgiveably wasteful. Open competition for financial support between the Center . . . and other universities ultimately means everyone loses because no one gains as much alone as might be gained through an intelligent and intensive joint effort (*Report of the President*, 1969).

New York City councilmen and Comptroller Abraham Beame, on the one hand, and Republican Mayor John Lindsay's office, on the other, have been engaged in a protracted conflict over the noncompetitive awarding of research contracts to, among others, the New York City–RAND Institute. New York educational institutions harbored highly qualified urban authorities. For example, Robert Weaver, former Secretary of Housing and Urban Development and a Harvard economist, was dean of the Bernard Baruch School of Business, and sociologist Henry Cohen, a high official in Mayor Robert Wagner's administration, was director of the New School for Social Research's Center for New York City Affairs. Both happened to be Democrats and were cited in the *New York Times* as regretting the lack of involvement by local universities in the study of city problems. RAND staff members gave a course at the New School; held an NSF grant jointly with the State University of New York at Stony Brook; sponsored a weekly seminar for city urbanologists; and used many local university consultants— mainly younger people, not chosen for their political influence.

Nonetheless, local institutions did not regard that as a satisfactory apportionment of city funds. In November 1970, a City Council committee reported:

. . . The [City] university, in response to this subcommittee's request, . . . has proposed the creation of an Urban Research and Service Center.

The purpose of the center would be to develop the city's own think tank and perform studies for city agencies. . . .

The university has a greater stake in the solution of the city's problems than do private consulting firms. . . . The university, moreover, can probably command a greater breadth of knowledge of social problems generally, and the city's problems in particular, than can private organizations.

The university believes that it can furnish a research and analytical service at a cost of $1-million a year, as compared with the $2-million being spent for Rand alone. . . .

The university envisions that under presently existing formulas the state would pick up one-half of the cost of all funding. At present, the state makes no contribution to the city's management and scientific studies ("Excerpts," 1970, p. 25).

As of June 1971, the crisis was unresolved; the RAND office was still functioning, but at a reduced level.

After a fixed-price competition in 1965, the Air Force awarded to the University of Dayton a $465,000 contract for flight load and related turbulence studies. The rival bidder, Technology, Inc., a Dayton firm, believed that, when all the costs were considered, its bid was lower. It protested the award to the Comptroller General of the United States:

Significant subsidies direct and indirect are received from government by universities. Accordingly, it is unreasonable to expect that a private enterprise could compete with a subsidized entity. . . . To ask industry to do so is tantamount to asking them to perform a useless act. . . . The attitude of the Comptroller General toward requiring bidders to perform useless acts in proposing bids without any possibility of acceptance has been stated repeatedly in numerous opinions. . . .

It is furthermore clear that a university—a non-profit entity—cannot and will not be held to the same standard of care, conduct and performance, and fiscal responsibility to which private enterprise will be held. Accordingly, implicit in this is the inescapable conclusion that the private company and the university are not and cannot be evaluated on the same basis. . . .

The Acting Comptroller General acknowledged the "cogent arguments" but dismissed the protest because "at the present time there is no policy pronouncement by the Department of Defense . . . which precludes competition between profit and nonprofit organizations when seeking Government contracts."[4]

In 1961, Oak Ridge National Laboratory Director Alvin Weinberg requested permission from the AEC to work for the Interior Department on the desalination of seawater. Regarding the laboratory's entrance into nonnuclear fields as an unwarranted extension of its function, the nuclear committee of the National Association of Manufacturers protested to the AEC, but the protest was summarily dismissed. "According to reports, one AEC commissioner read to the committee passages from the AEC's 1960 report extolling the laboratories [i. e., in our usage, the AEC's R & D centers under nonprofit and for-profit management] as national assets. Another stated that, as time went on and the needs of the atomic energy program might well lessen, the resources and staff of laboratories like Oak Ridge should be made available for other jobs of national importance. . . ." The Commission and the Joint Committee on Atomic Energy have repeatedly defended AEC centers against industry charges of "unfair competition" (Orlans, 1967, p. 109).

In 1970, the Navy assigned to the nonprofit Center for Naval Analyses some $1.5 million of work for its Tactical Analysis Group which had previously been done by profit-making companies. The Navy was dissatisfied with the coordination of multiple contractors and yet fearful that giving all the work to one company might create a conflict of interest in a subsequent hardware contract based upon that company's studies. However, the for-profit Planning Research Corporation claimed that it could do the work for $1 million. It protested to the White House and attacked the "unfair competition" entailed in administrative awards to R&D centers:

The Federal government should see to it that no more FCRC's [R&D centers] are formed unless the fundamental characteristics involving sensitive [classified] long-range unfettered research are required. . . . The recently (1968) established Urban Institute is greatly suspect in this regard. New policy should be established precluding the FCRC's from work for private sector companies or government offices other than their sponsor offices. (Correlatively, current policy allowing procurement officers to give FCRC's sole-source contracts without justification should be disallowed.) . . . If the rules of the competitive bids are reasonable, some of the originally sponsored work will be lost by the FCRC's . . . (Planning Research Corporation, 1970).

**UNIVERSITIES
ARE THEIR
OWN
ENEMIES**

If independent institutes are adversaries of universities, competing with them for the same limited financial resources, then university administrators have often been their own worst enemies by having helped create the institutes with which they later competed. The story of the Stanford Research Institute has many similarities to that of the Cornell Aeronautical Laboratory, the Syracuse University Research Corporation, and other largely independent institutes formed by a university to conduct classified, applied, and proprietary work for the government and industry. In each case, it was hoped that the university would gain income and peripheral benefits from the institute such as jobs for graduate students, research opportunities for faculty, and perhaps an augmented teaching staff. But the independence that enabled these institutes to operate without the constraints of academic departments induced them to expand without major involvement in the instructional process. Repeatedly, the peripheral benefits turned out to be no greater (and in some cases less) than those obtained by other universities from independent R&D centers and institutes in the vicinity.

The question of income is more moot. At Stanford, the university received only a small return from its investment until the disposition of the institute. Most universities managing federal centers have also received little discernible income from them. However, some reason that center overhead is a substantial form of indirect subsidy; and the Universities of California and Chicago have received fees from the AEC that may include an element of net income or "profit."[5] Albert Biderman goes so far as to suggest that until changes in procurement regulations reduced the ability of universities to "bootleg" support for academic functions from institute funds, these funds contributed significantly to the growth of academic departments. The Illinois Institute of Technology, he states, enlarged its buildings and faculty partly on funds derived from the Illinois Institute of Technology Research Institute.[6]

Nonetheless, few universities foresaw the rivalry that faculty would face from institutes and the isolation of these institutes from educational affairs. Legal control did not guarantee operating control, where the interests of university and institute diverged.

The driving source of that divergence was the need of full-time, tenureless research staff to sustain themselves.

More effective models of university control and the integration of research and instruction are afforded by the Mellon Institute and the Denver Research Institute.

After its merger with the Carnegie Institute of Technology in 1967 to form the Carnegie-Mellon University, a program of integration was set in motion under which the Mellon Institute can no longer be said to have an independent existence. Its endowment was merged with the university's; many staff members were given faculty appointments and assumed teaching duties; those who did not want to teach have gradually departed. Today, the Mellon resembles other university research-and-teaching institutes — down to the infinitely tedious and protracted faculty committee meetings which debate at length questions resolved by administrative fiat at independent institutes.

The director of the Denver Research Institute "is a member of the Dean's Council and in many respects is given the same status as a dean of one of the academic colleges." In January 1971, John Welles advises, the heads of four of the institute's seven divisions were also chairmen of university departments; about 45 of the institute's 150 full-time professional staff held joint appointments in academic departments. Departmental and institute offices and classrooms are commingled, and interaction between institute staff and faculty "has always been encouraged in such things as academic committee memberships, informal meetings, participation in campus professional societies, conferences, symposia, etc. . . ."[7] Altogether, the integration of institute and university activities at Denver contrasts markedly with the physical and professional separation of Stanford Research Institute and Stanford or the Cornell Aeronautical Laboratory at Buffalo and the Cornell campus at Ithaca.

Interinstitutional strife in the urban field is partly a consequence of too many men chasing too little money; partly, of the difficulty of isolating the central intellectual objectives of research in the interlinked web of urban problems (and, concomitantly, of establishing one or another set of intellectuals as the central authorities on these problems); partly to the multiplicity of agencies with some jurisdiction over urban affairs; and partly, perhaps, to the more modest scale of these affairs, which afford less scope for useful, and necessarily expensive, large-scale research.

If there is some way to overcome these difficulties other than by an infusion of funds large enough to occupy all urban researchers, I do not know what it is. Since the dispersion of effort among many institutions is not likely to be as productive as its concentration in a few, it would be wise for the main contenders to agree on a division of functions and funds—but that is too much to expect.

Sheltered research programs for universities may be warranted when there is a demonstrable need to attract scholars to the university and to add departments and, perhaps, graduate students, in a given field (though the latter would seem better accomplished by direct graduate student aid). Considering the present surplus of Ph.D's, these conditions seem far less prevalent today than they were in the 1950s and early 1960s, when sheltered programs were instituted by NIH, NSF, and a number of other agencies. If anything, nonprofit institutes can now complain about being effectively excluded from such programs. They pose little threat to universities in the domain of pure research, and it is hard to see why the university should receive special shelter for applied R&D work. Universities can mitigate unreasonable competition from local institutes by exercising greater control over faculty consulting and seeing that institutes pay for university services which they utilize.

INEQUITABLE COMPETITION WITH FOR-PROFITS
A better case can be made for reducing, if not eliminating, the direct competition between for-profit and nonprofit organizations for federal R&D funds and rendering more equitable the terms under which it occurs. The reduction of sole-source competition is more difficult, but at least the frequency with which it occurs and the reasons for it should be published.

In fixed-price bids, no allowance for differential tax status is apparently made by federal agencies (though some agencies allow for-profit firms a larger fee than nonprofits). This inequitability could readily be rectified by government contract regulations.[8] Following the Air Force award to the University of Dayton, Technology, Inc., requested changes in the Armed Services Procurement Regulations: (1) that "no competitive proposals . . . be solicited from not-for-profits if the supplies or services have been previously furnished by . . . industry"; (2) that no "proposals be accepted from universities or other not-for-profit entities for furnishing of other than basic or applied research, experimental or developmental work"; and (3) that bids by for-profit firms "be considered as equal in the factor of price . . . [if] no greater than 120 percent" of the bid of a nonprofit organization.[9] Without holding any brief for the 120 percent figure, the basic ideas seem reasonable: to disqualify nonprofit organizations from entering bids on routine testing for which commercial facilities are available; and to allow in bidding for the taxes that for-profit firms pay. However, it does not appear that the Department of Defense heeded these suggestions.

The American Council of Independent Laboratories (ACIL), an association of small for-profit testing laboratories, has diligently pressed the issue of unfair competition by visits and letters to the president and trustees of offending organizations and to other influential potential sympathizers. Despite the unabashed self-interest of its members, ACIL has made a number of cogent points which have embarrassed some nonprofit organizations' posture of public interest, and it has successfully combated flagrant cases of nonprofit commercialism. For example, according to Douglas Dies, ACIL executive secretary, some years ago the University of Miami was listed by the Aluminum Door Manufacturers Association as a testing laboratory. When this was brought to the attention of the university president, the testing equipment was sold to the professor using it and he then left the university.[10]

Of the "oft-repeated charge" that applied research institutes engage in "routine commercial testing, consulting, and market research," Victor Danilov writes:

Commercial testing laboratories—through the American Council of Independent Laboratories—have made such an issue over this point that the institutes now refuse to perform almost all except the most sophisticated types of testing. . . .

While routine testing has become almost a dead issue, there still is considerable pressure to dislodge all forms of management consulting and market research from not-for-profits.

It was such pressure that caused IIT Research Institute to discontinue management consulting as part of its not-for-profit contract services. The entire division was made a wholly owned, tax-paying affiliate in 1964 (Danilov, 1966, p. 6).

However, market analyses and "technico-economics" are major and expanding activities of applied research institutes; and, as Richard Lesher observes, "There is a fine line of distinction between consulting and research, especially in areas such as economics and management sciences . . ." (Lesher, 1963, p. 135).

The ACIL advocates:

Results of all research carried on at either educational institutions, tax-favored institutes or foundations . . . should be available to the public through prompt publication in appropriate scientific and technical journals and/or placing copies of reports in public libraries. They should not be kept confidential nor accrue to the sole benefit of a private sponsor. . . .

Inspection, sampling, analysis and testing for commercial purposes are in no case proper functions or activities for educational institutions or affiliated institutes.

Studies for the use of a private party or corporation do not constitute public service and therefore should not be a function of a tax supported or a tax-favored institution . . . (*Commercialism of Research,* 1968).

The first and last recommendations attack proprietary research for industry by nonprofit organizations, utilizing publication as the test of whether research is in the public interest and merits tax exemption. Similarly, NSF has recommended "that Federal tax-exemption privileges for nonprofit research institutes be modified, along the lines of more precise distinction between research performed for the restricted use of clients and research freely and publicly dedicated to society" (*Basic Research,* 1957, p. 53). As noted earlier, the taxability of income from proprietary research by nonprofit institutes is a mystery wrapped in an enigma hidden within IRS regulations.

THE SPECIAL CASE OF R&D CENTERS

Finally, what about the "unfair competition" of federal centers, which receive more federal funds than all other nonprofit institutes? The Planning Research Corporation (PRC)—itself an enterprise of former RAND staff—has attacked the "competition" of Department of Defense "think tanks," which, PRC contended, were no cheaper, no more objective, no better qualified, or no more public-spirited than independent, for-profit research firms.

But PRC did not discuss *the* critical function of R&D centers: their *continuing, primary* commitment to the study of *one* agency's problems. To suggest that the tasks assigned to a think tank be broken up and contracted out to the lowest bidders is to suggest that there is no value in the continuity of experience and the special "family" relationship represented by the model of the initial RAND–

Air Force contract. In fact, that contract was the one exception cited by PRC in its roundhouse attack on R&D centers. "Most of the work performed by . . . [these centers] (except perhaps for the sensitive long-range unfettered research such as done under the RAND Corporation's original contract . . .) can more efficiently and with at least the same degree of objectivity be performed by sufficiently available professional service organizations in the purely private sector."

To argue that the original function of RAND—of maintaining an intimate, confidential, enduring, but relatively independent evaluatory and advisory relationship with one government agency—is unnecessary is, in effect, to argue that intelligent, informed, and independent Air Force staff are largely unnecessary. For, unless it is seriously proposed to contract out critical functions of the executive branch of government (which some ideologues of "free enterprise" may well strive to do), the meaningful alternative to organizations like RAND is not contracting with a number of for-profit companies but enlarging and improving the analytical staff of government. The traditional criticism of the Department of Defense's analytical centers has been that they have weakened the public service by assigning to private experts functions that should remain in the public sector, where public officials are accountable for them. Thus, David Lilienthal, first chairman of the AEC:

[Scientific experts] . . . are paid by us, from our taxes, but they are not accountable to us or to Congress in the same way as are government employees, such as Generals or Secretaries of Defense. For the most part, they are shielded from public view by being employees of so-called "private" corporations which operate predominantly on government contracts. In substance I wonder why they are any different from direct federal employees as to responsibility, and yet they are freed from the accountability—and the salary limitations—of those who are in direct federal service. I can think of few things that over a decade can be more demoralizing to the strength and dignity of the federal career service than this: the creation and proliferation of a body of super civil servants, men who perform governmental functions yet who are independent of government and its obligations, men recruited and paid and supervised as if they were in private employment, but actually doing the government's work. For they are virtually immune from the tough, essential, and distinguishing characteristic of democratic processes of public life, the essence of which is direct accountability, in the open air, to public lay scrutiny.[11]

From this standpoint, nonprofit analytical centers already represent a victory for the private sector of society by removing to it, or halfway toward it, functions which, in a stricter view, should be lodged in public institutions. To move these functions fully into the normal commercial sector would be *prima facie* improper unless the commercial company were so organized and bound to one agency and to prescribed standards of conduct as to lose *its* competitive characteristics and (like NASA's Bellcomm and the AEC's Sandia) become distinguishable from the nonprofit centers mainly by its nominally for-profit management. This is not to assert that *all* functions R&D centers recently have assumed are identical to their core function. Indeed diversification poses many unresolved issues of public policy.

Unlike RAND, MITRE, or Oak Ridge, the Urban Institute took only two years to obtain substantial income from additional agencies. Faced with the danger that its initial sponsor, the Department of Housing and Urban Development, would withdraw, it rapidly obtained major support from other government agencies and the Ford Foundation. The implications of this transformation have not, to my knowledge, been discussed by the Congress or any other public body. There is no precedent for the formation by the executive branch of government of a permanent nonprofit organization designed to serve not one but any agency. The closest parallel may be the National Academy of Sciences, but that was established by act of Congress. (The Office of Education was authorized to establish an unspecified number of regional educational laboratories by a 1965 statute.)[12]

It may be that because of the dispersion of governmental responsibilities for domestic problems, more R&D centers should follow the Urban Institute or the emerging RAND precedent, or report administratively directly to the Office of the President, in the manner of presidential commissions.[13] But the formation of a permanent, privileged policy institute with exceptionally wide-ranging scope and high-level entree is sufficiently important — holding as many dangers as opportunities — to warrant full and open public discussion. How should the core function of an institute ranging over half the government be defined and who should monitor its work? Though some policy "scientists" have been enthusiastic about such an institute, one center president expressed reservations which I share:

. . . if we know anything by now about American politics, about the policy process and about research it is that *no* one or a small set of institutions can be allowed to have a "permanent, privileged" position of access to the higher reaches of government. No President or high official in his right mind would ever permit it and if he were to, he should be prevented by Congress. Of the essence is pluralism in channels of data, analysis, and advice, and openness in the process.

The Planning Research Corporation's argument against the administrative rather than competitive assignment of R&D is questionable, especially at a time when, by all accounts, competition for R&D funds is intensive and vast amounts of time and paper are wasted in the manufacture and processing of futile proposals. "The cost of multiple bids is enormous and can easily (for the sum of competitors) exceed the total value of the contract . . . ," one informant observed. "The government ultimately pays for this cost. For small institutes with untidy accounting, it's either sweated out of the staff 'on its own time' or partly time taken out of contracts but never shown, of course." If any more competition is needed, it should be genuine, and not spurious. Unfortunately, no regulation can impose genuine competition upon weak or guileful officials who prefer a charade of spurious bids. And no regulation should stop strong officials from exercising their judgment about whether a competitive or negotiated procedure is warranted. They can be required to justify that judgment not only in a confidential contract file but to the Congress and the public.

The pros and cons of competitive bidding are well summarized by a study group of the Commission on Government Procurement:

As R&D budgets have been reduced in some agencies, the number of serious bidders in competitions may have risen. Although such competition presumably results in the lowest prices for a specific contract, there may be costs or penalties not readily apparent which should be evaluated. Specific concerns involve the cost to the government for numerous expensive proposals on a contract only one can win; the cost of tying up productive resources in an unproductive exercise; the cost of interrupting technological continuity of incumbent contractors who cannot meet severe competition. All of this may result in an overall loss of efficiency and economy in R&D; on the other hand, it may be essential to retaining competition and avoiding the high costs which could result if restrictions on competitive procedures for R&D procurement led to a greater use of sole-sources contracts ("Study Topics," 1971).

To mitigate futile and enhance genuine competition, John Welles of the Denver Research Institute has suggested that the government "make better use of requests for qualifications. . . . For example, information could be requested concerning relevant past projects, sponsoring agencies, dollar amounts and time schedules, project monitors, and descriptions of the objectives of the work together with summaries of results obtained . . . procurement offices could then be more selective in generating lists of qualified bidders." Such a procedure, he believes, "should help to reduce the number of proposals submitted, to restrict submissions to qualified bidders, and to save time and money for both proposers and government evaluaters."[14] The procedure seems sensible enough to be worth a fair trial.

When an R&D center becomes a for-profit organization, the substance or shadow of public interest is formally replaced by the private interests of owners and officers. But their experience and qualifications and perhaps some of their capital were acquired from the government. Therefore the government's consent and public explanation should be required. To afford rival organizations a day in court, the sponsoring agency should hold an open hearing before reaching its decision. In the unlikely event that a center would insist on going for-profit against its wishes, the agency could withdraw its contract, require (in most cases) restitution of center assets, and even seek a court order to block the move. Should the sponsoring agency approve the change, it may nevertheless require the center to take steps to protect the public interest. This happened when the System Development Corporation obtained the consent of the Air Force to go for-profit; some $4 million was paid to the Air Force in lieu of taxes forgone, and a nonprofit System Development Foundation was formed to receive the System Development Corporation assets (represented by shares that are to be sold to the public), which will be used to support R&D in computer technology.

There are, however, limits to the extent to which the government can legitimately go in restraining the movement of center staff into the commercial sector. Individuals who have worked for a center are always free to go into private business and, to that degree, exploit a public investment for private gain. That happened when some RAND staff members established the for-profit Planning Research Corporation. If such a move involves the misuse of privileged information, the government or the center can go to court to prevent it.

In a thoughtful 1969 report, the Comptroller General discussed the diversification of R&D centers:

> It appears that it would be somewhat incongruous to provide fees to a nonprofit organization to enable it to shift to other fields of endeavor when the organization has received the bulk of its financing from a Government agency and has developed its capabilities through Government support under a sole-source arrangement. To the extent that the services of that organization were needed by the agency, the potential loss of such services would be detrimental to the interests of the agency.
>
> If, on the other hand, the nonprofit organization were no longer essential to the agency, the nonprofit's shift to other fields of endeavor would result in competition with private industry, for Government or private business. Such competition would appear to be inequitable since the heretofore sponsored nonprofit organization would have an unfair advantage over an organization which has built up its own capital and facilities. Furthermore, under these conditions any claims that the Government might have on the net assets acquired by a nonprofit from fees might well be negated since such claims are effective only upon dissolution of the organization (*Need for Improved Guidelines,* 1969, p. 35).

The Comptroller General recommended that the Budget Bureau restrict the size and use of center fees to "the amount needed to enable the organizations to accumulate a reserve to provide operational stability during temporary reductions in contract work and to pay prudent business expenses not otherwise reimbursable." In this view, centers should not use their fees to find new sponsors. But if it is to be restricted, diversification must be attacked directly, for the fee is only one means by which it is achieved.

In sum, to relinquish negotiated contracting for competitive bidding would be to proscribe administrative judgment essential to responsible government. However, the diversification of center funding merits closer examination to ensure that the centers remain responsible to the government and that their work is not merely self-aggrandizing. Any change in center status deserves more public justification than it has received. A public hearing is warranted, and—as is the case of System Development Corporation[15] —special measures to protect the public interest should be taken before a center is permitted to become a for-profit organization.

11. University and Institute Research: Is the Balance Tilting?

I began this inquiry with the thought that the post-Sputnik decade of university ascendancy on the national research scene was ending, and that what universities might lose in dollars, men, and influence, nonprofit research institutes were likely to gain. Student disruptions and destructiveness, the rancor and politicization of faculty, and hostility to government policies simply made the university a less suitable place for dispassionate inquiry. As Alvin Weinberg has observed, "The university cannot be the prime home of basic science, or even of rationality, unless it can achieve some tranquillity . . . " (*National Science Policy,* 1970, p. 319).

UNIVERSITY RESEARCH UNDER SIEGE The student rebellions and the weakened sense of academic discipline, seriousness, civility, and community have many causes; but, to my mind, and to that of other analysts, one root cause has been the neglect by overbusy faculty not just of "teaching," an obligation that can be discharged by appearing in a lecture hall four or six hours a week, but of their students, their colleagues, and their institution. As federally sponsored research has contributed in no small measure to the overbusyness of faculty, so (were it as easy to restore as to undo a community) a reduction of research whose purposes are practical and businesslike, not scholarly, should help to restore peace on campus.

This was the viewpoint of S. J. Tonsor in a 1969 address that President Nixon praised as representing his own views:

Until there is a restoration of genuine educational purpose there will be no restoration of confidence by society in its institutions of higher education. That educational purpose does not lie in the first place in pure or applied research. . . .

In order to ensure circumstances in which teaching rather than research or community service are the primary objectives of the university, government at all levels must forego the temptation of easy recourse to the enormous resources of the university . . . both the government and the university would be better served under most circumstances were both basic and applied research in the national defense area done in autonomous research institutes. The same case can be made against the use of the facilities of the university for the solution of social problems.[1]

And the same viewpoint was expressed in the April 1970 report of the American Council on Education's Special Committee on Campus Tensions, chaired by Sol Linowitz:

All the constituent [academic] groups share concern over the appropriate role of the faculty. Their chief criticism is that the professorial role — particularly in major universities — has become so distorted in the direction of research and scholarly achievement that many faculty seriously neglect their teaching function. . . . In national surveys, . . . students complain repeatedly about lack of contact with faculty and faculty indifference to student needs. These complaints are especially common in major, research-oriented universities (*Campus Tensions,* 1970, p. H4204).

This analysis was endorsed by the President's Commission on Campus Unrest, the Scranton Commission, in its September 1970 report on the causes and, hopefully, the cures of student unrest:

One of the most valid criticisms of many universities is that their faculties have become so involved in outside research that their commitment to teaching seems compromised. We urge universities and faculty members to reduce their outside service commitments.

. . . some scholars are so heavily engaged in outside research that they have become virtually inaccessible to students and colleagues. In students' eyes, they are compromised by their dependence on nonacademic patronage and by their attachment to rewards more tangible than the discovery of truth. But most important, the existence of substantial outside commitments means that faculty members do not give to teaching and research a fair share of time, energy, or care.

We recommend that universities establish general guidelines governing both the acceptance of outside commitments by the institution and the outside activities of individual faculty members. The guidelines should restrict outside service activities — whether for government, industry, or the local community — that drain energies away from teaching and research (*Report of President's Commission,* 1970, pp. 14, 196–197).

Robert Nisbet has been explicit about what would and should be the consequences of giving not lip service but genuine force to recommendations of this kind:

I do not see how authority, scholarship, teaching, or any other vital aspect of the university can be long maintained without a substantial number of present structures and activities on the American campus being removed within the next ten years. On a rough guess I should think at least 75 per cent of all existing institutes, centers, and bureaus in the academic sphere of the university should be phased out.

It is not research, large or small, that I am concerned with seeing phased out of the university. Research, along with teaching, is what universities are all about. But *research in conjunction with teaching,* and of a scale that does not constantly threaten to dwarf the rest of the university! I am well aware that there is much research today that simply cannot be done except in vast, highly organized, bureaucratized centers. Very good. But let such research be done where it can be done more efficiently and without damage to academic community. And let those whose passions are directed toward this kind of research be free to move from the university (Nisbet, 1971, p. 67).

Nisbet's stringent prescription has been entertained, if not yet endorsed, in milder form by Defense Secretary Melvin Laird. To the question: "What discussions and evaluations are going on within the Department of Defense about . . . whether or not to put any further research facilities at the university campuses?" Laird responded:

I think this is much more far-reaching than this Department. I have . . . sponsored a great deal of legislation along with John Fogarty in cancer, heart, vocational rehabilitation, mental illness. I can go down a long list of buildings . . . on college campuses all over the United States. . . .

The point is, if Federal research facilities on the campus itself are causing administrators grave problems, there are other locations where these Federal research facilities can be built and they can be handled separately. They can be near the universities but not necessarily on their campuses. . . . I haven't come down on any firm conclusion on this, but I think before we go ahead with building any more facilities, we ought to study the problem very carefully so that we understand it thoroughly.

To the further question, "What kind of alternatives [to university campuses] are there?" Laird replied:

There's . . . the direction . . . Stanford has gone. Stanford is now incorporated, the Stanford Research Institute, entirely separate and completely divorced from the University administration, and from the Stanford University faculty . . . the Stanford Research Institute is a separate body completely divorced from Stanford. This has been done at several other universities. MIT has a movement in this direction and several of their facilities are being set up separately so that they are not involved with the university administration itself. All of these things need to be looked at from the standpoint of the importance of research, not only from the standpoint of Defense, but Health, Welfare, and many other areas.[2]

If any force is likely to interrupt the conquest of universities by the legions of research, it is the market. Several factors are operating to weaken the power of faculty to allocate their time to research, and to strengthen the hand of administrators seeking to exact more teaching from them. It appears that the Ph.D. shortage of the 1960s will be replaced by a job shortage in the 1970s. The financial plight of universities is forcing many economies and none is seized more quickly than to reduce the staff and get more teaching out of it. Economist-President Charles Hitch has made it painfully plain to the faculty of the University of California which way the economic winds are blowing: "There must be greater commitment of faculty of all ranks to the instruction of undergraduate students. . . . The teaching program must significantly involve faculty of all ranks in instruction at all levels, including the lower division. . . . Evaluation and documentation of teaching performance must be substantially improved. . . ." ("From President Hitch," 1970, p. 57). The sacred principle of tenure is being challenged from diverse quarters for diverse reasons. One must infer that the attack is being mounted because the time is ripe for it, for the professoriate is now in a weak position, economically and morally, to claim that its closed shop has been maintained (except coincidentally) in the interests of students or of the public.[3]

As project research often requires institutional funds to cover costs not met by the sponsor, some universities (such as Minnesota and California) are becoming reluctant to take on additional commitments. Institutions which, after protracted policy battles in the 1950s, on campus and in Washington, succeeded in getting a portion of tenured professors' salaries reimbursed from project funds, are now in special financial difficulties because of the curtailment of these funds and hope to wean themselves from dependence upon them.[4]

The hostility to military operations in Vietnam has made research sponsored by the Department of Defense vulnerable to attack by students and faculty, regardless of how informed or uninformed, logical or illogical, is the basis of attack. Insofar as applied institutes and R&D centers have indeed been of help in improving the effectiveness of Defense Department personnel, policies, weapons, strategy, and tactics, there is a certain logic for opponents of the Vietnam war to object to the university giving such help.[5] Accordingly, universities have been under pressure to stop classified and applied research for the military on and off campus. "Pressure" is too mild a word. It should be understood that, during the last few years, many campuses have endured repeated verbal and physical attacks by students, and, like unarmed cities, have waited for the next mob to gather and the next terrorist to strike.

While there is, to my mind, less logic to attacks upon the conduct on campus of unclassified basic research financed by the Department of Defense, that has not prevented either the Congress or revolutionaries from attacking some of that research—the Congress, that which was *not,* and revolutionaries, that which *was,* helpful to the department.[6] However, the congressional proscription of research with no "direct or apparent relationship" to defense needs has eased, and the universities have thus far successfully resisted other pressures to curtail Defense-sponsored basic research. While many institutions rely on Defense funds, fewer are now dependent on that department than on the Department of Health, Education and Welfare and the NSF, which, in 1971, together will provide an estimated 62 percent of all federal R&D funds at universities. The Department of Defense will provide only 13 percent of those funds.

Independent of recent pressures, classified research on campus had gradually been reduced during the 1950s and 1960s; by 1969, only 4 percent of Defense-financed research on campus was classified. Accordingly, at most campuses, it is now possible to bar classified research completely, and an increasing number of institutions have done so without significantly affecting their income from research.

EXPULSION OF DEFENSE LABORATORIES   Applied and classified research conducted for the Department of Defense at off-campus laboratories have presented more severe problems. Repeatedly, members of the university community and official committees appointed to investigate the future of such laboratories have recommended that the university (a) exercise more control over the laboratory and take a more vigorous part in shaping its program; (b) that the laboratory program be integrated more closely with university research and teaching, that faculty and students be given more opportunities for research and consulting at the laboratory, and that laboratory staff be involved more fully in academic affairs; (c) that the university convert classified work on military problems into unclassified work on civilian problems; and (d) that laboratory work of direct assistance to the war in Vietnam be stopped.

Thus, at Stanford, a majority of a university study committee recommended that the university end Stanford Research Institute work on biological and chemical warfare, counterinsurgency, and "military research primarily and directly related to the war in Vietnam, or elsewhere in the world, which is found to be morally offensive"; a minority called for "a strengthening of ties between Stanford and SRI" and "community control over Institute policy and activities . . . , so that the Institute can function in a manner more harmonious with an evolving University" ("Report of Stanford-SRI Study Committee," 1969).

At Johns Hopkins, a group of students urged the board to end classified research at the Applied Physics Laboratory and to "appoint a committee to formulate and supervise the conversion of APL's priorities from military research to research of social usefulness" (Armbruster, 1970, p. 4).

George Washington University adopted a faculty committee recommendation that "the university should support no research the immediate and obvious implications of which would facilitate the destruction of human life or the impairment of human capacities" (*Report of the Ad Hoc Committee,* 1969; Jeffery, 1969, p. 41).

At Cornell, the Engineering College faculty recommended that the university retain the Cornell Aeronautical Laboratory and "increase the educational interaction with the Laboratory."[7]

At Columbia, a university committee declared that the principles governing sponsored laboratories should be the same as those governing instruction. "Research, too, should be of a quality and character appropriate to a University; the University should decide what research should be done. . . . The university must remain master of its house and it alone should decide what is taught and who teaches it, what research is done and who shall do it."[8]

At MIT, an institutional panel on special laboratories recommended that "The laboratories and M.I.T. should energetically explore new projects to provide a more balanced research program. . . . The educational interaction between the special laboratories and the campus should be expanded. . . . M.I.T. should avoid projects involving the actual development of a prototype weapons system, except in times of grave national emergency." Noam Chomsky, a panel member, took an even dimmer view of laboratory representation: "The matter of research of an institutional character should be handled in the way that academic affairs are handled. A new department or program can be initiated only with faculty authorization . . . the same principle should be extended to research that exceeds a certain scale" (*First Report of Review Panel,* 1969).

At the University of California, a committee of the academic senate complained that Livermore and Los Alamos laboratories "are isolated from the academic community with which they should ideally conduct a vigorous intellectual interchange" and that the university had failed "to assume leadership over them, shape their policies, guide their development and tap their resources. . . ." The committee recommended that the university "should exercise leadership in the determination of the technical policies of the laboratories and should extend to them the processes of review, supervision, advice, and governance generally applicable on the campuses. The resources of the laboratories, in turn, should be made available to the academic community for teaching and research purposes to the fullest extent possible." The committee also asked that the laboratory directors be appointed by procedures "identical with those followed in the naming of a new chancellor" and that they be "exempt from outside veto"—i.e., that the government's concurrence not be required, as at present (*Report of Special Committee,* 1970).

The foregoing recommendations represent consistent, widespread, and humane views of many faculty and students. The only trouble is that (a) they do not represent the views of laboratory staff, who have often been incensed at the disposition of faculty to control their destiny without consulting them about it;[9] (b) they are often not acceptable to government agencies, who are responsible to the Congress and the President, not faculty and students; and (c) they are at present, in most cases, impracticable, because the money needed to convert large laboratories from military to civilian purposes is not available or, to be more precise, has not been appropriated.

Hence most university boards have disregarded or tempered faculty recommendations for laboratory control and conversion[10] or just cut the laboratory loose from the university. The overall result has been a loss in dollars to the university and a gain for the institutes. The following laboratories and institutes conducting research for the Department of Defense have broken their university connection:

1   In 1967, the Electronics Research Laboratories, a component of the electrical engineering department at Columbia University, was converted into the independent nonprofit Riverside Research Institute.

2   In 1968, the Institute for Defense Analyses, an independent nonprofit center advising the Secretary of Defense, whose trustees had been appointed by 12 universities, was reorganized to eliminate university membership and render the trustees self-appointing.

3   In 1969, the Hudson Laboratories, an R&D center managed by Columbia University for the Navy, were absorbed into the governmental Naval Research Laboratory.

4   In 1969, the Human Resources Research Office, a center which has conducted personnel and "human factors" work for the Army, shed George Washington University's administrative umbrella and was reconstituted as the Human Resources Research Organization, an independent nonprofit center with its own board of trustees.

5   Also in 1969, the Center for Research in Social Systems, operated by American University under an Army contract, ended its connections with that university and its status as an R&D center, becoming part of the American Institutes for Research, an independent nonprofit organization with offices in Pittsburgh, Palo Alto, and Silver Spring, Md.

6   The same year, as "the direct result of student unrest," the Research Institute of Temple University was expelled from the university by the Board of Trustees and obliged to drop "Temple" from its name. Now an independent nonprofit corporation with a staff of 25 and an annual volume of about $0.5 million, the unit has affiliated with the Franklin Institute. A "painful readjustment" is being attempted "from defense-oriented projects to those concerned with our environment."[11]

7   In 1969, some 20 professional personnel (not faculty) of the Stanford Applied Electronics Laboratory relinquished their university appointments and transferred their work to the Stanford Research Institute.

8   In 1970, SRI itself severed its ties with Stanford to become a self-governing nonprofit institute. Under the terms of the agreement, SRI is to pay Stanford 1 percent of its gross operating revenues each year until $25 million

is reached and thereafter, ½ of 1 percent in perpetuity. Within five years, SRI must also drop "Stanford" from its name.

At least two more significant changes may be expected:

1 MIT has announced that the Draper Laboratory (the former Instrumentation Laboratory) will be evicted and, in all likelihood, set up as an independent nonprofit organization with its own board of directors. The laboratory conducted some $55 million worth of R&D in 1969, mainly on guidance and control systems for NASA and the Navy. Unlike MIT's Lincoln Laboratory, it adjoins the campus and has had close ties with faculty and student research and teaching, especially in the Departments of Aeronautics and Astronautics and Electrical Engineering.

2 The proposed sale of the Cornell Aeronautical Laboratory to the for-profit EDP Technology, Inc., for $25 million was announced in 1968, but has been held up by legal action challenging the right of Cornell university thus to alter the laboratory's nonprofit status. Owned and controlled by the Cornell University board but operating independently very much in the manner of the Stanford Research Institute, the Buffalo laboratory performed some $33 million worth of R&D in 1968, including classified work for government and proprietary work for industry. In November 1970, the Supreme Court of New York ruled unanimously that the university could proceed with the sale. However, the Cornell University–EDP contract was allowed to expire by mutual consent and the future status of the laboratory remains uncertain.

THE FRAGILE FINANCES OF INSTITUTES Despite all of the foregoing developments, and a lowering of the esteem with which the academic community has been regarded in Washington and the nation, I am less confident at the conclusion of this study than I was at the outset that the university will soon yield its pride of place in research to nonprofit institutes. In 10 years (the more distant the time, the more likely the change) there may be a more even balance of money and influence between the two sectors. But in the near term, this is less likely. The reasons are historical (universities are entrenched, institutes, aborning); logistical (in virtually every field, far more Ph.D.'s are on campus); political (universities are more powerful, politically more experienced, have more alumni, are better organized and more united, and are legally freer to lobby); and practical (universities are larger, geographically more dispersed, more versatile, and, in truth, less dispensable). But to my mind, the most important single reason is economic: the University is an altogether stronger and more enduring corporate enterprise than the institute.

As an economic enterprise, the university is like a conglomerate or a city—the University of California, New York University, Northeastern University, and the State University of New York are larger and more diversified than many cities—whereas the institute is more like a small business or shop. The university may close a school, a department, or a program, but what university has gone out of business?[12]

The university can curtail many activities without affecting the heart of its operations or its revenue from student fees, endowment, private grants, and state and federal agencies, which have helped it to acquire major assets in the form of buildings, lands, and equipment; these assets in turn enable it to obtain loans to meet any deficits. In contrast, an institute is financially fragile. In financial trouble, it can only curtail less profitable projects which may be its *raison d'être*. Except for operating foundations and endowed institutes, few institutes have assets against which loans can be obtained. Their viability can depend upon the capital needed for two or three months' operations.

Thus, when the Human Resources Research Office parted with George Washington University, its principal asset was the value of the leave its staff had accumulated. The university had billed the Army on a leave-taken basis; the Army agreed to pay the Human Resources Research Office on a leave-accrual basis, which enabled it to meet expenses during the first month's independent operations in September 1969. When Electronics Research Laboratories staff left Columbia University to form the Riverside Research Institute, their initial assets were $74 *(sic)* plus their contracts. The government advanced payments, subject to a lien on Riverside Research Institute's property and cash. If I have this story right, the government gave up a first lien on the property so that the institute could arrange a line of credit with a bank. In these cases, the Department of Defense was helpful to its friends in a time of trouble, as it was when it agreed to the 1969 transfer of Stanford University staff to the Stanford Research Institute and paid SRI's higher overhead.[13]

It is not only former components of universities which must make their way in the world with surprisingly few assets; many other institutes are in a similar position.

Founded in 1946 in a psychology professor's basement, the American Institutes for Research grew until, in 1965, it constructed its own building. But, in 1967, a year of rapid growth, American Institutes for Research was short of working capital. It borrowed over $1 million from a bank and sold its building to the University of Pittsburgh, renting back office space. Under stricter management, American Institutes for Research paid off most of its loans, but in 1970, when government contract payments were delayed, it again had to borrow money to meet its payroll.

In 1968, the Hudson Institute reported assets of $810,000, gross income of $1,233,000, and expenses of $1,368,000. The institute has been seeking funds to pay for the staff time to explore new ideas and to convert project reports into publishable books. Having failed to secure a substantial foundation grant, it has launched a campaign to raise $25,000 to $50,000 a year in contributions from "alumni" of its seminars.

Bowen Dees, who became president of the Franklin Institute in 1970, has testified to the financial plight of applied research institutes:

These organizations have little general support from gifts or endowment income, and must pay virtually all their costs of operation from contract revenues . . . in today's research climate, it is proving increasingly difficult for these groups to survive.

. . . I know there exist arguments for either letting these organizations die out or transforming them (in certain cases where this seems feasible) into commercial research laboratories. . . . I am distressed by our national tendency to look upon institutions sometimes as we do upon "no-deposit, no-return" bottles: Use them, then discard them (*National Science Policy,* 1970, pp. 205–206).

James Watson, the Nobel Laureate director of Cold Spring Harbor Laboratory of Quantitative Biology, laments: ". . . lacking an endowment we cannot expect first rate senior scientists to choose Cold Spring Harbor as their homes unless real security can be offered to them and their families." The $42,000 raised in annual contributions from 12 sponsoring universities and research institutions was "indispensable" for modest improvements to the library and instructional laboratories.

Since we lack endowment, we would have to stay in an essentially static state if our income were largely restricted to research grants. No business manager, no matter how astute, can collect enough overhead to permit expansion. Thus the continued financial support of our current sponsors plus the addition of new sponsoring universities and industrial organizations will be necessary ingredients for innovative direction (*Director's Report,* 1969).

Nor have endowed institutes escaped the need for economies. The Brookings Institution has projected a 1971 deficit of $400,000, with expenditures of $5.9 million; in 1970, the National Bureau of Economic Research had a $558,000 deficit, with $2.8 million expenditures; the Wistar Institute, an estimated deficit of $157,000 on a $2.9 million budget. After deficits of $1.2 million in 1968 and $1.8 million in 1969, which were met from capital, the Sloan-Kettering Institute has had to undergo "radical budget surgery."

Faced with . . . a probable deficit of $2.6 million for 1970, the trustees have set a deficit ceiling of $1.6 million and required expenditures to be cut by $1,000,000. As a result, seven out of 69 laboratories have had to be closed, while nine others have taken cuts of 20% to 30%. Both professional and technical staffs have been reduced and further curtailment next year is inevitable ("Research Crisis," 1970, p. H4150).

The chronic financial instability of institutes can only be aggravated by the provisions of the 1969 Tax Reform Act against accumulation of income. Indeed, the senior financial officer of one R&D center which has constructed a building from accumulated fees observed that "there is a question if building a building is part of our corporate purpose." The IRS may also question the practice of buying nearby property as an investment or as a defense against rising land costs. In brief, the tax law makes it difficult for an institute to bolster its financial position.

DEATH AND TRANSFIGURATION It might be thought that higher educational institutions have so many problems of their own that they can offer little comfort to an institute which is ailing financially or intellectually. However, a considerable number of independents have become affiliated with, merged with, or been converted into universities.

1 Perhaps the most celebrated case is the Rockefeller Institute for Medical Research, which became Rockefeller University in 1954. This change was not made for economic reasons; the institute had an endowment in excess of $100 million. Nonetheless, since becoming a university, the Rockefeller has tempered its aversion to government money. In 1954–55, it received only $57,000 in research grants; in 1968–69, $5.5 million, and, during the next two years, the amount of federal support increased by almost 10 percent per year. This turn toward the government was due, of course, not

to greediness but to the greater expense of operating a university with graduate students and a broadened program of instruction and research.

Apparently, the change was motivated by a wish to revivify the institute, which, though highly distinguished, was no longer unique. Leading universities were now also engaged in high-quality biomedical research and the bloom was on the rose of graduate education. Would not brilliant graduate students transform a fine institution into an exciting one? Detlev Bronk, who was largely responsible for the move as incoming president in 1953, recalls:

When I first came here, the tables [in the dining hall] were lined up like rows of tombstones in a military cemetery, eight people to a table and usually the same people from the same laboratory at the same table. Nearly everybody had been advised by the head of his laboratory not to talk about his current project lest some outsider get on to it. That kind of insularity was prevalent among research institutes. They were ingrown. They did not perpetuate themselves. They tended to grow selfish. But with young people around the walls have to come down (Kobler, 1970, p. 46).[14]

Some qualified observers contest this explanation, holding that the Rockefeller was better off as an institute than as a university, that it had not fallen from its scientific pinnacle nor did it need rejuvenating. The graduate students are not all brilliant; some lack elementary knowledge and require coaching. The institute had been a community, lean but quick-footed; the university became a showplace. In their view, due to the well-meaning but misguided motives of Bronk and board chairman David Rockefeller, the institute succumbed to all-too-common American lures: novelty, growth, and grandiloquence.

2 The Mellon Institute's 1967 merger with the Carnegie Institute of Technology to form the Carnegie-Mellon University is a similar case. Again, there were signs of insularity and stuffiness, a slowing down in the circulation of men and ideas through doors that too few outsiders opened. Like the Rockefeller, the Mellon was solvent, with a comfortable endowment. Still, the Mellons had apparently wearied of the need repeatedly to endow the institute, and there were financial advantages to becoming an educational institution. "Mellon officials, including President Paul C. Cross, candidly say that research institutes such as Mellon have found it progressively more difficult to obtain the federal funds necessary for extensive research. They explain that many programs are specifically earmarked for educational institutions, and that in other programs, universities are often given a competitive advantage in obtaining research funds. At Mellon it has become apparent that the institute would do better financially if it had a university label" (Nelson, 1967, p. 674).

3 The transfer by the Navy of the Center for Naval Analyses contract from the Franklin Institute to the University of Rochester in 1967 may appear anachronistic. However, protests against the military had not yet become *de rigueur.* Nor should we be so blinded by events at places like Harvard, MIT, Cornell, Columbia, Pennsylvania, and Stanford as to forget that many universities continue to accept classified research and reject attempts to expel it. Thus, Rochester President Allen Wallis has rejected a faculty recommendation to give up the CNA contract and has made his policy stick.[15] So far as CNA staff were concerned, the new contract represented an improvement; they gained more independence in setting program objectives and were less involved in "fire fighting." However, as Rochester received no fee, CNA had very little money to invest in the diversification which it and the university sought (the little that it had came from the university's general funds and a few non-Navy contracts).

4 The Woods Hole Oceanographic Institution obtained the power to grant graduate degrees in 1967 and awarded its first doctorate in 1969. It now has a joint degree program with MIT and a joint graduate level program with Harvard. The explanations *Science* reporter Luther Carter gave for the change were similar to those advanced for the Rockefeller: though a first-class research institution, Woods Hole was no longer unique, since universities had developed comparable research programs; and "Woods Hole fears that, without a steady infusion of able graduate students, its intellectual vigor and competence will decline." Much of the $2.5 million that had to be raised for the first five years' costs of the educational program were expected to come from federal programs for educational institutions. ". . . [F]or the first time, WHOI will be able to participate in some government grant-in-aid programs for which it has been ineligible in the past. WHOI hopes to receive [funds . . .] from the National Science Foundation and . . . the U.S. Office of Education" (Carter, 1967 pp. 115–117).

5 The Graduate Research Center of the Southwest, founded in 1962, retitled the Southwest Center for Advanced Studies in 1967, became the nucleus of the University of Texas at Dallas in September 1969. From its inception, the center could grant degrees, but didn't, partly because of the hostility of neighboring universities. The center's first president, Lloyd Berkner, had headed Associated Universities, Inc., the pioneer university research consortium. An energetic, persuasive, and successful entrepreneur, Berkner had large visions of the expanded industry and employment that the center would bring to Dallas and the Southwest. However, Berkner died and so did some of the visions. From 1962 to 1968, the center raised $22.5 million in gifts and grants mainly from individuals and firms in the Dallas area, and $19.3 million in sponsored research funds. But the center's ambitions exceeded its funds. It was rescued by the state legislature at the cost of its independence. Writing on stationery titled "The University of Texas at Dallas" with no mention of the erstwhile center, Acting President Francis S. Johnson states:

As a part of the state system, we are now charged with the responsibility of developing a general educational institution. However, we are restricted by legislative action not to accept undergraduates before 1975 and then only at the junior and senior level. There are some suggestions that these restrictions may be changed. In the meantime, we are embarking formally on graduate programs in certain areas of science and broadening our planning for future activities. . . . It is not clear how our relations with other universities will develop in the future. Since we will grant our own degrees, we will be more competitive and it may be more difficult to maintain cooperative programs. However, we are still carrying on cooperative programs and will welcome any new ones. [16]

6 A clear case in which an institute affiliated with a university to gain financial stability is that of the Virginia Institute for Scientific Research. A small nonprofit institute which has conducted basic and applied research in biochemistry, biology, chemistry, and physics, it began operations in 1949. In 1969, its revenues were $210,000 and its net worth $395,000, down from $487,000 in 1967. The director's report for 1969 explains:

On September 15, 1969, the Institute became affiliated with the University of Richmond. This major event was the final result of discussions beginning in 1966 to carry out the Trustees directive to affiliate with an educational institution in order to perpetuate, insure the stability, and broaden the usefulness of the Institute. . . .

The year 1969 saw much publicity given to the concern of the scientific community for the decline in support of scientific research. The institute has felt this decline in support severely as potential sponsors have delayed consideration of funding research proposals or have declined to support work which in past years would have received more consideration. National priorities in research have changed with recognition of the mixed blessings of technology, and in the last two years of the Institute's existence, we have been unable to make the adjustments required by changing fashions. These adjustments must now be made. . . .

The institute was located near the university, whose provost, Robert Smart, was a member of the board. As of October 1970, final arrangements had not been worked out, but the university had agreed "to underwrite the operations of the Institute as required." The institute had made provisions for faculty to conduct research in its laboratory; biology classes had been held there; and some institute staff had been appointed as adjunct professors to teach courses or to direct graduate student research.[17]

7   The Charles F. Kettering Research Laboratory of Yellow Springs, Ohio, founded in 1953, has been separated from the Charles F. Kettering Foundation and will affiliate with, and later move to, the campus of Wright State University at Dayton. The laboratory has a professional staff of 50 and engages in research in photobiology, cell differentiation, and nitrogen fixation.[18] Were it "to remain dependent upon funding from the Foundation indefinitely," E. H. Vause, executive vice-president of the foundation, writes, "its growth would be terminated as the limit of our financial capability was reached." As Wright State is "a new and rapidly growing institution," affiliation is seen as a way to foster the growth and research quality of both the institute and the university.[19]

8   RAND has begun an experimental program of graduate education which may lead to the award of Ph.D.'s in policy analysis, conceivably by the California Institute of Technology or the University of California at Los Angeles or by RAND itself. In December 1970, a workshop in international development and courses in macroeconomics and game theory were being given on a quarter basis to 11 students, all members of the RAND staff, with master's degrees. Inquiries had been made at the Western Association of Schools

and Colleges to see if the work could be accredited at a degree-giving institution. RAND officials and trustees are by no means agreed upon the wisdom of enlarging and formalizing the program. Charles Wolf, head of the RAND economics department, has given these reasons for the experiment:

> . . . the national need [for] . . . manpower properly trained for interdisciplinary research; the possibility that a policy research organization like Rand might have special capabilities for helping to meet this need . . . ; the keen interest of some of Rand's best staff members in undertaking the effort; the benefits from upgrading the Rand staff who participate as students . . . ; and the benefits from having a small and select group of graduate students working at Rand in the follow-on phase. . . .
>
> The [staff] committee [which Wolf chaired] decided that these positive arguments outweighed the non-negligible negative ones: the complexities, distractions, and fragmentation that such a program might entail for our principal research endeavors; the uncertainties . . . [about] whether . . . rigor and relevance could be achieved . . . ; and . . . prospective funding problems if we decide to expand and sustain the program (Wolf, 1970, pp. 6–7).

One informant estimated the present cost of the program at $50,-000 a year. Some of that might be offset by cheap labor of graduate students, but the program is now too limited for RAND to be reclassified as an educational institution by either the IRS or the Office of Education, and thus receive the financial advantages which such an institution enjoys.[20]

It should be noted that, in the present study, I have accepted the Office of Education's criteria of "higher educational institution," since the Office of Education's list of these institutions is published annually and is used by NSF in its R&D surveys. The IRS criteria require not the awarding of degrees, but just regular classes, faculty, and students. Under the 1969 Tax Reform Act, the advantages of being classified as an educational institution rather than a "private foundation" are so pronounced that many research-cum-educational institutions have applied for the former status. Among these are the Brookings Institution, the Carnegie Institution of Washington, the Wistar Institute, the Center for Advanced Study in the Behavioral Sciences, and the Institute for Advanced Study (which, as of December 1970, had had its application approved).

SUMMING UP I have found it futile to compare the growth of R&D expenditures on campus with that at nonprofit institutes because the precise composition of each sector in surveys has been too erratic. However, there has been no striking difference since 1945; if anything, the academic sector has grown slightly faster. Many of the administrative changes that have been enumerated represent shifts *within* the institute sector as I have defined it (from R&D centers or applied institutes under university management to independent centers or institutes). And, as has been noted, the institute tub leaks into both the academic and commercial sectors.

Despite all the furor it has aroused, the volume of Department of Defense research expenditures on campus has held up remarkably. Of 524 campuses surveyed by the American Council on Education's Committee on Campus Tensions, only four reported that they had discontinued any research for the military in the 1968–69 academic year; none would acknowledge that this was the direct result of a protest or incident. That may be too sanguine a version of history, but Deputy Defense Secretary David Packard shares it: "I am not particularly troubled that a few university faculties have chosen not to support defense-funded research. . . . There are many other universities where defense support is welcome, and there are many scientists and engineers to do the work."[21] There are some signs of what might be called a "Southern" or "hinterland" strategy, in which Department of Defense funds have been shifting from turbulent to quieter campuses.[22]

R&D centers were hit by the curtailment of government expenditures several years before the campuses were. Except for a few organizations (e.g., the Population Council) specializing in "hot" fields, most institutes have had to effect economies and are, at best, now only holding their own. Whatever the long-term consequences of campus disturbances, nonprofit institutes have not yet benefited financially from them.

Some institutes hope, as one official said, that "when the spigot is opened, much more will come our way than to the universities." Shortly after "16 scientists, four technicians, and four secretaries packed their belongings and moved in a group from the Applied Electronics Laboratory . . . on the Stanford University campus to the . . . Stanford Research Institute" in the spring of 1969 ("How Students," 1969, p. 24), SRI President Charles Anderson said:

The environment on many university campuses throughout the country has been changing quite dramatically in the last few years. I know of numerous instances where scientists have become uncomfortable and are seeking other places. . . . These places might well be found in industry and in private research institutions and, perhaps, even in government laboratories.

As these men decide that they would rather conduct their professional activities in places other than the university, it is only natural that the kind of contract support that is involved in their work would follow them.

In addition, some qualified people who normally would gravitate to a university might now prefer to stay away from the campus. . . . If a trend such as this should develop, it would also tend to draw government contracts away from the campus. . . .

My guess is that the first movement will be in the applied research areas — particularly applied research funded by the Department of Defense, because that work is the most immediate target of student radicals. But I also expect that basic research involving scientific theory will leave, because you just don't take one segment of a research area away and continue with all the rest of it. It seems likely that these things will follow together in a package.

This isn't going to be something that will happen as an overwhelming movement overnight, but more as an erosion, perhaps over a period of several years (Anderson, 1969, p. 22).

Such a development is possible. It may even be desirable. I believe that it would be wise for the government to reduce its dependence upon universities, especially for large-scale research, and for universities, in turn, to pound less often and less loudly on the doors of research agencies. But wisdom does not always prevail in governmental or academic affairs.

Part Five

Conclusion

12. An Assessment

To some, large research installations represent the wave of the future, creating the new knowledge and technology necessary for the effective functioning of an advanced industrial society. Knowledge is now supposed to be producible from scientists on demand, like gum pellets from a vending machine. The atomic bomb, radar, guided missiles, earth satellites, and moon rockets demonstrated that, given enough money, scientists and engineers can accomplish difficult technical tasks in a remarkably short time. Many forces contributed to these achievements, but one was the assembling of scientists, engineers, technicians, and supporting staffs in laboratories funded by the federal government and managed by private institutions. Combining private talents and public funds in this manner has had enough technical success and political appeal — meeting public needs while acknowledging and, indeed, gratifying the traditional American distrust of government — to seem applicable to almost any national problem.

I have argued that the formula is too glib and that proponents should demonstrate, and not merely assume, that a new research institute is required for the solution of a problem.

When the government establishes a new research center, should it be independent or under university management?

After the war, university management was preferred for many large laboratories developing military and nuclear technologies. Sometimes, the university assumed management reluctantly, as a patriotic responsibility, under government pressure. David Lilienthal recalls that, in 1947, the University of California Regents were "anxious to be relieved" of the Los Alamos weapons laboratory contract, but, as chairman of the AEC he persuaded them to continue it because laboratory staff on that remote mesa valued the association as a means of maintaining their academic status.

Nonetheless, like other observers,[1] Lilienthal now questions the arrangement. Indeed, after suggesting that excessive involvement in government programs has interfered with teaching and scholarship, he asks if universities "too deeply committed" to withdraw should not convert themselves into research institutes by "lopping off entirely what has become the minor function of teaching . . . " (Lilienthal, 1963, pp. 77, 80).

One cannot examine the reasons that have been given for and against the university management of applied R&D centers without concluding that policy on this issue has been governed less by academic principles than by practical circumstances. In 1954, the Hancher Committee of the American Council on Education stated that classified research by universities was justified "only by the demands of national security. . . . [W]e nevertheless recognize that our institutions have a public responsibility to handle such research if they are uniquely qualified to do the work." That was sufficiently equivocal to permit any institution to do what it pleased. Elsewhere, the committee said:

Numerous large research projects with military objectives are now managed by educational institutions. These projects are vitally important and must be carried out. It is essential, however, to so manage these projects that they do not improperly or seriously disrupt the educational programs of other institutions through unreasonable competition for manpower and particularly through excessively high salary temptations. . . .[2]

Evidently, it was the danger that federal funds would be used to raid faculty and to raise salaries unduly that really distressed the committee.

In 1958, NSF was also equivocal. No, it said, large-scale applied work should not be conducted "within" universities; but, yes, it might be conducted "outside" the departments. (How a large-scale project could be squeezed into a department was not explained.)

. . . it is suggested that Federal agencies carefully consider other alternatives before placing large-scale applied research and development projects within institutions of higher learning. Where a Federal agency finds it necessary to obtain such work from a university over a period of time, it is generally desirable that it be done through the device of a research center constructed and supported by the Government, and staffed and managed by the university but kept outside the academic departments (*Government-University,* 1958, pp. 27–28).

The next year, President Eisenhower's Budget Director accentuated the negative and made one of the stronger official statements against university-managed applied centers. Government agencies, he said, "should consider other feasible alternatives and contractors before requesting an institution of higher learning directly to administer a large-scale applied research and development facility under an operating and management contract, particularly if the work is concerned with development and testing" ("Use of Management," 1959).

The President's Science Advisory Committee soon responded to this budgetary threat with the forceful document, *Scientific Progress, The Universities, and the Federal Government,* known as the Seaborg Report:

Since the beginning of World War II there have developed a number of major research installations which are supported by Federal money and operated by universities or groups of universities. . . . We believe that this particular form of partnership between government and universities deserves encouragement and improvement.

We specifically reject the view that such large operations . . . are inevitably alien to the university. We believe that great fields of research like nuclear physics simply must not be cut off from universities just because they now require very large instruments and correspondingly large staffs of specialists and technicians. The very difficulties of such large laboratories, in our view, are an argument for strengthening their connection to the universities (*Scientific Progress,* 1960, p. 21).

The reference to "groups of universities" and "nuclear physics" endorsed government support for expensive basic research installations such as those managed by Associated Universities, Inc. Supporters of the university management of R&D centers commonly cite centers devoted to basic research, whereas opponents cite those engaged in applied research and development; the broader policy is then subsumed under the stronger but narrower case. However, the Seaborg report contested the distinction between basic and applied research:

. . . one striking characteristic of our scientific age has been the disappearance of the barriers between pure and applied science. . . . Basic and applied science today are distinguished less by method and content than by motivation. Part of the strength of American science stems from close attention to intellectual intercourse between basic and applied scientists.

Very often, indeed, the same man can be both "pure scientist" and "engineer," as he works on different problems or on different parts of one problem. We do not believe in any artificial separation between basic and applied research or between science and engineering (*Scientific Progress,* 1960, p. 4).

Of course, a committee chaired by Chancellor Glenn Seaborg of the University of California's Berkeley campus did not intend to rebuke the AEC for entrusting to the Universities of California and Chicago facilities engaged not only in very pure research but also in very practical work on nuclear weapons and reactors. The Bell report *Government Contracting for Research and Development* submitted to President Kennedy 17 months later concurred: "University-associated research centers are well suited to basic *or applied research. . .* " (my italics).[3]

And so did President Howard Johnson of MIT in 1967, when he extolled

. . . the continued achievement of our two large special laboratories, the Lincoln Laboratory and the Instrumentation Laboratory. They serve their primary purpose of providing major additions to the nation's operative defense and space programs, and, in another dimension, they provide appropriate problems for productive research by our students and faculty. Their purpose is a good one, and their process productive for our scholarship ("Report of the President," 1967, p. 5).

Faculty and student protests at MIT, occupations of buildings, a "strike for peace," and general institutional turmoil commencing in the fall of 1968 and reaching one peak in March 1969 and another in January 1970 wreaked a forceful change in that opinion. In April 1969, Johnson appointed a review panel; and in May 1970, he announced a decision to separate the Instrumentation Laboratory from MIT (which had not yet occurred by June 1971).[4]

Is it unduly cynical to conclude that most of the arguments for and against the management of Defense laboratories by universities have been an intellectual gloss on political realities?

In contrast to the turbulence on campus, life has been comparatively peaceful at most institutes. The absence of students has spared them that source of disruption, and their authoritarian structure and lack of staff tenure have doubtless inhibited protest. But staff subsisting on defense research will not view it as do students and faculty who have other means of support. At many institutes, research for the Department of Defense is a way of life that is not changing very quickly or radically.

One question I was asked to address in this inquiry was (I paraphrase): "Have research institutes found new ways of organizing knowledge, less rigid than those of the university, which may give them a leadership position in the future generation of knowledge?" That is not the sort of question that can be answered in a word. Nonetheless, I will answer "No," in the sense of generating a distinctive order of knowledge previously unknown to man, but "Yes" in a more humdrum and essentially administrative sense: the institute is better able than a university department to generate knowledge which is reliable and timely or requires the coordinated and protracted work of many men. Perhaps it would be better to say that institutes have found new ways of organizing not knowledge but professional men. If the knowledge which they and universities produce differs, it is because of differences in the purposes, organization, and financing of the two institutions. Modern science and social science have long since passed the day when every investigator did all his own work. An accelerator, a computer, or even a typewriter requires staff to man it, and often to digest its product — Wolfgang Panofsky, director of the Stanford Linear Accelerator Center, has called this last type of personnel "data reducers."[5] The institute is simply an organization providing such services to the investigator and to research sponsors. Among its services, of course, is the full-time labor of professional men from different disciplines, who can be assigned to tasks as needed.

In contrast, the research of faculty is voluntary[6] and must be accommodated to the requirements of teaching; and interdisciplinary research runs against the grain of departmental organization. Campus institutes may foster interdisciplinary work, but must constantly contend with faculty independence and departmental interests. As Alvin Weinberg observes, campus institutes "suffer from a mismatch between the social ethos of the university and the social ethos of the institute: the one is individual and democratic, the other collective and hierarchical. When the institute acquires a collective and hierarchical character, which I believe is necessary for its success, its tie with the university department becomes more tenuous" (Weinberg, 1970, p. 1070). A campus institute with full-time professional staff is a disenfranchised colony ruled by academic landlords. To my mind, the principal objection to a university institute is the peonage of its staff, while the virtue of an independent institute is the self-respect it gives them.

The principal practical problems of institutes are intellectual isolation and financial instability.

Few of even the largest institutes enjoy the cultural and library resources, the variety of intellectual activities, and the round-the-clock discussions characteristic of universities.[7] To remain alert, an institute can offer fellowships and other hospitality to graduate students and faculty, facilitate contacts with neighboring campuses, and promote the kind of atmosphere which encourages an interest in ideas and distinguishes a genuine intellectual organization from a business.[8] If some institutes have difficulty distinguishing the two, so, unfortunately, do some universities.

Should anything be done about institutes' chronic financial insecurity? A special value of applied and project institutes is precisely their responsiveness to the research marketplace; were they more secure, they would presumably become less responsive. The marketplace occupies a peculiar place in American demonology: we extol its virtues while seeking to escape its risks. And the federal government is a principal means by which friendly and defeated nations, industries, educational institutions, hospitals, orchestras, and a hundred thousand other faltering causes seek to escape the unkind mercies of the market.

I do not think that nonprofit research institutes, as a class, should be sheltered from the exigencies of the intellectual marketplace any more than they are at present. Which is not to say that present tax laws and government policies affecting institutes are ideal.

There are basic obstacles to improving these policies. Anyone can establish an institute in his home and apply for an NSF grant the next day—and people do. Any new law or program which dealt liberally and generously with institutes as a class would undoubtedly lead to a rapid increase in their number. Accordingly, government policies toward institutes should be selective. But to formulate policies which are both selective and equitable requires far more information about institutes than is now available.[9] In this area, as in many others, good policy and good information go hand in hand.

As noted previously, the 1969 tax act should lead to better financial reporting by nonprofit institutes; the IRS plans to centralize their returns in its Philadelphia office, where they will be available for public examination. IRS should improve form 990A, and institutes, in turn, should complete it adequately.[10] At present, many questions are inapplicable, or are answered so inconsistently that they fail to yield much meaningful information. For example, the Wistar Institute's 1969 return is blank except for the entry "00" on lines 10 and 17. Nor could IRS find a recent return submitted by the American Institutes for Research, the Brookings Institution, the Institute for Advanced Study, the Research Triangle Institute, the Southwest Research Institute, the Syracuse University Research Corporation, or the Urban Institute, among others. I cannot say where the fault lies.

Many R&D centers and institutes publish no annual report or publish one so late that it is only of historic interest. The Kitt Peak National Observatory and the Brookings Institution reports for 1968 were so long delayed that they prepared biennial reports for both 1968 and 1969. As of 1970, the Bioscience Information Service, the Child Research Center of Michigan, the Electromagnetic Compatibility Analysis Center, the Eppley Foundation for Research, the Infectious Disease Research Institute, the Interscience Research Institute, the Lincoln Laboratory, the Los Alamos Scientific Laboratory, and the National Opinion Research Center published no annual reports at all.

That has also been true of many private foundations. The Foundation Library Center, with offices in New York and Washington, was formed to encourage foundations to give a fuller public accounting of their activities. Though the center has had limited success at that,[11] it has made foundation reports, tax returns, and other information readily accessible to the public. It would be helpful if the center could do the same for at least the larger nonprofit institutes.

Alan Pifer has proposed that regular block grants be given by the government to financially weak nonprofit organizations doing work of national importance.[12]

A few institutes, such as the Center for Advanced Study in the Behavioral Sciences and the Institute for Advanced Study, have already received substantial ad hoc block grants from NSF; the Sloan-Kettering Institute was awarded a pioneering five-year institutional grant from NIH. Institutes also receive, as an additional "free" or block grant, a small percentage of the sum of their NIH project grants.

Contractual fees have given many R&D centers a vital operational freedom and enabled some to build up financial reserves. As the Sloan-Kettering grant has been attacked by a congressional committee and the size of center fees has been criticized by the Comptroller General, executive agencies must, however, be chary about both devices.

Another form of block support is the overhead allowance, which can have powerful and prompt effects on institute finances. Bruce Smith observes that the Air Force's 1961 refusal to reimburse contractors for the depreciation of buildings "sent a shiver of apprehension through RAND officials" (Smith, 1966, p. 134). One informed congressional staff member declared that the Bureau of the Budget rules for calculating overhead had been so liberalized that institutes as well as universities "may be making a profit on . . . [their] government work." Institute administrators, however, contend that too many government officials fail to understand institute finances: they assume that the salaries of institute staff, like those of professors, are financed from sources other than research projects; that institutes can cost-share; and that most institutes are endowed or grown fat on fees, like (they imagine) Battelle, Aerospace, and RAND.

Of course, institutes would like to receive "unrestricted" funds which they are free to use as they please. Unfortunately or fortunately, they are less likely to receive such funds from the government than from private donors; and, regardless of how much they receive, their needs are likely to exceed their income.[13]

Since institutes have been less important, as a group, than universities or industry, they have been relatively neglected in the formulation of government research policies.[14] The programs and cost policies of NSF and the Public Health Service have been designed for universities and hence, institute officials complain, are inadequate for institutes.[15] However, as these agencies have enlarged their applied research programs, they have been paying more attention to institutes' needs. Thus, the Department of Health, Education and Welfare has recently prepared a special administrative handbook for institutes and other nonprofit organizations. These are grouped into six classes, according to their financial independence and management quality. A "financially dependent" organization, to which stricter management controls apply, is one which "received 80 percent or more of its total revenue from grants *and* contracts awarded directly or indirectly (i.e., through subcon-

tracts or similar arrangements) by *all* Federal agencies. . . ."[16]
Management is graded as follows:

1 Excellent management, to which "relaxed management systems" are applied "by requiring reports less frequently and in less detail, reducing the scope and frequency of audits, removing or reducing prior approval requirements and relaxing certain other requirements."

2 No serious management deficiencies, in which "It is expected that the vast majority of grantees will be found," to which normal policies are applied.

3 Serious management deficiencies: "These organizations will be subject to certain special requirements, controls, or limitations pertaining to the particular management deficiencies disclosed in the review. . . . They will be given a prescribed period of time to correct the deficiencies. . . . Special requirements will be rescinded when all deficiencies have been corrected. If the deficiencies persist, further action will be taken on a case-by-case basis, including the withholding of support where necessary" (*A Program for Improving the Quality*, 1970, **2**, p. 11).

Many institutes are small and inexperienced and their administrative practices could be improved. Occasionally, as in the case of the National Opinion Research Center and the American Institute of Biological Sciences (a professional association), glaring management errors have been made. Thus, the HEW program should help promote the prudent management that will be even more necessary should a system of major block grants be instituted.

If government policies have been unsatisfactory to institutes, they are in part to blame because they have done little to propose better policies.[17] To do so, they must first agree on what they would propose, but institutes are so varied in organization, finances, and purposes that this will be no easy task. Most institute directors have preferred to operate as individuals or in ad hoc informal groups; they have not felt a sufficient community of interest to organize a comprehensive national association to discuss their common problems, to develop professional and administrative standards, and to concert policies.

Some of the main circles of interest may be indicated by the few formal and informal groups of institute representatives that I have been able to discover. The one formal national association is the Association of Independent Research Institutes, consisting of some 60 biomedical research institutes whose ninth annual meeting was held in October 1970. Each institute is represented at meetings "by the two persons having chief responsibility for the scientific direction of and for the administrative direction of the institute respectively." Membership is open to any nonprofit institute "whose principal purpose is to conduct independent scientific investigations in the biological and medical sciences and whose research budget is in excess of $100,000 annually."

The purpose of this Association is to contribute to the advancement of research and research facilities in the health related sciences (1) through visits to various member institutes and discussions of the objectives, management, and accomplishments of the scientific programs in these institutes, (2) by arranging and conducting meetings for the exchange of information and experiences among members on problems common to the independent research institutes, (3) by bringing speakers before the members who may contribute to the solution of common scientific or business problems of the research institutes, and (4) by other means and devices which shall from time to time be determined by the members.

The Association may from time to time carry out studies to determine what is needed to advance the scientific efforts of the independent research institutes and may, on request, make the results of such studies known to appropriate representatives of the U.S. Public Health Service, other U.S. Government agencies, voluntary health agencies, or any other non-profit agencies or foundations (Association of Independent Research Institutes, 1969).

The Conference of Institutional Administrators, composed in 1969 of the senior administrative officers of some 22 nonprofit organizations in the Washington, D.C., area, has met monthly since 1961. The Brookings Institution, Carnegie Institution of Washington, Center for Applied Linguistics, National Planning Association, Resources for the Future, and Urban America belong, but most other participants represent scientific, educational, and professional associations. Senior professional personnel and directors of Washington policy research institutes met monthly for luncheon discussions for four years at Brookings until the spring of 1971 when the informal group apparently expired. The directors of applied research institutes have met periodically, as one member said, "to cry on each other's shoulders." The directors of some AEC centers have got together over the years and the directors of the Office of Education's regional educational laboratories have begun to follow suit. The Office of Education group even plans "to employ staff to deal with inter-lab program coordination and dissemination on a full-time basis . . . " (Bailey, 1970, p. 14).

Alan Pifer has suggested that a council of nonprofit organizations be established to serve their interests much as the American Council on Education serves the interests of colleges and universities.[18] Such a body would, I believe, provide a much needed forum for discussion and a source of information for the public as well as nonprofit institutes. Nonetheless, institute directors have been reluctant to establish a large formal association. Some are positively hostile to the idea and perhaps the most characteristic response is that of a director who said that if someone else organized such an organization, he would join, but he would not spend *his* time organizing one.

Perhaps that is as good a note as any on which to end this monograph. It remains to be seen what common purposes independent research institutes will be able to define: if, like universities, they will come to play a distinctive role in scientific and intellectual affairs, or if the several kinds of institutes described in this narrative will continue to go their separate ways.

13. Recommendations

It may be useful to draw together the principal recommendations that have been scattered throughout this monograph.

A precondition of better policies toward nonprofit institutes is better knowledge about them. The necessary knowledge consists partly of information and partly of understanding. Considering the growing importance of nonprofit institutes, both types of knowledge are sadly lacking. In contrast to the excellent and voluminous (if often highly repetitive) literature on universities, that on research institutes is, with a few exceptions, surprisingly thin and unenlightening.

Both governmental agencies and institutes themselves have a primary responsibility to remedy this situation. The IRS should improve its reporting forms, making the questions more relevant to institutes, and then see that they are actually completed and available for public examination. Institutes should answer the questions not, as many now do, legalistically, with the minimum number of disclosures, but informatively, attending to the purpose as well as the letter of the law and regulation.

Pursuant to its new statutory authority, the NSF has begun to publish statistics on most government obligations to individual R&D centers and certain other institutes. While this is a good start, the number of institutes surveyed should be increased; all government obligations should be included; and nongovernmental obligations should also be reported. Too many institutes have neglected their public information responsibilities. All should issue annual reports and make their public work readily accessible. More should follow RAND's system of filing unclassified reports with depository libraries. It would also be helpful if the Foundation Library Center extended its services at least to larger institutes or if a similar organization were formed for institutes.

But information without understanding is sterile. Public understanding of the advantages and limitations of the institute mode of research must rest on public discussions by spokesmen for institutes, rival institutions, and (often neglected in professional discourse) the constituencies most affected by the results of institute research. A professional association of institute administrators and staff should, I believe, be formed to promote such discussions, to foster better professional and administrative practices, and perhaps also to formulate and represent institute interests.

"Everyone talks about 'policy,'" remarked President Nixon's science adviser Lee DuBridge on one occasion (I paraphrase), "but what they really mean is 'money.'" In that sense, government "policy" toward research institutes should remain highly selective, since institutes have highly diverse capabilities and government officials should always exercise their judgment about the merit of awarding individual grants and contracts to particular institutes.

Nonetheless, broad financial and administrative policies have been adopted for designated types of institutes (such as R&D centers and operating foundations) and, as institutes grow in number and importance, the number of such policies is also likely to grow. Government administrative and cost principles designed for academic or industrial organizations may not be satisfactory for independent institutes; if these institutes can make a significant contribution to the government's objectives, they should do so under equitable terms. Government agencies should recognize nonprofit institutes as a legitimate and useful sector of the national R&D enterprise and make appropriate provisions for dealing with them.

However, the government should deal equitably with for-profit organizations as well. Direct R&D competition between for-profit and nonprofit organizations is not uncommon and has apparently been increasing. Its wisdom is questionable but when it occurs, contracting officers should, in evaluating bids, make a fair allowance for the different tax status of the two types of organizations.

The amount of competition for government R&D funds has increased to the point that large sums — ultimately reimbursed by the government, in overhead or hidden professional time — are wasted on futile proposals. While genuine competition must be preserved, spurious or formalistic competition should be reduced by tighter screening to ensure that applicants are qualified for the task before they are invited to enter a bid.

The taxability of the income derived by nonprofit institutes from proprietary work for industry has long been in dispute: some institutes have, and others have not, paid tax on it. This confused and unjust situation is a small scandal; a clear ruling by the IRS is overdue.

The largest volume of federal R&D conducted by nonprofit institutes is undertaken by centers under university or independent management, such as RAND, MITRE, and the Lincoln, Los Alamos, Argonne, Brookhaven, and Jet Propulsion laboratories. These centers have been attacked from many quarters. Congress has placed budgetary ceilings on Department of Defense centers and has subjected them to repeated critical scrutiny. Though for-profit companies favored, and played a part in, the creation of independent centers like RAND and the Aerospace Corporation to prevent the conflicts of interests that were posed when these centers were divisions of individual manufacturing companies, some now attack such centers as privileged preserves sheltered from normal competition for the government dollar. Many scientists believe that the large sums expended on such "big science" centers as the National Accelerator Laboratory, the Stanford Linear Accelerator Center, or the National Radio Astronomy Observatory would be better spent on the small-scale projects of individual investigators. Other critics charge that "think tanks" serve the interests of their patrons rather than the public and, further, contribute to the devaluation and demoralization of the civil service.

There is much merit to some of these criticisms and, even where there is little, the resultant discussion serves a constructive purpose in clarifying the role of the centers and government policy toward them. Indeed, it is regrettable that discussion has focused almost exclusively on Department of Defense centers; greater attention should be paid to the AEC centers, which receive far larger sums, and also to the centers of the NSF and the Office of Education.

Doubtless, a diligent inquiry will conclude that the work of one or another center should be terminated, curtailed, or redirected. But I believe that the centers as a whole serve purposes that are not merely useful but virtually indispensable to basic scientific research; to the applied sciences, social sciences, and engineering;

and to the independent evaluation of government programs. They provide vital strands in the cords that link science to technology, ideas to action, and government to the public interest.

The management by universities of centers and other laboratories engaged in large-scale applied research and development for the Department of Defense, the AEC, and, in some cases, private industry has been challenged by radicals who abhor this service to the "military-industrial complex" and by conservatives and liberals who believe it interferes with the university's more essential functions of education and scholarship. Of late, a number of these laboratories have severed their university ties. Over the years, various committees have issued statements about the wisdom or unwisdom of having universities manage such centers. I do not think that either policy can be defended strictly on grounds of logic, academic principle, or the national interest, if only because the character of the centers (e.g., the Center for Research in Social Systems and the Livermore laboratory) and of higher educational institutions (e.g., Brandeis and the Illinois Institute of Technology) is so diverse. The management decisions of individual universities and government agencies appear to have reflected specific opportunities and practical realities more than general principles, and that situation will presumably continue. I believe that students have a legitimate grievance at their neglect by overbusy faculty; that faculty involvement with all sorts of extraneous activities — of which applied research is only one — should be reduced; and that the government should make fewer calls of this kind upon the professoriate. The tighter academic job market may prove more effective than student pleas in extracting more teaching from faculty. And independent institutes can perform well a goodly portion of any work that, as a result, is not done by universities. But it would be rash to conclude that universities should or will soon forgo all large-scale government R&D. If more exercise greater discrimination about the work they accept, rival universities are as likely as institutes to pick up any rejected work.

The consortium device — a nonprofit organization composed of representatives of numerous universities — has proved so convenient for the management of government-funded basic research installations that insufficient attention has been paid to its drawbacks. The number of members of some consortia is preposterously large and a marked duplication can be noted in their membership. A study of existing arrangements should be conducted so that the best practices can be more widely adopted, and formalistic but nonfunctional or disfunctional memberships can be reduced. Serious consideration should also be given to Albert Crewe's suggestion that a code or convention be adopted governing equitable access by all scientists to national research facilities. That might separate the question of effective administration from that of political representation in consortia.

Though R&D centers perform vital functions, not all their functions are vital. Accepting the widespread American equation of growth with progress and confronting budgetary ceilings of their principal agency sponsor, many have sought to diversify their activities and sponsors. The irrepressible urge to expand and diversify poses problems for all institutes, endangering their financial stability and attenuating their professional competence. Candide's counsel, "we must cultivate our gardens," would be good advice for all, but all will not heed it, and the endowed institutes that have done so have been threatened by intellectual stultification. Nonetheless, the main justification for the establishment of centers by the government has been that they furnish important professional services not available from existing institutions, a crucial element of which has been their special, continuing relationship with their sponsoring agency. Insofar as this relationship is jeopardized by the proliferation of sponsors and ad hoc projects, diversification threatens the purposes for which centers were established.

It would be unreasonable to say that all diversification should cease and that centers should not tackle important new problems for new sponsors. But it is not unreasonable to call for a closer review of this process and, if it is sanctioned, a new rationale for the government's support of centers which, working for many agencies, no longer maintain a special relationship with one. Perhaps the best solution would be for the government to conduct an inquiry, including a public hearing, to determine if a center should work primarily for its initial sponsor or diversify more extensively and be formally dropped from the center rolls and (with any safeguards necessary to protect the public interest) join the freer world of other institutes. A similar procedure has been adopted in sanctioning the conversion of some nonprofit institutes into for-profit companies. However, public hearings have not been held. They should be, so that critics receive their day in court, and an adequate public justification of the final decision should then be issued.

In conclusion, nonprofit institutes have institutional advantages in bringing together persons from different disciplines for a concentrated and, if necessary, protracted attack on a technical or social problem, undistracted by students, considerations of financial profits, or the restraints of government bureaucracy. However, they can also be politically weak, financially insecure, and intellectually narrow. Though convenient and responsive R&D organizations, their organizational form by itself affords no assurance that their R&D will succeed. The thirst for organizational solutions to enduring human problems—perhaps derived from the effective organization of industrial production and distribution—can lead to an overvaluation of research and research institutes. We should not expect from knowledge more than we can expect from men.

Notes

PART ONE   *Chapter 1*

1   So classified by the IRS.

2   Nonprofit organizations not mainly engaged in research—hospitals, foundations, professional associations, museums, and botanical gardens—and nonprofit trade associations and research institutes of private industry will not be considered here.

3   Palmer (1968). This directory sells for $39.50; six supplements issued from December 1968 through September 1970 cost an additional $32.50.

PART TWO   *Chapter 2*

1   The only centers omitted are those financed by the U.S. Office of Education (National Science Foundation, 1970*a*).

2   The original definition was devised before the foundation itself had financed any centers devoted solely to basic research, and at a time when more AEC centers were more heavily engaged in classified work than is true today. A practical political advantage of the center concept to the cause of academic science is to reduce the volume of government expenditures in the "university proper" sector of the national R&D accounts.

3   Nevertheless, four "regional educational laboratories" receiving less than $500,000 from the Office of Education in 1969 were classified as federal research centers (National Science Foundation, 1970*b*, p. 55).

    The full definition of what are now termed "Federally Funded Research and Development Centers" states that they

". . . are R&D-performing organizations exclusively or substantially financed by the Federal Government that are supported by the Federal Government either to meet a particular R&D objective, or, in some instances, to provide major facilities at universities for research and associated training purposes. Each center is administered by [a university, nonprofit organization, or, in the cases of seven AEC centers, industrial firm]. . . .

"In general, all of the following qualification criteria are met by an institutional unit before it is included in the Federally Funded Research and Development Centers category: (1) its primary activities include one or more of the following: basic research, applied research, development, or management of research and development (specifically excluded are organizations engaged primarily in routine quality control and testing, routine service activities, production, mapping and surveys, and information dissemination); (2) it is a separate operational unit within the parent organization or is organized as a separately incorporated organization; (3) it performs actual research and development or R&D management either upon direct request of the Federal Government or under a broad charter from the Federal Government, but in either case under the direct monitorship of the Federal Government; (4) it receives its major financial support (70 percent or more) from the Federal Government, usually from one agency; (5) it has or is expected to have a long-term relationship with its sponsoring agency (about five years or more), as evidenced by specific obligations assumed by it and the agency; (6) most or all of its facilities are owned or are funded for in the contract with the Federal Government; and (7) it has an average annual budget (operating and capital equipment) of at least $500,000" (National Science Foundation, 1969*a*, p. 97).

4   See JPL Study Committee (1970, p. 1) and Welles et al. (1969, p. 332).

5   The Franklin Institute managed the Center for Naval Analyses from 1962–67; the Illinois Institute of Technology Research Institute has managed the Air Force Electromagnetic Compatability Analysis Center since 1961; and since 1968 the Stanford Research Institute and the Syracuse University Research Corporation have managed small educational policy research centers for the Office of Education. Three Defense Department contract organizations once, but no longer, classified as research centers have also been managed by preexistent nonprofit institutes — the Army's Fuels and Lubricants Research Laboratory by the Southwest Research Institute, the Navy's Oceanographic Research Laboratory by the Woods Hole Oceanographic Institute, and the Army's Center for Research in Social Systems by the American Institutes for Research.

It is no accident that the Battelle Memorial Institute, which since 1965 has operated the AEC's Hanford Laboratory, then renamed the Pacific Northwest Laboratory, is the nation's wealthiest nonprofit institute, with 1969 assets estimated at $238 million. One condition of the AEC award of that management contract to Battelle was its investment of some millions of its own funds to diversify the laboratory's activities (Orlans, 1967, p. 25).

6   The Brookhaven, Argonne, Oak Ridge, Ames, Lawrence, and Los Alamos Laboratories. Of the six (or, rather seven, counting separately the Lawrence

Radiation Laboratory at Berkeley and at Livermore), only Oak Ridge—
originally, the Clinton Laboratories managed by the University of Chicago
—has ever been operated by private industry.

7 The Oak Ridge Institute of Nuclear Studies, a nonprofit organization of
14 Southern universities, was founded in 1946 mainly to promote education
in the new nuclear fields and to encourage faculty to conduct research at
the Oak Ridge National Laboratory. When negotiations to extend the
Monsanto contract snagged in 1947 because of what the AEC regarded
as unreasonable demands by the corporation, the AEC considered asking
the University of Chicago to return. ORINS thereupon entered its own bid
for the contract, while Commissioner Lewis Strauss suggested that the
laboratory scientists "themselves form a corporation to serve as the contractor"—an interesting idea that came to naught. After some investigation, the AEC decided that ORINS "was not yet prepared to assume so great
a burden" and negotiations with Chicago advanced toward a seemingly
successful conclusion. However, in a last-minute switch due to several
factors including Commission Chairman David Lilienthal's growing apprehension about Chicago Chancellor Robert Hutchins' "logical over-
simplifications" and "superficial" pronouncements on nuclear affairs, the
laboratory contract was awarded to Union Carbide, which was already
operating the enormous Oak Ridge gaseous diffusion plants (Hewlett &
Duncan, 1969, pp. 77–78, 99, 103–104, 121–124).

At Argonne (and in subsequent Midwest scientific enterprises) the domi-
nance of the University of Chicago, which does not have a school of engineering, had been resented by the many great public universities in the area
which do have such a school. In 1946, 29 Midwest institutions (including
the Battelle Memorial Institute and the Mayo Foundation) elected a Board
of Governors for Argonne, which "reviews the research programs and
operating budgets presented by the Director and must approve them before
they are submitted by the contractor to the government" (Daniels, 1948,
p. 178). This cumbersome arrangement, virtually identical with one that
was reinstituted in 1966, was terminated in 1948 when the laboratory became more heavily engaged in classified reactor work (Orlans, 1967,
p. 61).

8 May 1970 interview with a physicist who was not quoting Groves but
summarizing the gist of his response. Groves may have got the idea from a
1946 report of an advisory committee of seven leading scientists who
recommended that a number of universities be represented on the board of
each of the four regional laboratories (Hewlett & Anderson, 1962, p. 634).
The original Associated Universities, Inc., charter stated that "The principal
office of the corporation is to be located at Columbia University," but the
provision was dropped when the charter was amended in February 1952
(Associated Universities, 1963, pp. 35–36).

9   A reader notes, "There is apparently no difference in the effectiveness of IDA after this change. . . . Once IDA had used the universities which sponsored it as a recruiting device for their initial staff (and in the early rounds of turnovers in staff), the universities ceased playing any significant role in IDA's management" (May 1971 communication).

10 An account of this episode will be found in Greenberg, 1964, and 1967, chap. 11.

11 See "48 Universities," 1969, pp. 4–5.

12 See *The Rand Corporation, The First Fifteen Years,* 1963.

13 Bruce Smith observes that "there is no evidence to support the view, which subsequently gained some currency, that the company reluctantly accepted the Project RAND contract at the government's urging out of lofty patriotism. It seems clear that the company in a general sense sought the contract, though the specific timing and initiative for activating the project in the fall of 1945 rested principally with General Arnold and Dr. [Edward L.] Bowles" (a special consultant for science and technology to Secretaries of War Henry Stimson and Robert Patterson, General George Marshall, and Arnold). This general interpretation is supported by Collbohm, who has testified that "The proposal was initially made by industry personnel who had worked with the military services and with the Office of Scientific Research and Development during World War II" (Smith, 1966, pp. 39–40; and *Systems Development and Management,* 1962, part 3, p. 920).

14 Groves himself was consulted during this formative period. "The model of the Manhattan District was considered . . . but was set aside" (*The Rand Corporation,* 1971, p. 3).

15 However, the basic technology of the airplane remained untouched by wartime gains in the technology of bombs, communications, guidance, and detection. "The Army needed airplanes at once; there was no time to nurse along something that was not even on the drawing board. Hence, at the twilight of the Second World War, the . . . [Army Air Force's] frontline arsenal was based on aeronautical concepts that had been known, and successfully applied, before the outbreak of hostilities. . . . [Contrariwise, the Germans] had developed and successfully employed both jet-powered aircraft and rockets" (Komons, 1966, p. 3).

16 Smith adds, "Arnold had known and worked with Douglas for some time and their two families were related by marriage. One of General Arnold's three sons . . . had married Donald Douglas' daughter in 1943 after his graduation from West Point" (1966, p. 42–43).

17 In recent years, the Savannah River Laboratory has also been listed as an

R&D center under the management of a profit-making firm. The reasons for this reclassification are not clear.

18 This version of the genesis of the Aerospace Corporation is drawn from a "Brief History" contained in *Systems Development and Management,* 1962, part 3, pp. 1127–1135.

19 The "Case of the Missing Centers" deserves Sherlock Holmes's attention. In 1961, NSF listed 12 Department of Defense centers under the management of for-profit companies; in 1968, none. Where did they disappear to? Some, such as four engaged in the development of the ill-fated nuclear-propelled plane, were closed down but others evidently persist as straightforward industrial R&D ventures, having escaped the oft-invidious designation of "center." This has happened, it is said, because the congressional committees monitoring Defense affairs have maintained a strict vigil over nonprofit centers, which they regard as adjuncts of the department that must be closely controlled. Contrariwise, for-profit centers are deemed part of the private sector, which merits greater freedom.

20 Further discussion of the conflict-of-interest problem and of measures the AEC has taken to cope with it will be found in Orlans, 1967, pp. 20, 30–31, 57, 214.

21 By Herbert Roback, Staff Administrator for the Military Operations Subcommittee of the House Committee on Government Operations, in *Systems Development and Management,* 1962, part 5, p. 1758.

Chapter 3

1 This was largely due to Raymond Ewell (now vice-president for research at the State University of New York in Buffalo), the first permanent head of the NSF office responsible for these statistics, who was influenced by his experience on the staff of the Stanford Research Institute.

2 Some might also regard IITRI as a "dependent" institute like the Denver Research Institute; that seems to have been truer in its earlier years, when there were closer physical and professional links with Illinois Tech.

3 There are innumerable others. A description of many such organizations will be found in Palmer, 1955. In another publication, Palmer attempts to distinguish "independent research centers" (those I have termed "applied research institutes"), "specialized research institutes" engaged in applied research in specific industries and trades or in biomedical fields, separately incorporated "university-affiliated research organizations" such as the Purdue and Ohio State research foundations, and "unincorporated institutional units." Though the distinctions seem reasonable and useful, it is virtually impossible to define them with sufficient precision and constantly to obtain enough information to maintain an accurate and current classification of all such organizations (Palmer, 1956, pp. 31–42).

4   For this account and the history of other applied research institutes, I have relied to a considerable extent upon the unpublished dissertation of Richard Lesher, 1963, pp. 64–102.

5   According to William Hamor, "The Research Around Us in Mellon Institute," *Commonwealth,* July 1947, as cited by Lesher, 1963, pp. 77. While the Mellon Institute, like the Franklin Institute's Bartol Research Foundation, conducted a substantial amount of basic research, the bulk of its work remained proprietary.

6   Armour has undergone as many name changes as an English lord. Initially the Research Foundation of Armour Institute of Technology, it became the Armour Research Foundation of the Illinois Institute of Technology in 1945 and the Illinois Institute of Technology Research in 1963.

7   This account is based upon a 52-page "Report of the Stanford-SRI Study Committee" issued by Stanford University as a *Campus Report Supplement* on April 14, 1969.

8   The main terms of the separation agreement were:

SRI will continue to function as a non-profit research organization, but will be legally separated from the University. . . .

SRI will continue to use the name "Stanford Research Institute" for a period not to exceed five years.

Stanford Trustees will relinquish control of the Institute and will no longer be general members of SRI with authority to elect the SRI Board. Instead, this function will be assumed by the SRI Board itself which will have the power to fill vacancies as they occur and to exercise complete responsibility for Institute policies. . . .

Beginning in 1971, SRI will pay to the University one percent of its gross operating revenues each year until a total of $25 million has been reached. [It was estimated in May 1971 that the payment for 1971 would be approximately $500,000.] Thereafter, payments will continue indefinitely at a rate of one-half of one percent of gross revenues.

. . . successful performance of the agreement is dependent upon the continued financial viability of the Institute and . . . important consideration will be given that factor in the application of contract provisions ("Final Agreement," 1970, pp. 1–2).

9   From the proposal to establish a Syracuse University Applied Research Center, as it was then named ("A Short History of SURC and Discussion of SURC-ASU Relationships," November 1969, Syracuse University, 29 pp. plus eight exhibits, multilithed). The rest of the SURC story, including

the remarks of Chancellor Tolley and the SURC vice-president which follow, is also drawn from this source.

Chapter 4

1   Elihu Root, chairman of the Carnegie Institution board from 1913–1937, expressed the same idea:

Science has been arranging, classifying, methodizing, simplifying every-thing except itself. . . . It has organized itself very imperfectly. Scientific men are only recently realizing that the principles which apply to success on a large scale in transportation and manufacture and general staff work apply to them . . . ; that the effective power of a great number of scientific men may be increased by organization just as the effective power of a great number of laborers may be increased by military discipline. . . . A very great mind goes directly to the decisive fact, the determining symptom . . . ; but there are few such minds even among those capable of real scientific work. All other minds need to be guided away from the useless and towards the useful. That can be done only by the application of scientific method to science itself through the purely scientific process of organizing effort (quoted by Bunker, 1938, p. 729).

2   *Relatively* fixed because the progressive rise in market values has enabled many foundations to increase their annual outlays either from income or capital, while their total assets also continued to rise or at least hold stable. However, the more recent fall in stock prices, coming cruelly after many uni-versities and other nonprofit organizations had heeded the advice of Ford Foundation president McGeorge Bundy to switch from bonds to stocks, has put them in a severe budgetary bind. The foundation has recently under-written a "Common Fund for Nonprofit Organizations" to help nonprofit organizations invest their funds wisely (see Crowl, 1971, p. 1).

3   These formula grants are calculated as a small percentage of the total funds awarded in research project grants. In fiscal year 1968, for example, NIH awarded to each institution 10 percent of the first million dollars of its non-federal research expenditures plus 5 percent of the first, and 3 percent of the second, million dollars of federal research expenditures, as well as a base grant of $25,000.

4   "In the last 2 complete fiscal years, . . . Sloan-Kettering investigators applied for 34 separate grants, of which only 20 were approved by NIH's scientific review bodies. . . . If projects are unacceptable to NIH on the basis of an adverse scientific review by its nongovernmental consultants, what justification is there for giving the grantee discretion to finance these same projects from a single cost-sharing grant?" (*The Administration of Research Grants,* 1967, pp. 39–40).

Chapter 5

1 Written statement submitted during a December 1970 interview.

In its 1970 annual report, SRI formulates the matter as follows:

> The Institute is a nonprofit corporation that paid Federal income tax at prevailing corporate rates on its unrelated business taxable income for years prior to 1969. The management has reviewed the applicable regulations and has determined that the Institute had no such income in 1969 or 1970. Taxable years after 1960 are being examined by the Internal Revenue Service. Management believes that based on its interpretation of the applicable regulations, it has adequately provided for Federal income tax liabilities (SRI, 1971, p. 25).

2 The IRS publication *How to Apply for Exemption for an Organization* conveniently provides two draft articles of incorporation for those wishing to form nonprofit corporations.

3 See Internal Revenue Service, No. 1969-6, pp. 58–68; No. 1970-4, pp. 43–7.

4 Remarks of Randolph W. Thrower before American Bar Association Section on Taxation, Dallas, Texas, August 19, 1969.

5 For example, the articles of incorporation of the National Bureau of Economic Research state that "The Executive Committee, under the general direction of the Board . . . shall at all times guard against any attempt or tendency to make the Bureau an agency for propaganda"; those of the Stanford Research Institute, that SRI "shall not carry on propaganda or otherwise attempt to influence legislation"; and those of the Institute for Policy Studies, that "No part of the Corporation's assets shall be used in attempting to influence legislation by propaganda or otherwise, Nor shall this Corporation participate in, or intervene in any manner, . . . in any political campaign."

6 See Goldwater, 1970; "Senator Hawk," 1970, p. 15; and "Dole Cites," 1970.

7 In order to maintain its status as a "public organization," the Battelle Memorial Institute asked the AEC to be relieved of its responsibility for the construction and operation of a fast-flux test facility at Richland. Battelle President S. L. Fawcett stated that "The Federal Tax Reform Act of 1969 . . . places limits . . . on the amount of financial support which exempt organizations like Battelle . . . may receive from a single bureau (source) and still retain their status as a . . . public organization. . . . [D]isproportionately massive support from any one bureau of government could seriously affect an organization's public status" (Battelle press release, January 30, 1970).

Chapter 6

1   In addition to Harding, who died before he could serve, the original trustees included Battelle's mother; Bishop John W. Hamilton, a relative of Gordon Battelle and president of American University; Earle C. Derby, a Columbus industrialist; Joseph H. Frantz, a business associate of Battelle's father; and Harry M. Runkle, a lawyer and business associate of Gordon Battelle (Thomas, 1963, p. 9).

2   For example, John Walsh writes, "One major lesson to be drawn from the Camelot reversal is that social sciences research would profit from the kind of apparatus constructed in the years when physical and life sciences began receiving major support from federal agencies. SORO, for example, lacks the support of a distinguished board like the RAND Corporation, or a consortium of universities like that which backs the Institute for Defense Analyses" ("Social Sciences," 1965, p. 1213).

3   One way to keep board members better informed about institute affairs, it has been suggested, is to appoint several officers or staff to the board. This is the case at RAND, where three officers are members of the board.

4   June 1970 letter and phone conversation. To be eligible for TIAA-CREF, a research institute "must be tax exempt under Section 501 (c) (3) of the Internal Revenue Code; its primary function must be educational or scientific research; its research must be basic, except in instances where applied research is conducted by grant or contract from governmental agencies; its research projects may be sponsored by foundation grants or government contracts, but not by commercial organizations; and if research is directed to governmental expenditures, efficiency in government, zoning, urban renewal and tax reductions, eligibility will ordinarily be denied. Action organizations are not eligible" ("Eligibility for TIAA-CREF," 3 pp., undated).

5   For example, in May 1971, the pronunciamento of a committee chairman forced at least one center to make substantial cuts in its expenditures for the fiscal year ending June 31, 1971. In effect, it faced the alternative of not spending money it had already spent during the preceding 10 months or firing staff without notice and rehiring them on July 1. Similarly, a cut in fiscal 1971 funds—that is, in funds for the 12-month period starting July 1, 1970—imposed by the House Subcommittee on Defense Appropriations in October 1970 obliged the Center for Naval Analyses to cut its staff by 10 percent early in 1971.

6   More precisely: in 1970, the turnover, or termination rate, was 18.7 percent; the total professional staff was reduced 7 percent.

7   Glass, 1968*a* and 1968*b,* both Department of Defense reports issued on

a restricted basis and therefore not directly quotable. A more detailed account of their findings is contained in Welles et al., 1969, pp. 379ff.

8   "No!" a reader asserts. "It is simply that *all* Navy and most Army centers are university-managed. . . ."

9   Conflict of interest regulations also restrict the freedom of center staff to invest their personal funds.

Chapter 7

1   A diligent RAND reader of this manuscript writes, "RAND should be included explicitly in the first group rather than let the reader think it may be in the latter one. Over 190 libraries in the U.S. and abroad have subscription collections of unclassified Rand publications (and more than three quarters of Rand publications are unclassified). In 1970, 226,000 copies of Rand publications were distributed to external readers." The RAND system of depository libraries is commendable and should be copied by more institutes and research sponsors. However, (setting aside the problem of classified material), all research "reports" are not real "publications," and there is a significant difference in the accessibility of the two forms. *Reports* comprise a paraliterature accessible to the cognoscenti, whereas *publications* are a genre handled by all the traditional media of scholarly communication—publishers, bookstores, libraries, journals, indices, etc.

2   In a September 13, 1965, interview, General Leslie Groves said that the AEC laboratories have been good because they had "unlimited money. I started them that way, because it didn't pay to have a $1,000 motor if you could get a better one for $1,500." Money may have been one factor, but, of course, there were others, such as the importance and excitement of their work and the distinction of their wartime leaders.

3   Don E. Kash of the University of Oklahoma reports the number of members of the National Academy of Sciences at nonprofit institutes in 1969 as: Carnegie Institution of Washington, 15; Institute for Advanced Study, 5; and one each at the following: Institute for Cancer Research, Kitt Peak Observatory, Lawrence Radiation Laboratory, Lowell Observatory, Ortho Research Foundation, RAND, Salk Institute, Scripps Clinic and Research Foundation, Sloan-Kettering Institute (personal communication, October 1970). In 1965, the Rockefeller University had "three Nobel prize winners and 36 members of the National Academy of Sciences among its 40 or so full professors and 10 emeriti" (Walsh, 1965, p. 1,695).

   With the kind cooperation of John Voss, executive officer of the American Academy of Arts and Sciences, I made a count, in April 1971, of the number of AAAS members at various nonprofit research institutes. The results were as follows: Rockefeller University, 31; Institute for Advanced Study,

20; Carnegie Institution of Washington, 9; Woods Hole Oceanographic Institution, 7; Brookings Institution, 4; Brookhaven National Laboratory, 3; Aerospace Corporation, 3; Oak Ridge National Laboratory, 3; Mount Wilson and Palomar Observatories, 3; Jackson Memorial Laboratory, 3; Marine Biological Laboratory, 2; Worcester Foundation for Experimental Biology, 2; Lawrence Radiation Laboratory (Berkeley), 2; Institute for Defense Analyses, 2; Center for Advanced Study in the Behavioral Sciences, 2; Salk Institute, 2; and one each at the Argonne National Laboratory, Aspen Institute for Humanistic Study, Associated Universities, Carnegie Endowment for International Peace, Central Institute for the Deaf, Cold Spring Harbor Laboratory, Committee for Economic Development, Hale Observatories, Humanities Research Institute, Institute for Southern History, Jet Propulsion Laboratory, Kitt Peak National Observatory, Los Alamos Scientific Laboratory, Lawrence Radiation Laboratory (Livermore), Lowell Institute, National Bureau of Economic Research, National Center for Atmospheric Research, R. S. Peabody Foundation for Archaeology, John B. Pierce Foundation Laboratory, Stanford Linear Accelerator Center, University City Science Center, and Yerkes Observatory.

4   For the two most recent studies, see Cartter, 1966, and Roose & Anderson, 1970. Similar comprehensive studies were conducted in 1924, 1934, and 1957.

5   "The main reason that the DoD's study of [the] quality of its laboratories has been kept fairly secretive," writes one reader, "is that our friend, Admiral Rickover, complained loudly and publicly that any such study was hogwash because it represented merely a public opinion poll of semi-informed or uninformed people. No Secretary of Defense enjoys tangling with Rickover."

6   ". . . it wasn't a particularly surprising report," one informant wrote. "But Piore worked very hard on the detailed agency-by-agency, laboratory-by-laboratory, problems which the panel discovered and highlighted. For example, Piore and several others met monthly with [Director of Defense Research and Engineering John Foster, Jr.] . . . for more than a year to review DoD's progress in changing certain policies at several laboratories and in straightening out a number of administrative jungles that were inhibiting laboratory operations."

7   The task force, chaired by Ruben Mettler, stated its belief that "the time is ripe for a comprehensive review of the role and future plans of the Federal laboratories, with a view towards reaffirming the mission and plans of some, redeploying some in whole or in part, and closing down others, if necessary" (*Science and Technology,* 1970, p. 31). McElroy's remarks will be found in *National Science Policy,* 1970, p. 242.

8 The Hudson Institute disclaims not only corporate but individual responsibility for one category of its product, the informal paper whose circulation is "entirely a matter of the individual's initiative. Since such papers are often intended to provoke discussion, they do not necessarily reflect the considered judgment even of the author" (Hudson Institute, 1969, p. 7).

9 A reader comments, "I am not sure that it's simply the 'professional standards' which determine the quality of manuscripts. There is another factor which might be called the intellectual leadership's style. For example, would Brookings ever publish a Hudson-type paper? Most of the staff at Hudson are as familiar with scholarly standards, and as respectful of originality, as the professional staff at Brookings. But because Herman Kahn's style is so different and because the Hudson Institute is scrambling in a much fuzzier intellectual area, their output is marked by an entirely different outlook on the function of the output itself." The point is well taken.

10 "As of September 1956, RAND had issued 49 formal recommendations to the Air Force and 36 had been accepted either fully or in part" (Smith, 1966, p. 202, footnote 6).

11 Franklin Research Laboratories, May 1970 leaflet.

12 The gratuitous advice, a reader notes, "usually comes from people who have been paid to get knowledgeable in one of the defense centers and who then go on another payroll to challenge the policies or programs which they studied 'within the system.' There's nothing the matter with this; it's quite similar to the service-to-the-doves which [Defense Secretary Robert] McNamara's detailed 'posture statements' represented."

13 Board Chairman David A. Shepard and President Henry S. Rowen, "Foreword," *Rand Annual Report 1968,* and the same report, p. 5; *The Institute of Public Administration,* brochure, 1969, p. 9; *The Impact of Battelle,* the president's report, Battelle Memorial Institute, Columbus, Ohio, 1969, p. 2; *Center for Policy Research,* brochure, New York, 1970; *The Corporate Environment, 1975–1985,* Hudson Institute, Croton-on-Hudson, New York, January 1971, p. 41.

PART FOUR *Chapter 8*

1 This proposal was purportedly a spoof, but there is little aside from the opening "Why not? . . ." to distinguish it from all the others.

2 Setting aside other administrative divisions and units, NIH contained, in the fall of 1970, 10 institutes: the National Cancer Institute, National Eye Institute, National Heart and Lung Institute, National Institute of Allergy and Infectious Diseases, National Institute of Arthritis and Metabolic Diseases, National Institute of Child Health and Human Development, National Institute of Dental Research, National Institute of Environmental Health Sciences, National Institute of Neurological Diseases and Stroke, and National Institute of General Medical Sciences; elsewhere, the Public Health Service harbored the large National Institute of Mental Health, separated from NIH in 1967. All these institutes administer extramural programs and all but the Institute of General Medical Sciences also support research by their own professional staff.

3 The answer was given in a report by Roger E. Levien (1971, p. v) which states: "The pending legislation leaves unanswered a wide range of questions concerning the NIE. This planning study was undertaken to develop a more detailed picture of what the NIE might become."

4 A pathetic example of unrealistic hope was the introduction by Chicago Congressman Roman Pucinski, shortly after the strangulation murder of eight Chicago nurses, of a proposal for six centers for research on the criminally insane, in order to understand and prevent such crimes (see the eighth item in our list of proposed institutes.)

5 A prize example of the institute as a religion is offered by the "World Institute" of Julius Stulman, whose mystic, utopian vision of the humanizing role of knowledge (and the messianic role of researchers) differs from that of Harold Lasswell, Kenneth Boulding, Karl Deutsch, and more hardheaded scholars mainly in its nakedness.

This Organism, THE WORLD INSTITUTE, an international body, would be composed of the very best men and women, brought to the fore, operating principally on a rotating basis, from anywhere in the world, from every discipline, who have been able to break out of their disciplines and work together in an organismically interdisciplinary manner symbiotically with the best of our growing technological abilities, at the peak of availability and performance in flow and change. It would be set up to funnel the latest information and creative abilities from everywhere around the world through affiliated institutions and established facilities.

This methodology should make available abilities far in excess of any which can accrue by presently known methods. It would enable man to discern *new natural laws* which cannot now be easily observed, and offer him the ability to judge the consequences of actions in the multiple effects "of quantum jump metamorphical changes."

The outpouring of continuous information is evaluated in-depth, broken down to its component parts in the movement of information flow, computerized, cross-referenced, and constantly interrelated and reevaluated. Such information, the maximization of mankind's knowledge, newly coded for effective use internationally, would be made available for continued review, research, or direct application in fully presented, well-integrated, "role-playing" programs at phased levels of conditioned acceptance. . . .

Mankind will be ushered forward into a new age. . . . (Stulman, 1970, p. 62).

Chapter 9

1 The diversification efforts of AEC laboratories are discussed at some length in my book on AEC contracting for research and development (Orlans, 1967, pp. 101–115).

2 "Beginning in fiscal year 1965, the House Committee on Appropriations initiated appropriation restrictions which had the effect of imposing ceilings on the funding [Department of Defense] . . . centers could obtain from their primary sponsors. . . . The Senate Armed Services Committee gave the explanation that . . . [centers] weakened in-house competence. The related view that . . . [centers] encroach on the authority and responsibility of government agencies had previously been expressed by the House Defense Appropriations Committee. The aspect of cost has been a recurring theme. . . . So has concern over . . . [their] noncompetitive nature. . . . Many of the center managers interviewed considered Congressional ceilings a reaction to the management excesses of a few . . . [centers] or to a mistrust by Congress of the 'expertise of think tanks.' In short, they considered the ceilings to be a disciplinary device . . ." (Welles et al., 1969, pp. 7–8).

3 ". . . [T]he details of the actual process are somewhat messier," comments a reader who has been closely involved in that process. "DoD has considerable freedom to spend its R&D money with respect to various kinds of contractors. Thus when a center is 'decenterized,' the DoD does not lose money from its total budget nor does the FCRC component of the total budget necessarily lose money; rather, what usually happens is that the same money goes from the same source to the same recipient in a new status" (May 1971 letter).

4 "The new restrictions — or ceilings — on defense center budgets were relaxed in FY70 and have *not* been reimposed," writes the foregoing reader. "In effect, the Congress bought Foster's [John S. Foster, Jr., director of defense research and engineering] argument that the DoD was managing the FCRC's in such a way that the prior, apparently mindless growth of centers had been stopped and that their programs were being reviewed more carefully. Thus Congress did not impose a ceiling on the FCRC component of the Defense R&D appropriation" (ibid.).

5 "These figures change from time to time, of course, and the ones that are quoted are for the period September to October of this year" (October 29, 1970, letter from A. E. Hayward, Office of the Director of Defense Research and Engineering).

6 March 4, 1969, letter of Secretary of Defense Melvin R. Laird and March 5 memorandum of John S. Foster, Jr., for The Presidents of Defense

Department–Sponsored Federal Contract Research Centers, "Policy on Non-Defense Activity."

7   John S. Foster, Jr., remarks before American Nuclear Society, Seattle, Wash., June 18, 1969.

8   In addition to the Air Force, these were listed as the Department of Defense (presumably, the Office of the Director of Defense Research and Engineering), Advanced Research Projects Agency, Project AGILE (on counterinsurgency), International Security Affairs (again, in the Office of the Secretary of Defense), Defense Atomic Support Agency, The Atomic Energy Commission, National Aeronautics and Space Administration, Agency for International Development, National Institutes of Health, National Library of Medicine, Department of Transportation, Department of Housing and Urban Development, Office of Economic Opportunity, New York City, California Committee on Regional Medical Programs, Ford Foundation, Carnegie Corporation, Resource Analysis, Good Samaritan and Children's Hospital, and the New York and American Stock Exchanges.

9   As one RAND publication puts it, "The broader perspective gained from working for the Office of the Secretary of Defense and the Defense Agencies, the National Security Council, Central Intelligence Agency, and the State Department cannot help but enhance Rand's value to its principal client, the Air Force" (*The Rand Corporation*, 1971, p. 35). But that takes a rosy view of the matter, for its special relationship also enhanced RAND's value to the Air Force.

10   "Soon after the new corporation took over the Project RAND contract it was notified by the Air Force that as a result of a general budget squeeze the Project would have to be scaled down to an annual rate of $3,000,000 by FY 1951, instead of $4,000,000. As matters turned out, this cut was never made. . . . But at the time of notification, the Air Force suggested that the Corporation seek compatible work elsewhere to make up the difference.

"Fortunately, Project RAND had earlier added a group of physicists to its staff . . . to keep the Project posted on progress in nuclear technology, as a complement to its work on weapon systems research for the Air Force. Consequently, Project RAND was brought into contact with the Atomic Energy Commission and some of its laboratories. It was logical for Rand . . . to approach that agency as a potential sponsor. In late 1949 an agreement, similar to the arrangement with the Air Force but on a smaller scale, was worked out with the AEC.

"This contract marked The Rand Corporation's first venture into diversification" (*The Rand Corporation*, 1971, pp. 10–11).

11   Unidentified quotations in this section are drawn from interviews at RAND.

12   "Do you consider, Mr. Collbohm, that RAND will continue to be in the
foreseeable future, as it has been in the past, primarily an Air Force
contractor?" Herbert Roback, staff administrator for the Military Operations Subcommittee of the House Committee on Government Operations
asked. "We hope so," was the reply and to Roback's further question, "You
are not interested in building up a diversified operation as such?" Collbohm
responded "No. As a matter of fact, I do not think it would work too well.
I think that the Air Force . . . started right out with a philosophy and a
policy as to how to handle the type of an organization that RAND is, that
is practically perfect, I would say. And it would be very, very undesirable
for the country as a whole, if this relationship should be changed" (*Systems
Development and Management,* 1962, part 3, p. 952).

13   "The 'goal' of fifty-fifty military–non-military funding has less operational
meaning than your language suggests," a reader comments (though I do not
see any operational implication in that language besides the need to acquire
a lot of nonmilitary money). "For one thing the 'quality' of the support
available would be crucial. If it couldn't be made available on terms that
were satisfactory that goal wouldn't be reached. Also implicit in that was
the notion, as in the case of the New York Institute, that much of the domestic research would probably be separately organized and administered."

14   "It seems to me that . . . apparent 'disaster' may be socially preferable to
an apparent success . . . ," one RAND reader comments. "There would
have been very little social value in seeing to it . . . that this particular
client was 'satisfied.'" Another writes, "In fact, some significant changes
were made in police operations as a result of the work. Of course there
was a 'failure' in the relationship. But . . . the possibility of the resump-
tion of work with the police is not negligible—when the 'consultants'
issue which has held up payments on the city's contracts with consultants
is resolved."

15   "Government officials in Washington have already suggested that Rand
was the possible source of the leaked documents. Last week the Pentagon
reclaimed the two copies of the report in Rand's possession, and said they
could possibly be the basis of criminal action. One of the sets was at Santa
Monica and the other at Rand's Washington, D.C. office. Rand said it was
storing the volumes for individuals, but refused to name them.

". . . Top executives of the 'think tank,' most of whose work is highly
classified research for the Department of Defense, reportedly are concerned
that its security clearance might be lifted—which would virtually put it
out of business.

"Relations between Rand and the Department of Defense have become
strained over the last several years, since Rand researchers have been
increasingly critical of government policy on Vietnam in their reports"
(Aarons, 1971, p. A12).

16   Payment was stopped not only on the contract with RAND but on that with McKinsey and Co. and other consultants on the ground that these had been awarded improperly without public hearings, competitive bidding, and approval by the Board of Estimate. Legal action to force payment was instituted by McKinsey and Mayor Lindsay's office. Comptroller Beame's action was upheld by the lower and appellate courts; as of June 1971, the mayor's office was appealing the latter decision to the Court of Appeals, the highest state court (see Tolchin, 1971, p. 14).

17   "A $500,000 consultant study of the Police Department by the Rand Corporation was termed a 'failure' and was abruptly terminated, Council President Sanford D. Garelik said yesterday.

"Mr. Garelik, at the time the study was made, in 1968–69, was the chief inspector, the department's highest-ranked uniformed officer. He declared that the study has been 'tossed out,' adding that the Rand engineers had had no background in police operations. . . .

"Mr. Peter Szanton, President of New York City Rand Institute, conceding the failure of the study of the Police Department, explained the reasons for the cancellation" (Ranzal, 1970).

Commenting on this damaging account, Szanton wrote "I conceded no such thing and could not have done so since no 'study' of the Police Department existed, and the analytic work was in no sense a failure. We engaged in some 14 or 15 separate studies for the Department, no fewer than 7 of which were the specific subjects of Mr. Garelik's remarks and my responses. What failed, I was at some pain to point out, was not 'the study' or any of the studies, but rather the relationship between the Institute and the Police Department" (unpublished October 7, 1970, letter to the editor of the *Times*).

18   Characteristic of the debate were the divergent views expressed about the value of RAND's work for the Fire Department, which is widely accepted as its most successful work in New York.

"By evaluating on paper complicated deployment patterns that would be virtually impossible to test in actual practice, the model, developed by the New York City–Rand Institute, has already fostered two new fire-fighting procedures that have saved the city $7 million in the last year," Fire Commissioner Robert O. Lowery said yesterday.

"We can save at least another $7 million a year as we implement the procedures in more sections of the city," the Commissioner said. . . .

However, Michael J. Maye, president of the Uniformed Firefighters Association, gave a sharply contrasting view yesterday. Calling the $7 million savings "purely a paper figure," he asserted that the $600,000 spent for computer studies "might better have been spent on more manpower and the replacement of relic equipment we are being forced to use."

Mr. Maye contended that the fireman's work load had tripled in the last 10 years and that the Fire Department has been able to claim greater efficiency and cost savings "only by overworking the fire fighter" (Mc-Fadden, 1971, p. 26).

Other news accounts and letters detailing the pros and cons of the controversy over RAND's New York City work will be found in, among other issues, the *New York Times* of July 1, 8, 16; October 7, 29; November 16, 24; and December 3 and 21, 1970.

In addition to their work on rationalizing the system of responding to fire alarms and helping to introduce "slippery water," which enabled the same-sized hose to deliver a larger volume of water, RAND staff are particularly proud of their work for the Housing and Development Administration. This laid the foundation for reforming New York City's rent control law. Peter Szanton states that it "was a clear and important success, and is so recognized not only by the Housing Administrator but by virtually all members of the intellectual community who followed New York housing matters closely" (April 1971 letter; see also Lowry, 1970).

Chapter 10

1 "In August 1969, Robert H. Finch, then Secretary of Health, Education and Welfare, sent a memorandum to his agency heads saying he wanted them to avoid negotiated or sole source contracts and to use competitive bidding whenever possible" (Mathews, 1970, p. 11). It is unclear if this represented an isolated instruction of one cabinet officer or, as seems more likely, a broader policy of an administration disposed to favor free competitive enterprise.

2 The Washington office is, of course, not peculiar to universities. Indeed, as universities have more associations serving their interests than do the more competitive and less well-organized nonprofit institutes, they need to maintain fewer individual offices. In 1970, the following were among the nonprofit institutes which maintained offices or operating divisions in the Washington area but whose principal facilities were located elsewhere: Aerospace, Associated Universities, Inc., American Institutes for Research, Armour Research Foundation, Battelle, Cornell Aeronautical Laboratory, Gorgas Memorial Laboratory, Hudson Institute, Institute of Public Administration, Midwest Research Institute, MITRE, Organization for Social and Technical Innovation, RAND, Russell Sage Foundation, Southwest Research Institute, Stanford Research Institute, Tax Foundation, Twentieth Century Fund, Universities Research Association, W. E. Upjohn Institute for Unemployment Research. In addition, the greater Washington area is the headquarters of innumerable centers and institutes

such as the Applied Physics Laboratory, the Center for Naval Analyses, the Human Resources Research Organization, the Institute for Defense Analyses, the Research Analysis Corporation, the Brookings Institution, Bureau of Social Science Research, Carnegie Institution, and Resources for the future.

Albert Biderman notes that "The Washington area has by far the largest concentration of non-university scientists and social scientists. The weakness of Washington-area universities, taken together with the special advantages of proximity to the sources of government funds, has had much to do with the development of the non-university research institution" (May 1971 communication).

3   Quoted, with minor changes, from Gilmore, Ryan, & Gould, 1967, p. 117. Two educational policy centers were eventually established, at the Stanford Research Institute and the Syracuse University Research Corporation.

4   Letter of June 18, 1965, to Comptroller General of the United States from Robert N. Katz, attorney of Washington, D.C., on behalf of Technology, Inc., and reply of Frank H. Weitzel, Acting Comptroller General, by letter of July 13, 1965.

5   "It appears that M.I.T. benefits financially from the special laboratories [the Draper and Lincoln labs] in the following way: the special laboratories use many M.I.T. facilities; under existing government regulations, they are charged for the use of these facilities, e.g., libraries, infirmary, accounting office. Were the laboratories to be severed from M.I.T., many of these common functions would not become appreciably less expensive to operate. To maintain M.I.T. on-campus facilities at their pre-divestment levels, the Institute would have to assume the laboratories' share of the operating expenses. Thus, M.I.T. benefits from the special laboratories in the reduction of overhead expenses by an estimated $7 million annually" (Kabat, 1969, p. D-7).

Former AEC Commissioner Loren Olson stated in 1963 that "The University of California and the University of Chicago are, by the standards of the AEC's controller, at least, making at least a half a million dollars a year profit" on their management of AEC centers; university officials disagree (cited in Orlans, 1967, p. 199, footnote).

6   May 1971 communication.

7   January 1971 letter from John G. Welles, head of the Industrial Economics Division at the Denver Research Institute and senior author of *Contract Research and Development Adjuncts of Federal Agencies,* Denver Research Institute, March 1969.

8 The president of one applied research institute writes, "The profit element for all types of contracts, including fixed-price and cost-plus-fixed fee, is negotiated in accordance with the Weighted Guidelines policies and techniques set forth in Armed Services Procurement Regulation 3–808. Under this system fees to profit and nonprofit organizations are initially determined on the same criteria, but then if a nonprofit organization is involved the fee so determined is reduced by three percentage points. . . . If there is any 'inequity' we feel it is against us" (May 1971 letter).

9 September 27, 1965, letter from Robert N. Katz to Colonel Reagan Scurlock, chairman, Armed Services Procurement Regulation Committee, Department of Defense.

10 October 1970 interview. Reference to the same episode appears in an article by Elinor Langer: "Representative of the kind of work that agitates ACIL members are the testing of primary aluminum windows and sliding glass doors performed at one southeastern university and the testing of a variety of fans at an institution in Texas" ("Industrial R&D," 1964, p. 274).

11 Lilienthal, 1963, pp. 87–88. "Noble statement if public servants are really so held accountable," comments a Defense center staff member. "I doubt it very much. One criterion of our work — to distinguish it from staff support (i.e., doing the government's administrative work on contract — which is illegal although some outside groups do it more than others) is that it produces an identifiable report (whose technical adequacy we can vouch for). Bellcom did and MITRE does appreciable staff support and we very little."

12 Title IV of the Elementary and Secondary Education Act of 1965 authorized $100 million to be spent over a five-year period "for the construction and operation of regional centers for research in education. Such centers may be constructed by the Commissioner of Education or through grants to universities, colleges, or other public and nonprofit institutions" (*Congressional Record* of April 7, 1965, cited by Bailey, 1970, p. 11).

13 Other precedents are President Hoover's Research Committee on Social Trends and President Franklin Roosevelt's National Resources Planning Board. Like presidential commissions, both were sheltered by their impermanence.

14 Letter of June 1, 1971 to the Commission on Government Procurement.

15 ". . . discussions were held with the Internal Revenue Service," writes an SDC official, "the Secretary of the Air Force, certain key Congressmen, and the California Attorney General before a scheme was approved which allowed us to convert to a for-profit status. . . . [T]he [System Development] Foundation is attempting to realize the asset represented by SDC and to dispose of that asset in accordance with the rules governing foundations."

Chapter 11

1   Tonsor, 1969, p. E 3728. This address was distributed by President Nixon to his principal staff and officials concerned with government policy toward higher education with the note that "this happens to be my view. . . . I want everyone who has anything to do with education to read this speech carefully and to follow this line in their public pronouncements" (*The Chronicle of Higher Education,* May 5, 1969, p. 3).

2   "Informal meeting with Secretary of Defense Melvin R. Laird and newsmen at the Pentagon Wednesday, September 2, 1970 — 11:00 AM" (transcript).

3   "Today the concept of tenure for faculty members is under attack — the most concerted attack in recent years, according to Bertram H. Davis, general secretary of the AAUP [American Association of University Professors].

"At least five state legislatures now have bills before them to limit or at least to re-examine tenure at state institutions. In addition, several institutions of higher education have initiated their own studies of tenure. . . .

"Many students and administrators seeking academic reform and greater emphasis on teaching oppose tenure because they see it protecting faculty members who want to avoid undergraduates.

"At several new and experimental institutions, . . . short-term contracts have been substituted for tenure. . . .

"Mr. Davis feels that the current economic crisis will force many institutions to offer tenured positions far less frequently than in the recent years of expansion, when the offer of tenure was an important recruiting device" (Scully, 1971, pp. 1,4).

4   An account of this battle is given in my book *The Effects of Federal Programs on Higher Education* (1962, pp. 205–220). I then concluded that "universities are making a mistake when, in effect, they put their faculty on the federal payroll. . . . Immediately, they stand to gain; but over the long run, it may be feared, they stand to lose two important assets: the ability to pay their faculty from independent sources of income, and, thereby, their ability to say 'no' to the government" (pp. 219–220). Harvey Brooks observes that "With the current cutback in federal re-

search funds in universities, the past practice of paying a portion of faculty salaries out of research grants has greatly aggravated the current financial plight of many institutions, which became committed to a larger faculty than they could realistically support out of their own local resources (mostly tuition, endowment, or state or local government funds)" (*National Science Policy,* 1970, p. 949).

MIT is a good example of such an institution. A recent faculty report notes that "In fiscal 1969, 35 percent of MIT's nine-month academic salaries were paid out of research grants. . . . Although faculty members are under no formal obligation to raise the funds for a portion of their own salaries, they know that if everybody stopped doing so the Institute would face a critical financial problem. . . . In the near future the percentage of faculty salaries coming from research grants will probably shrink, but over the long run we should pursue a conscious policy of reducing the percentage of faculty salaries drawn from research grants. At the same time, the faculty must understand that any such commitment may involve a reexamination of work loads among various areas of the Institute"—i.e., presumably, that faculty may have to devote more time to teaching (*Creative Renewal,* 1970, pp. 40, 45, 46).

5   I should perhaps note that I do not agree with this logic, but that is neither here nor there for the purpose of this narrative; this is not the first time in human history that what seems logical to one man seems emotional to another.

6   The "Mansfield Amendment" in the defense authorization act for 1970 specified that "None of the funds authorized to be appropriated by this Act may be used to carry out any research project or study unless such project or study has a direct or apparent relationship to a specific military function or operation." Contrariwise, the self-styled "revolutionary cadres" who blew up the Army-financed basic mathematics research center at the University of Wisconsin in August 1970 argued that the center "did the vital basic research necessary for the development of conventional and nuclear weapons, chemical weapons, small arms and bullets" etc. ("Communiqué from the Underground," 1970). Of course, both the Congress and these revolutionaries are wrong. Much of the basic research which the Department of Defense has sponsored on campus (before and after passage of the 1970 authorization act) has no "direct or apparent relationship" to any "specific military function or operation." Thus, when Princeton University's Special Committee on Sponsored Research recently "tried to determine whether it could find a difference between the character of research supported by DoD and that funded by the National Science Foundation and other civilian agencies" it concluded that "In the science and mathematics departments, we have found no clear distinction," and again:

"One of the most striking discoveries during this first review of Princeton's science and mathematics departments was the virtual impossibility of discerning consistent differences between research sponsored by DoD and research sponsored by other agencies" (Special Committee on Sponsored Research, 1970, pp. 11, 38).

7   As noted in the minority report of the Curtiss Committee on Cornell Aeronautical Laboratory–Cornell University Relations, April 1968.

8   Untitled mimeographed report of 43 pages, dated May 31, 1968, submitted to "Dear Mr. President" (of Columbia University) by a committee of seven faculty members, Louis Henkin, chairman. (It is astonishing how poorly identified are some of these nonscholarly products of scholars.)

9   The only reference to the welfare of laboratory staff that I have noted in a dozen faculty reports was by Jonathan Kabat, a student member of the MIT panel. In a lengthy and informative minority report, Kabat suggested that "given the urgency and importance of the problem of conversion, M.I.T. should undertake to salary all [laboratory] people involved at the present levels of income (with provisions for standard increases) until satisfactory long term arrangements can be made." He did not, however, go on to suggest the increased fees that students should pay, the decreased salaries faculty should receive, and other institutional economies that should be effected to cover the $11.7 million annual cost of work in three laboratory programs that he recommended be halted immediately.

10   An exception has occurred at the University of Washington, where President Charles Odegaard has attempted to follow the recommendations of a faculty committee that classified research be reduced at, and closer ties established with, the Applied Physics Laboratory, an R&D center conducting underwater ordnance research for the Navy. When this policy was announced, APL director Joseph Henderson "was retired," and associate director Jack Robertson resigned. "Robertson is convinced that the Lab will close within two years, since the Navy hasn't got much unclassified ordnance research to contract for and it won't contract for classified research under the conditions agreed to with the University. He predicted a $1.2-million decline in contracts" in fiscal year 1971, from the $3.2 million level of 1970 ("Lab Loses Leaders," 1969, p. 13).

11   The quoted passages are drawn from a March 1971 letter from Germantown Laboratories President A. V. Grosse; additional information about the laboratories was kindly provided by Franklin Institute Vice-President Joseph Feldmeier.

12 A few colleges have done so, but, to my knowledge, no university, though a number of private institutions, such as the Universities of Buffalo and Pittsburgh, have bartered their assets for a more public status, and most are dependent upon some form of public revenue.

13 "SRI received a subcontract for the balance of the term of the university's contract, but when it came time for renewal, the Air Force put the contract out for competitive bid," a reader explains. "This is because the authorizing regulation which empowers an agency to negotiate with an educational institution is different from the authority which enables an agency to negotiate with other nonprofit organizations. Hence, there can be no transfer of a contract from one organization to another, but rather the contract with the nonprofit institution must be initiated as a new contract and as such exposed to the normal competitive procurement policies of the agency."

14 Elsewhere, Bronk explained that, in the early 1950s, "a career of teaching and research in a university had become more desirable than life in an intellectually limited research institute that lacked the vital stimulus of eager graduate students. . . . In 1952, when more graduate schools of the highest quality were an urgent national need, the trustees determined. . . . [to create] a graduate university" (Corner, 1964, p. vi).

15 After the faculty senate recommended in April 1969 that the university relinquish the CNA contract, "The Senate resolution was immediately supported by an intensive campaign by Students for a Democratic Society, by an unsuccessful student strike, and by threats of violence, coercion, disorder, and disruption that continued until Commencement. It was followed also by a referendum among River Campus undergraduates on the question whether CNA should be 'on campus,' in which 38 per cent voted 'No,' 25 percent voted 'Yes,' and 37 percent did not vote."

Responding to the senate resolution, President Wallis stated that 'loyalty to the United States precludes harassing it when it is in difficulty. . . . Thus, even if it were in the University's long-run interest to sever our connection with CNA, now would not be the time to do it. . . . [T]here has been generated an atmosphere of coercion, recrimination, threats, and in general of high pressure politicking, in the sense of attempting to mobilize the force of numbers rather than to rely on the forces of reason and persuasion. Had the merits of the case seemed to me and my associates to support the recommendation, it would then have been a serious question whether the long-run harm to the University of appearing to give in to such pressures would not have been so great as to preclude accepting the recommendation" (August 29, 1969, memorandum of Allen Wallis to Faculty Senate on Center for Naval Analyses).

16 Letter of September 18, 1970. An account of the center's problems is given by Carter (1968, pp. 1251–1254). No hint of these problems is contained in an ebullient paper presented in April 1965 by the center's vice-president at a Purdue symposium on Science and Public Policy: Evolving Institutions" (see Triolo, 1966, pp. 139–148).

17 From J. Samuel Gillespie, Jr., Director, Virginia Institute for Scientific Research (1970), and letter of October 5, 1970.

18 News item in *Chemical and Engineering News,* June 8, 1970, p. 61.

19 June 1970 letter.

20 These advantages have recently led the Massachusetts General Hospital

. . . to seek a state license as an educational institution, in addition to its hospital license, in an effort to gain broader financial support.

"If state approval proves possible, the hospital would become eligible for funds now granted only to educational institutions," said Dr. John H. Knowles, MGH general director. "Wide varieties of private foundation and government support could become a reality. . . ."

If the MGH move is successful it could have far-reaching financial effects for other teaching hospitals. It could even help restrain the mounting cost of hospitalization for the public, in that some costs of educational programs in hospitals "find their way onto the patient's bill," Knowles said (Black, 1971, p. 4).

21 The American Council on Education Survey, conducted as part of the inquiry of its Committee on Campus Tensions, is reported in the *Congressional Record—House,* May 11, 1970, daily edition, p. H 4207. Packard's remark was made in the course of an address at the convention of the Instrument Society of America, Philadelphia, October 26, 1970.

22 "Despite increasing student and faculty protests, most American universities have not decreased their research for the Department of Defense. . . .

"Several major universities, such as Caltech, Harvard, Princeton, Northwestern, and the University of Pennsylvania, *did* cut their volume of defense contracts sharply from fiscal 1967 [to 1968]. But other schools—the Universities of Florida and Alaska, and Oregon State, and Louisiana State—have filled the void" ("No Drop in Campus Research," 1969, p. 20).

PART FIVE *Chapter 12*

1 For example, Don Price: ". . . when for lack of any more appropriate institution to turn to, the Government persuaded the University of California to take on Los Alamos and when it persuaded MIT to take on a whole series of institutional entities which MIT was not particularly eager to take on, and did only under great pressure, and I was one of those who had some hand in applying that pressure as a junior staff officer of the Defense Department, it was taking advantage of the handiest machinery that was in existence, but at the cost of distorting the role of those institutions.

"And I think that some things of that kind, some technological work of that kind in the future might better be shifted either to quite private independent corporate entities or taken on within the structure of Government itself" (*National Science Policy,* 1970, p. 13).

2   *Sponsored Research Policy,* 1954, p. 14. Members of this committee, chaired by President Virgil Hancher of the State University of Iowa, included Professor Robert Bacher of the California Institute of Technology, Vice-President James Corley of the University of California, and President James R. Killian of the Massachusetts Institute of Technology.

3   *Report to the President,* 1962, p. 11. It may be noted that two of the Bell committee's seven members had also been members of the Seaborg panel (Alan Waterman, director of the National Science Foundation, and Seaborg himself, who by this time had become chairman of the Atomic Energy Commission) and a third, President Kennedy's science advisor Jerome Wiesner, had been a member of the Science Advisory Committee which issued the report.

4   "A decision to cut loose from Draper while retaining ties to Lincoln . . . was announced to the faculty 20 May by President Howard W. Johnson. The decision constitutes, in effect, a declaration that M.I.T. wants to get out of developing specific weapons systems (as at Draper) but will continue working on broader military problems (as at Lincoln).

"M.I.T. decided to begin the tortuous and lengthy process of divesting itself of Draper because it had failed in the short run to find the money needed to implement a policy of 'converting' the two laboratories toward a greater civilian emphasis. . . .

"Draper Laboratory, with nearly 2,000 employees, had a budget of $53.6 million in the year ending 30 June 1969. . . . When divestment . . . is complete, a year or more from now, M.I.T. will lose some $5 million a year in compensation for administrative functions. This pours into M.I.T.'s general treasury and helps support such activities as the library and health services. . . .

"The almost continual crisis began in the fall of 1968 when a soldier absent without leave was harbored in the M.I.T. student center for a few days until police arrested him. The incident crystallized antiwar feeling among many M.I.T. students and faculty who had shied away from protest until then. Among the results were the all-day discussion of the dangers of science held at M.I.T. and other campuses on 4 March 1969 and a demonstration against Draper Lab's work on Poseidon in which demonstrators burst into Johnson's office. . . .

"The fall term of 1969 opened with an announcement that Draper would step down as head of the laboratory (which was to be renamed for him) on 1 January, 6 months earlier than planned. But radical pressures continued to rise. Demonstrators disrupted a General Electric recruiting session on 29 October, blocked one entrance to a Draper Laboratory building on 4 November, and occupied Johnson's office for several days in January, causing $6000 damage before they left" (McElheny, 1970, pp. 1074–1075).

5 "We are now generating a third kind of physicist, who . . . I will call a 'data-reducer.' Usually, he has received a better education in theory than most experimentalists but is neither a creative theoretician nor an experienced designer of complete experiments. Such physicists start their research, for example, by taking pictures in a bubble chamber exposed to a high energy particle beam; they are not involved in the design or operation of the bubble chamber or accelerator. They subject these pictures to analysis, generally with extensive use of computers, and then draw physical conclusions. As a result, in addition to becoming conversant with current problems in modern physical thought, they learn a great deal about modern data-processing techniques. . . .

". . . The increasing number of degrees given to data-reducers is a consequence of increasing specialization . . ." (Panofsky, 1968, p. 196).

6 ". . . universities do not *assign* professors to research projects in the way an employee is assigned in industry [and many institutes]. If more than one faculty member is to work on a project, the initiative must usually come from faculty. The university is therefore hampered in what it can do inside the normal structure. When large projects are undertaken, non-faculty are usually hired to do most of the work" (Robinson, 1971, p. 105, his italics).

7 "I think most people with experience at both Rand and a university would disagree," protests a RAND staffer. "There is more interaction and intellectual discussion at Rand than at most universities, although this may be true only of Rand."

8 "It has always been mystifying to me as to why the presence of students is supposed to contribute to an intellectual atmosphere," a reader comments. "There is an unwarranted intellectual smugness to academicians that may be traceable to the ease with which ideas can seem to impress impressionistic youngsters."

9 Some of the kinds of information that would be useful have been noted on pp. 102–106.

10 Cf. Joseph Goulden: "The 990-As, because they are written by lawyers and tax accountants for their opposite numbers in the government, are

mysterious accumulations of numbers which, standing alone, tell little of what a foundation does or how it earns and spends its money" (1971, p. 73).

11 "Of the 30,242 foundations on the IRS list, only 140 issue printed reports on an annual or biennial basis. . . . Only seven of the ten largest foundations publish such reports. . . . About one-third of the 261 foundations with assets of over $10,000,000 publish reports, and the Foundation Center thinks 'this is a scandal'" (Goulden, 1971, pp. 74–75).

12 "Would a new central mechanism in Washington, created with a broad charter, to act as a sort of analogue to the National Science Foundation, prove feasible as a device for channeling general support grants to the nongovernmental organizations? It would seem so in theory, but there would be many problems that might make the idea unworkable. A more practical approach, but one that also contains potential dangers for the organization seeking funds, would be to have each federal agency decide for itself which organizations it considered essential for its purposes and then determine the amount of general support each should receive. . . . [S]uch a process would have to be rigorously selective, with a wary eye open for possible incompetents and self-servers. The process would also have to be based on criteria politically defensible to Congress and the public" (Pifer, 1966, p. 15).

13 ". . . regardless of the funds available, the needs for research will always exceed them" (Calkins, 1966, p. 4).

14 Contrariwise, Defense R&D centers have received more attention than their importance warrants. They would like nothing better than to be neglected by the Congress for awhile.

15 "The federal government and voluntary health agencies . . . can never fully provide the operating and development costs of a private research institute. They do not support all the research and training projects, nor do they pay for all expenses of any given project. Likewise they do not finance the purchase of all research equipment or the construction of all research space, nor do they provide reserve and emergency funds" (*Boston Biomedical Research Institute Research Programs,* 1970 brochure, p. 18).

It is fair to add that the cost policies of contracting agencies like the Department of Defense have generally been more satisfactory to institutes than those of granting agencies like the National Science Foundation and the Public Health Service. And, of course, a basic reason for the formation of independent institutes by universities and university faculty has been the ability thus to obtain a fee and to recover fuller costs than in on-campus research.

16 *A Program for Improving the Quality,* 1970, p. 51. See also the same citation, vol. 1; and *A Guide for Non-Profit Institutions,* 1967.

17 Similarly, private foundations were in part to blame for defects in the 1969 tax act. As one foundation executive wrote, "the need for more information about nonprofit organizations . . . became a matter of great concern during the recent legislation on foundations, where we found ourselves unable to provide the relevant committee staffs and committee members with the kind of taxonomy that would have enabled them to arrive at a better definition of the term private foundation" (June 1970 letter to author).

18 Pifer has also discussed the problems of nonprofit organizations in the 1967, 1969, and 1970 annual reports of the Carnegie Corporation.

References

Aarons, Leroy F.: "Witness Says Ellsberg Used Her Xerox," *Washington Post,* June 25, 1971.

The Administration of Research Grants in the Public Health Service, ninth report by the Committee on Government Operations, U.S. House of Representatives, H. R. Rep., No. 800, 90th Cong., 1st Sess., October 20, 1967, pp. 39–40.

American Institute for Economic Research: *Auditor's Report,* Exhibit B, December 31, 1968.

Anderson, Charles: "Research: A Retreat from the Universities?" *Scientific Research,* November 24, 1969.

Armbruster, Robert J.: "APL: Asset or Anachronism?" *The Johns Hopkins Magazine,* April 1970.

Associated Universities, Inc.: *Organization and Objectives,* New York, December 31, 1963.

Association of Independent Research Institutes: *Constitution and By-Laws,* 1969. (Mimeographed.)

Bacon, Donald W.: "Working with the IRS: The New Exempt Organizations Program in Audit," *The Tax Adviser,* vol. 1, no. 1, pp. 69–72, January 1970.

Bailey, Stephen K.: "Emergence of the Laboratory Program," *Journal of Research and Development in Education,* vol. 3, no. 2, pp. 5–17, 1970.

Basic Research, A National Resource, National Science Foundation, Washington, 1957.

Baxter, James P.: *Scientists Against Time,* Little, Brown and Company, Boston, 1946.

The Behavioral Sciences and the Federal Government, National Academy of Sciences, Washington, 1968.

Black, Herbert: "MGH Seeks License as Educational Institution," *The Boston Globe,* February 1, 1971.

Bloom, Benjamin S.: "Research and Development Centers: Promise and Fulfillment," *Journal of Research and Development in Education,* vol. 1, no. 4, pp. 181–89, 1968.

Brim, Orville G., Jr.: "Diversity in Social Research Organizations," Russell Sage Foundation, September 1, 1967. (Draft.)

Bunker, Frank F.: "Cooperative Research, Its Conduct and Interpretation," in *Cooperation in Research,* The Carnegie Institution of Washington, 1938.

Calkins, Robert D.: "Remarks," in *Government and Critical Intelligence,* an address by President Lyndon B. Johnson marking the fiftieth anniversary of the Brookings Institution, Washington, September 29, 1966.

Campus Tensions: Analysis and Recommendations, Report of the Special Committee on Campus Tensions, Sol M. Linowitz, chairman, April 26, 1970, *Congressional Record—House,* May 11, 1970, daily edition.

Carroll, James D.: "Science and the City: The Question of Authority," *Science,* vol. 163, no. 3870, February 28, 1969.

Carter, Luther: "Dallas: Larger Education Role Proposed for Research Center," *Science,* vol. 162, no. 3859, December 13, 1968.

Carter, Luther: "Oceanography: Woods Hole and MIT Pool Their Resources," *Science,* vol. 157, no. 3793, September 8, 1967.

Cartter, Allan M.: *An Assessment of Quality in Graduate Education,* American Council on Education, Washington, 1966.

Chase, Francis S.: *The National Program of Educational Laboratories,* Office of Education, Washington, 1969.

Chemical and Engineering News, vol. 48, no. 24, June 8, 1970.

Chronicle of Higher Education, May 5, 1969.

Clapp, Stephen: "The Intellectual Bombthrowers" (an article on the Institute of Policy Analysis), *Washingtonian,* December 1969.

Coddington, Dean C., and J. Gordon Milliken: "Future of Federal Contract Research Centers," *Harvard Business Review,* March–April 1970.

Commercialism of Research at Universities, American Council of Independent Laboratories, Inc., Washington, March 1968.

"Communiqué from the Underground Number One—the Marion Delgado Collective," in "Text of F.B.I. Affidavit Charging Four in University of Wisconsin Bombing," *New York Times,* September 4, 1970.

Congressional Record—House, July 14, July 20, 1966; May 11, 1970, daily edition.

Congressional Record—Senate, November 20, 1967; October 1, 1968; June 19, July 9, November 11, 1969; April 13, 1970, daily edition.

Corner, George W.: *A History of the Rockefeller Institute, 1901–1953,* The Rockefeller Institute Press, New York, 1964.

Creative Renewal in a Time of Crisis, Report of the Commission on MIT Education, Massachusetts Institute of Technology, Cambridge, Mass., November 1970.

Crewe, Albert V.: "Science on a Regional Scale," in Boyd R. Keenan (ed.), *Science and the University,* Columbia University Press, New York, 1966.

Crowl, John A.: "Ford-Aided 'Common Fund' to Provide Colleges with Professional Investment Management," *The Chronicle of Higher Education,* April 26, 1971.

Cumulative List of Organizations Described in Section 170(c) of the Internal Revenue Code of 1954, revised to December 31, 1968, Internal Revenue Service, Washington, 1969.

Daniels, Farrington: "The Argonne National Laboratory," *Bulletin of the Atomic Scientists,* vol. 4, no. 6, pp. 177–179, June 1948.

Danilov, Victor J.: "Contract Research in the United States," unpublished talk given in Brussels, October 20, 1969.

Danilov, Victor J.: "The Not-for-Profit Research Institutes," *Industrial Research,* February 1966.

Director's Report, Cold Spring Harbor of Quantitative Biology Annual Report 1969, Cold Spring Harbor, Long Island, N.Y., 1969.

"Dole Cites Anti-War Drive, Asks Tighter Lobbying Rein," *Washington Evening Star,* August 21, 1970.

Dressel, Paul L., F. Craig Johnson, and Philip M. Marcus: "The Proliferating Institutes," *Change,* vol. 1, no. 4, pp. 21–24, July–August 1969.

Dupree, A. Hunter: *Science in the Federal Government,* The Belknap Press, Harvard University Press, Cambridge, Mass., 1957.

"Eligibility for TIAA-CREF," Teachers Insurance and Annuity Association of America — College Retirement Equities Fund, New York, 3 pp., undated.

Enke, Stephen: *Think Tanks for Better Government,* TEMPO, General Electric Company, Santa Barbara, Calif., December 1967.

"Excerpts from Report of the City Council's Subcommittee on Consultants," *New York Times,* November 16, 1970.

"Final Agreement Is Announced on Separation of University, SRI," *Campus Report,* Stanford University, Palo Alto, Calif., January 14, 1970.

Finney, John W.: "U.S. Will Examine Its Laboratories," *New York Times,* September 4, 1964.

First Report of Review Panel on Special Laboratories, Massachusetts Institute of Technology, Cambridge, Mass., May 31, 1969.

"The First Thirty-five Years *and* Plans for the Future," *Economic Education Bulletin,* vol. 8, no. 8, August 1968.

"48 Universities Form Consortium for Space Research," *Higher Education and National Affairs,* July 18, 1969.

Foster, John S., Jr.: "Remarks before American Nuclear Society," Seattle, Wash., June 18, 1969.

"From President Hitch: Statement on Improvement of Undergraduate Teaching," *University Bulletin,* University of California, Berkeley, Calif., November 9, 1970.

Gillespie, J. Samuel, Jr.: *Annual Report of the Director of the Institute,* Virginia Institute of Scientific Research, Richmond, January 30, 1970.

Gilmore, John S., John J. Ryan, and William S. Gould: *Defense Systems Resources in the Civil Sector,* Denver Research Institute, University of Denver, Denver, July 1967.

Glass, E. M.: *Summary of Findings and Conclusions of a DoD Study on Compensation Practices of FCRC's* and *Summary of Findings and Conclusions of a DoD Study on Executive Compensation in FCRC's,* Department of Defense, Washington, 1969*a* and 1968*b.*

Goldwater, Barry: "Outside 'Whiz Kids,'" *Northern Virginia Sun,* January 26, 1970.

Good, C. W.: "Administration of Sponsored Research," in George P. Bush and Lowell H. Hattery (eds.), *Scientific Research: Its Administration and Organization,* American University Press, Washington, 1950.

Goulden, Joseph: *The Money Givers,* Random House, Inc., New York, 1971.

Government-University Relationships in Federally Sponsored Scientific Research and Development, National Science Foundation, Washington, 1958.

Grant, James D.: "The Future of Nonprofit Research and Development Organizations," *California Management Review,* Summer 1965.

Green, Philip: "Science, Government, and the Case of RAND," *World Politics,* vol. 20, no. 2, pp. 301–326, January 1968.

Greenberg, D. S.: "The MURA Accelerator: Compromise for the Mid-West," *Science,* vol. 143, no. 3605, pp. 450–452, January 31, 1964.

Greenberg, D. S.: *The Politics of Pure Science,* New American Library, Inc., New York, 1967.

A Guide for Non-Profit Institutions, Establishing Indirect Cost Rates for Research Grants and Contracts with the Department of Health, Educa-

tion and Welfare, Department of Health, Education and Welfare, Washington, November 1967.

Haskins, Caryl P. (ed.): *The Search for Understanding,* Carnegie Institute of Washington, Washington, 1967.

Hewlett, Richard G., and Oscar E. Anderson, Jr.: *The New World, 1939–1946,* Pennsylvania State University Press, University Park, Pa., 1962.

Hewlett, Richard G., and Francis Duncan: *Atomic Shield, 1947/1952,* Pennsylvania State University Press, University Park, Pa., 1969.

"Honoraria," *Policies/Procedures Guide,* The RAND Corporation, September 1, 1961, revised August 20, 1967.

"How Students Forced a Move at Stanford," *Scientific Research,* November 24, 1969.

Hudson Institute: *Report to the Members,* Croton-on-Hudson, N.Y., 1969.

"Industrial R&D: Competition from Universities, Non-Profits, Alarms Independent Laboratories," *Science,* vol. 144, no. 3616, April 17, 1964.

"The Institute for Policy Studies," *Congressional Record—Senate,* October 20, 1969, daily edition, p. S128130.

Institutions for Effective Management of the Environment, Report of the Environmental Study Group to the Environmental Studies Board of the National Academy of Sciences–National Academy of Engineering, part 1, January 1970.

Internal Revenue Service: *Supplement to Publication No. 78 (Rev. 12-31-68): Cumulative List of Organizations,* Washington, No. 1969-6, pp. 58–68 and No. 1970-4, pp. 43–47.

Internal Revenue Service Code, Reg. 1501(c) (3)- 1(b), Commerce Clearing House, 1967.

Jeffery, David: "Up Front at Foggy Bottom," *The George Washington University Magazine,* Washington, August 1969.

Joint Committee on Atomic Energy: *The Future Role of the Atomic Energy Commission Laboratories,* Joint Committee Print, 86th Cong., 2d Sess., October 1960.

Journal of Finance, vol. 24, no. 2, May 1969.

JPL Study Committee: *The Jet Propulsion Laboratory and the Caltech Campus,* Report to President Harold Brown, California Institute of Technology, Pasadena, Calif., March 11, 1970.

"Juvenile Institute Urged in Congress," *New York Times,* November 25, 1969.

Kabat, Jonathan P.: "Personal Addendum," in *First Report of Review Panel* *on Special Laboratories,* Massachusetts Institute of Technology, Cambridge, Mass., May 31, 1969.

Klaw, Spencer: "The Perils of Running a Nonprofit," *Fortune,* vol. 74, no. 6, p. 158ff., November 1966.

Knowledge into Action: Improving the Nation's Use of the Social Sciences, Report of the Special Commission on the Social Sciences of the National Science Board, National Science Foundation, Washington, 1969.

Kobler, John: *The Rockefeller University Story,* The Rockefeller University Press, New York, 1970.

Komons, Nick A.: *Science and the Air Force,* Office of Aerospace Research, Arlington, Va., 1966.

"Lab Loses Leaders in Retirement Row," *Scientific Research,* November 10, 1969.

Leavitt, William: "ANSER: USAF's 'Short-Order' Think Tank," *Air Force/ Space Digest,* August 1967.

Lesher, Richard L.: *Independent Research Institutes and Industrial Application of Aerospace Research,* Ph.D. dissertation, Graduate School of Business, Indiana University, Bloomington, Ind., 1963.

Levien, Roger E.: *Independent Public Policy Analysis Organizations — A Major Social Invention,* The RAND Corporation, Santa Monica, Calif., P-4231, November 1969.

Levien, Roger E.: *National Institute of Education: Preliminary Plan for the Proposed Institute,* The RAND Corporation, Santa Monica, Calif., February 1971.

Lillienthal, David E.: *Change, Hope, and the Bomb,* Princeton University Press, Princeton, N.J., 1963.

Lowry, Ira S.: *Reforming Rent Control in New York City: The Role of Research in Policy Making,* The RAND Corporation, Santa Monica, Calif., November 1970.

Mathews, John: "Marland's Pact's History Shows HEW Aides Split," *Washington Evening Star,* October 16, 1970.

McElheny, Victor K.: "MIT Administration Makes Public Its Intentions on Disposition of Draper and Lincoln Laboratories," *Science,* May 29, 1970, pp. 1074–1075.

McElheny, Victor K.: "Radio Astronomy: NSF Scrutinizing Proposals for Six Major Instruments," *Science,* vol. 157, no. 3790, pp. 782–784, August 18, 1967.

McFadden, Robert D.: "Computer Helps Fire Department," *New York Times,* February 21, 1971.

National Science Foundation: *Directory of Federal R&D Installations for the Year Ending June 30, 1969, A Report to the Federal Council for Science and Technology,* Washington, 1970*a*.

National Science Foundation: *Federal Funds for Research, Development, and Other Scientific Activities, Fiscal Years 1968, 1969, and 1970,* vol. 18, Washington, 1969*a*.

National Science Foundation: *Federal Funds for Research, Development, and Other Scientific Activities,* vols. 15–19, Washington, 1966–70.

National Science Foundation: *Federal Funds for Science: Federal Funds for Scientific Research and Development at Nonprofit Institutions 1950–51 and 1951–52,* vol. 1, Washington, 1953.

National Science Foundation: *Federal Support of Research and Development at Universities and Colleges and Selected Nonprofit Institutions, Fiscal Year 1968,* Washington, 1969*b*.

National Science Foundation: *Federal Support to Universities, Colleges, and Selected Nonprofit Institutions, Fiscal Year 1969,* Washington, 1970*b*.

National Science Foundation: *National Patterns of R&D Resources, 1953–70,* Washington, 1969*c*.

National Science Foundation: *Scientific Activities of Nonprofit Institutions 1966,* Washington, 1969*d*.

National Science Policy, Hearings before the Subcommittee on Science, Research, and Development of the Committee on Science and Astronautics, U.S. House of Representatives, 91st Cong., 2d Sess., July 7, 8, 21, 22, 23, 28, 29; August 4, 5, 11, 12, 13; September 15, 16, and 17, 1970.

Need for Improved Guidelines in Contracting for Research with Government-Sponsored Nonprofit Contractors, report to the Congress by the Comptroller General of the United States, February 10, 1969.

Nelson, Bryce: "Carnegie University: New Institution Emerging in Pittsburgh," *Science,* vol. 155, no. 3763, pp. 673–76, February 10, 1967.

Nelson, Sidney G.: *The Creation, Evaluation, and Selection of Research Projects in Not-for-Profit Research Institutions,* unpublished thesis, Business School Library, Ohio State University, Columbus, 1968.

New York Times, March 4; July 1, 8, 16; October 7, 29; November 16, 24; December 3, 21, 1970.

Nisbet, Robert: "The Future of the University," *Commentary,* vol. 51, no. 2, February 1971.

Nixon, Richard M.: "Regulation Governing Payment of Compensation to Officers or Employees of Federal Contract Research Centers," *Federal Register,* February 13, 1970.

"No Drop in Campus Research for DoD," *Scientific Research,* February 3, 1969.

"Notice," *Research at 200GEV,* Universities Research Association, Washington, August 1967.

Orlans, Harold: *Contracting for Atoms,* The Brookings Institution, Washington, 1967.

Orlans, Harold: *The Effects of Federal Programs on Higher Education,* The Brookings Institution, Washington, 1962.

Palmer, Archie M. (ed.): *New Research Centers,* a Periodic Supplement to *Research Centers Directory,* Gale Research Company, Detroit, issues no. 1-7, December 1968–December 1970.

Palmer, Archie M.: *Nonprofit Research and Patent Management Organization,* National Academy of Sciences–National Research Council, Washington, 1955.

Palmer, Archie: *Nonprofit Research and Patent Management in the United States,* National Academy of Sciences–National Research Council, Washington, 1956.

Palmer, Archie M. (ed.): *Research Centers Directory,* 3d ed., Gale Research Company, Detroit, 1968.

Panofsky, Wolfgang K. H.: "Big Science and Graduate Education," in Harold Orlans (ed.), *Science Policy and the University,* The Brookings Institution, Washington, 1968.

Pifer, Alan: "The Nongovernmental Organization at Bay," *Annual Report,* Carnegie Corporation of New York, New York, 1966.

Pifer, Alan: "The Quasi Nongovernmental Organization," *Annual Report,* Carnegie Corporation of New York, New York, 1967.

Planning Research Corporation: *Professional Service Companies: FCRC's Versus Private Sector,* February 27, 1970. (Offset.)

A Program for Improving the Quality of Grantee Management, Financially Dependent Organizations, Division of Grants Administration Policy, Office of the Assistant Secretary, Comptroller, Department of Health, Education and Welfare, vol. 2, June 1970.

Ramsey, Norman F.: *Annual Report,* University Research Corporation, Inc., January 30, 1970.

The Rand Corporation, The First Fifteen Years, The RAND Corporation, Santa Monica, Calif., 1963.

The Rand Corporation: Its Origin, Evolution, and Plans for the Future, The RAND Corporation, Santa Monica, Calif., February 1971.

Ranzal, Edward: "Garelik Calls Rand Study of City's Police a Failure," *New York Times,* October 7, 1970.

Reeves, Richard: "Think Tanks: Applied Research on Not-for-Profit Basis Is Paying Off Handsomely," *New York Times,* June 15, 1967, p. 46M.

"Regional Educational Laboratories: Agents of Change," *Journal of Research and Development in Education,* vol. 3, no. 2, Winter 1970.

Report of the Ad Hoc Committee on Sponsored Research, Robert W. Kenny, chairman, George Washington University, Washington, June 1969. (Mimeographed.)

The Report of the President to the Board of Trustees, The Washington Center for Metropolitan Studies, November 18, 1969.

Report to the President on Government Contracting for Research and Development, Prepared by the Bureau of the Budget and Referred to the Committee on Government Operations, U.S. Senate, 87th Cong., 2d Sess., Document No. 94, May 17, 1962.

"Report of the President 1967," *Massachusetts Institute of Technology Bulletin,* 1967.

The Report of the President's Commission on Campus Unrest, Washington, September 1970.

Report of the Special Committee on University Research at Livermore and Los Alamos, Academic Senate, University of California, Berkeley, Calif., 31 pp. (Undated; evidently Spring 1970.)

"Report of the Stanford-SRI Study Committee" *(Campus Report Supplement),* Stanford University, Palo Alto, Calif., April 14, 1969.

"Research Crisis: Cutting Off the Plant at the Roots," *Time,* February 16, 1970, reproduced in *Congressional Record—House,* May 11, 1970, daily edition.

Robinson, David Z.: "Government Contracting for Academic Research: Accountability in the American Experience," in Bruce Smith and D. C. Hague (eds.), *The Dilemma of Accountability in Modern Government: Independence Versus Control,* St. Martin's Press, Inc., New York, 1971.

Roose, Kenneth D., and Charles J. Anderson: *A Rating of Graduate Programs,* American Council on Education, Washington, 1970.

Rossi, Peter H.: "Researchers, Scholars and Policy Makers: The Politics of Large Scale Research," *Daedalus,* Fall 1964, pp. 1142–1161.

Science, vol. 156, no. 3776, May 12, 1967.

Science and Technology: Tools for Progress, The Report of the President's Task Force on Science Policy, Washington, April 1970.

Scientific Progress, The Universities, and The Federal Government, Statement by the President's Science Advisory Committee, The White House, November 15, 1960.

Scully, Malcolm G.: "Attacks on Tenure Mount; Limitations are Proposed in 5 States," *The Chronicle of Higher Education,* March 22, 1971.

"Senator Hawk vs. Senator Dove," *Newsweek,* vol. 76, no. 7, August 17, 1970.

"Sickles, Wineland Seek U.S. Studies," *Washington Post,* September 4, 1968.

Sieber, Sam D., and Paul F. Lazarsfeld: *Reforming the University: The Role of the Research Center,* Bureau of Applied Social Research, Columbia University, New York, 1971.

Singer, Max: *The Work of the Hudson Institute: A Background Statement,* The Hudson Institute, Croton-on-Hudson, N.Y., September 25, 1969.

Smith, Bruce L. R.: *The Rand Corporation,* Harvard University Press, Cambridge, Mass., 1966.

Smith, Bruce L. R., and D. C. Hague (eds.), *The Dilemma of Accountability in Modern Government: Independence Versus Control,* St. Martin's Press, Inc., New York, 1971.

"Social Sciences: Cancellation of Camelot After Row in Chile Brings Research Under Scrutiny," *Science,* vol. 149, no. 3639, September 10, 1965.

Special Committee on Sponsored Research: *Preliminary Report to the Council of the Princeton University Community,* Princeton, N.J., 1970.

Sponsored Research Policy of Colleges and Universities, A Report of the Committee on Institutional Research Policy, American Council on Education, Washington, 1954.

Stanford Research Institute: *SRI Annual Report 1970,* Menlo Park, Calif., February 1971.

Stern, Lawrence: "Institute Quizzed on Political Tie," *Washington Post,* April 15, 1965.

"Study Topics as of 1 February 1971," Research and Development Study Group, Commission on Government Procurement, Washington 1971. (Working paper, multilithed, unpaged.)

Stulman, Julius: "Beyond Crises: A 'Creative Ladder' for Oncoming Generations," *Fields Within Fields . . . Within Fields, The Methodology of the*

Creative Process, Man's Emergent Evolution, The World Institute, vol. 3, no. 1, 1970.

Systems Development and Management, Hearings before a Subcommittee of the Committee on Government Operations, U.S. House of Representatives, 87th Cong., 2d Sess., 1962.

Task Force Report: Science and Technology, a report of the President's Commission on Law Enforcement and Administration of Justice, prepared by the Institute for Defense Analyses, Washington, 1967.

Tax Reform Act of 1969, Hearings before the Committee on Finance on H.R. 13270, U.S. Senate, 91st Cong., 1st Sess., part 6, October 3, 6, 7, 8, and 22, 1969.

Thomas, B. D.: *The Legacy of Science, the Story of Battelle Memorial Institute,* The Newcomen Society in North America, Princeton, N.J., 1963.

Tolchin, Martin: "Beame Is Upheld on Consultants," *New York Times,* June 25, 1971.

Tonsor, S. J.: "Alienation and Relevance in Higher Education," Address at a Meeting of the Education Committee of the National Association of Manufacturers, Washington, April 1, 1969, in *Congressional Record,* May 7, 1969, pp. 11644–46.

Triolo, James S.: "A New Community of Scholars in the Southwest," in Boyd Keenan (ed.), *Science and the University,* Columbia University Press, New York, 1966.

"Use of Management and Operating Contracts," Bureau of Budget Circular A-49, February 25, 1959.

"USOE-Funded Research and Development Centers: An Assessment," *Journal of Research and Development in Education,* vol. 1, no. 4, summer 1968.

Utilization of Federal Laboratories, Hearings before the Subcommittee on Science, Research, and Development of the Committee on Science and Astronautics, U.S. House of Representatives, 90th Cong., 2d Sess., March 26, 27, 28; April 2, 3, 4, 1968.

Waks, Norman: *Problems in the Management of Federal Contract Research Centers,* The MITRE Corporation, Bedford, Mass., September 1970.

Walsh, John: "Behavioral Sciences: The View at the Center for Advanced Study," *Science,* vol. 169, no. 3946, pp. 654–658, August 14, 1970.

Walsh, John: "The Rockefeller University: Science in a Different Key," *Science,* vol. 150, no. 3704, pp. 1692–1695, December 24, 1965.

"Washington Science Outlook," *Scientific Research,* April 14, 1969.

Weinberg, Alvin M.: "Scientific Teams and Scientific Laboratories," *Daedalus,* vol. 99, no. 4, pp. 1056–1075, Fall 1970.

Weinberg, Alvin M.: "Social Problems and National Socio-Technical Institutes," in *Applied Science and Astronautics,* a report to the U.S. House of Representatives by the National Academy of Sciences, 1967, pp. 415–434.

Weinberg, Alvin M.: in *Yale Scientific Magazine.* vol. 37, 1963.

Welles, John G., Dean C. Coddington, J. Gordon Milliken, Catherine C. Blakemore, John S. Gilmore, and Terry Sovel Heller: *Contract Research and Development Adjuncts of Federal Agencies: An Exploratory Study of Forty Organizations,* Denver Research Institute, University of Denver, Denver, March 1969.

Wilson, Richard: "'Newsroom' Firing Poses Foundations Trouble," *Washington Evening Star, April 29, 1970, reproduced in Congressional Record* May 1, 1970, daily edition, p. E3825.

Wolf, Charles: *Policy Sciences and Policy Research Organizations,* RAND paper P-4457, September 1970.

Wolfe, Singleton B.: "Federal Policing of Exempt Organizations," *Twenty-Eighth Annual Institute on Federal Taxation,* New York University, New York, 1970.

Wolfle, Dael: "Unnecessary Research Institutes," editorial in *Science,* vol. 139, no. 3555, February 15, 1963.

Wolfman, Bernard: "Federal Tax Policy and the Support of Science," in Harry W. Jones (ed.), *Law and the Social Role of Science,* Rockefeller University Press, New York, 1966.

Bibliography

Advisory Committee for Assessment of University Based Institutes for Research on Poverty: *Policy and Program Research in a University Setting: A Case Study,* Division of Behavioral Sciences, National Research Council–National Academy of Sciences, Washington, 1971.

Air Force Relations with the Not-for-Profit Corporations, report of Air Force Systems Command Board of Visitors' Ad Hoc Group, U.S. Air Force, 1966.

Danhof, Clarence H.: *The Expanding Roles of Non-Profit Organizations as Contractors with Government: Some Research Needs,* Program of Policy Studies in Science and Technology, George Washington University, Washington, March 1968.

Danhof, Clarence H.: *Government Contracting and Technological Change,* Brookings Institution, Washington, 1968.

Dickson, Paul: *Think Tanks,* Atheneum, New York, 1971.

Federal Contract Research Centers, A Brief Historical Analysis, Management Analysis Memorandum, Office for Laboratory Management, Office of the Director of Defense Research and Engineering, August 21, 1967.

Glass, E. M.: *Evaluation of R&D Organizations,* Management Analysis Memorandum, Office for Laboratory Management, Office of the Director of Defense Research and Engineering, July 31, 1969.

Management Trends in Federal Contract Research Centers (FCRCs), Management Analysis Memorandum, Office for Laboratory Management, Office of the Director of Defense Research and Engineering, August 1, 1968.

Milliken, John Gordon: *An Analysis of Selected Management Problems of Federal-Auxiliary Contract Research and Development Centers,* Thesis submitted to the University of Colorado Graduate School, Boulder, Colo., 1969.

Observations on the Administration by the Office of Civil Defense of

Research Study Contracts Awarded to Hudson Institute, Inc., report to the Congress by the Comptroller General of the United States, March 25, 1968.

Ritchie, Ronald S.: *An Institute for Research on Public Policy: A Study Prepared for the Government of Canada,* Toronto, 1971.

Roback, Herbert: "The Not-for-Profit Corporation in Defense Contracting: Problems and Perspectives," *Federal Bar Journal,* Spring 1965, pp. 195–206.

Swatez, Gerald: *Social Organization of a University Laboratory,* Space Sciences Laboratory, University of California, Berkeley, Calif., April 1966.

Appendix A: Federally Funded Nonprofit R&D Centers, 1969

ATOMIC ENERGY COMMISSION*

University-Operated

Ames Laboratory (Iowa State University of Science and Technology)

Lawrence Radiation Laboratory (University of California)

Los Alamos Scientific Laboratory (University of California)

Plasma Physics Laboratory (Princeton University)

Stanford Linear Accelerator Center (Stanford University)

Operated by Nonprofit Institutions or University Groups

Argonne National Laboratory (University of Chicago and Argonne Universities Association)

Atomic Bomb Casualty Commission (National Academy of Sciences)

Brookhaven National Laboratory (Associated Universities)

Cambridge Electron Accelerator (Harvard University and Massachusetts Institute of Technology)

National Accelerator Laboratory (Universities Research Association)

Oak Ridge Associated Universities

Pacific Northwest Laboratory (Battelle Memorial Institute)

Princeton-Pennsylvania Accelerator (Princeton University and University of Pennsylvania)

* In addition to the nonprofit centers listed in the table, the Commission funded the following seven centers which were operated by for-profit firms: Bettis Atomic Power Laboratory (Westinghouse Electric), Knolls Atomic Power Laboratory (General Electric), Mound Laboratory (Monsanto), National Reactor Testing Station (Idaho Nuclear), Oak Ridge National Laboratory (Union Carbide), Sandia Laboratory (Western Electric-Sandia), and Savannah River Laboratory (duPont).

DEPARTMENT OF DEFENSE

University-Operated

Applied Physics Laboratory (Navy–Johns Hopkins University)

Applied Physics Laboratory (Navy–University of Washington)

Center for Naval Analyses (Navy–University of Rochester)

Center for Research in Social Systems (Army–American University)†

Hudson Laboratories (Navy–Columbia University)‡

Human Resources Research Office (Army–George Washington University)§

Lincoln Laboratory (Air Force–Massachusetts Institute of Technology)

Mathematics Research Center (Army–University of Wisconsin)†

Ordnance Research Laboratory (Navy–Pennsylvania State University)

Operated by Nonprofit Institutions

Aerospace Corporation (Air Force)

Analytic Services (Air Force)

Electromagnetic Compatability Analysis Center (Air Force–Illinois Institute of Technology Research Institute)

Institute for Defense Analyses (Secretary of Defense)

MITRE Corporation (Air Force)

RAND Corporation (Air Force)

Research Analysis Corporation (Army)

DEPARTMENT OF HEALTH, EDUCATION AND WELFARE, OFFICE OF EDUCATION

University-Operated

Center for the Advanced Study of Educational Administration (University of Oregon)

Center for Research and Development in Higher Education (University of California)

Center for Research and Development for Learning and Re-Education (University of Wisconsin)

Center for the Study of Evaluation of Instructional Programs (University of California)

Center for the Study of Social Organization of Schools and the Learning Process (Johns Hopkins University)

Coordination Center for the National Program in Early Childhood Education (University of Illinois)

Learning Research and Development Center (University of Pittsburgh)

Research and Development Center in Educational Stimulation (University of Georgia)

Research and Development Center in Teacher Education (University of Texas)

Stanford Center for Research and Development in Teaching (Stanford University)

Operated by Nonprofit Institutions

Appalachia Educational Laboratory

Center for Educational Policy Research (Stanford Research Institute)

Center for Urban Education

Central Atlantic Regional Educational Laboratory‡

Central Midwestern Regional Educational Laboratory

Cooperative Educational Research Laboratory‡

Eastern Regional Institute for Education

Educational Development Center

Far West Laboratory for Educational Research and Development

Michigan-Ohio Regional Educational Laboratory‡

Mid-Continent Regional Educational Laboratory

Northwest Regional Educational Laboratory

Policy Research Center (Syracuse University Research Corporation)

Regional Educational Laboratory for the Carolinas and Virginia

Research for Better Schools

Rocky Mountain Regional Educational Laboratory‡

South Central Region Educational Laboratory‡

Southeastern Educational Laboratory

Southwest Educational Development Laboratory

Southwest Regional Educational Laboratory

Southwestern Cooperative Educational Laboratory

Upper Midwest Regional Educational Laboratory

NATIONAL AERONAUTICS AND SPACE ADMINISTRATION

University-Operated

Jet Propulsion Laboratory (California Institute of Technology)

Space Radiation Effects Laboratory (College of William and Mary)

NATIONAL SCIENCE FOUNDATION

University-Operated

Arecibo Observatory (Cornell University)¶

Operated by University Groups

Cerro Tololo Inter-American Observatory (Association of Universities for Research in Astronomy)

Kitt Peak National Observatory (Association of Universities for Research in Astronomy)

National Center for Atmospheric Research (University Corporation for Atmospheric Research)

National Radio Astronomy Observatory (Associated Universities)

† Phased out as a federal research center at the end of fiscal 1970 (June 30, 1970).

‡ Phased out as a federal research center at the end of fiscal 1969 (June 30, 1969).

§ In fiscal 1970, became an independent nonprofit center renamed the Human Resources Research Organization.

¶ Became a federal research center in fiscal 1970.

SOURCE: National Science Foundation, 1970c, pp. 99–100.

Appendix B:
Federal Obligations
to 125 Centers
and Institutes, 1969

Rank	Federal funds, 1969 (millions)	Institute	Type	State	Main agency sponsor
1	$162,659	Lawrence Radiation Laboratory	a*	California	AEC
2	156,295	Jet Propulsion Laboratory	a	California	NASA
3	99,302	Los Alamos Scientific Laboratory	a	New Mexico	AEC
4	89,401	Argonne National Laboratory	a	Illinois	AEC
5	76,338	Aerospace Corporation	a	California	AF
6	61,379	Lincoln Laboratory	a	Massachusetts	AF
7	51,218	Applied Physics Laboratory	a	Maryland	Navy
8	49,613	Pacific Northwest Laboratory	a	Washington	AEC
9	48,855	Brookhaven National Laboratory	a	New York	AEC
10	32,702	MITRE	a	Massachusetts	AF
11	31,030	Stanford Research Institute	b	California	DOD
12	23,552	Stanford Linear Accelerator Center	a	California	AEC
13	20,438	RAND	a	California	AF
14	18,093	Cornell Aeronautical Laboratory	b	New York	DOD
15	16,015	Battelle Memorial Institute	b	Ohio	DOD
16	15,423	System Development Corporation	c	California	DOD
17	13,616	National Center for Atmospheric Research	a	Colorado	NSF
18	12,388	Institute for Defense Analyses	a	Virginia	DOD
19	9,961	IIT Research Institute	b	Illinois	DOD
20	9,915	Research Analysis Corporation	a	Virginia	Army
21	9,218	Center for Naval Analyses	a	Virginia	Navy
22	8,577	Ordnance Research Laboratory	a	Pennsylvania	Navy

23	Ames Laboratory	7,652	a	Iowa	AEC
24	Plasma Physics Laboratory	7,404	a	New Jersey	AEC
25	National Radio Astronomy Observatory	7,231	a	West Virginia	NSF
26	Southwest Research Institute	5,840	b	Texas	DOD
27	Kitt Peak National Observatory	5,564	a	Arizona	NSF
28	Riverside Research Institute	5,241	c	New York	DOD
29	Princeton-Pennsylvania Accelerator	4,970	a	New Jersey	AEC
30	Sloan-Kettering Institute	4,900	c	New York	HEW
31	Electromagnetic Compatibility Analysis Center	4,642	a	Maryland	AF
32	Mayo Foundation	4,321	, c	Minnesota	HEW
33	Syracuse University Research Corporation	4,175	b	New York	DOD
34	Atomic Bomb Casualty Commission	3,788	a	District of Columbia	AEC
35	Cambridge Electron Accelerator	3,555	a	Massachusetts	AEC
36	Southern Research Institute	3,527	b	Alabama	HEW
37	Research Triangle Institute	3,483	b	North Carolina	DOD
38	National Accelerator Laboratory	3,459	a	Illinois	AEC
39	Human Resources Research Office	3,445	a	District of Columbia	Army
40	Urban Institute	3,400	c	District of Columbia	HUD
41	Applied Physics Laboratory	3,205	a	Washington	Navy
42	Midwest Research Institute	3,089	b	Missouri	DOD
43	Hudson Laboratory	3,080	a	New York	Navy
44	Institute for Cancer Research	2,770	c	Pennsylvania	HEW
45	Research for Better Schools	2,700	a	Pennsylvania	OE
46	Southwest Center for Advanced Studies	2,667	c	Texas	NASA
47	Center for Urban Education	2,646	a	New York	OE
48	Southwest Regional Educational Laboratory	2,487	a	California	OE

Rank	Federal funds, 1969 (millions)	Institute	Type	State	Main agency sponsor
49	$ 2,485	Medical Research Foundation of Oregon	c	Oregon	HEW
50	2,484	Lovelace Foundation for Medical Education	c	New Mexico	AEC
51	2,457	Franklin Institute	b	Pennsylvania	DOD
52	2,307	Children's Cancer Research Foundation	c	Massachusetts	HEW
53	2,067	Oak Ridge Associated Universities	a	Tennessee	AEC
54	2,039	Worcester Foundation for Experimental Biology	c	Massachusetts	HEW
55	1,978	Jackson Laboratory	c	Maine	HEW
56	1,861	Center for Research in Social Systems	a	District of Columbia	Army
57	1,860	Oklahoma Medical Research Foundation	c	Oklahoma	HEW
58	1,763	Northwest Regional Educational Laboratory	a	Oregon	OE
59	1,746	Central Midwestern Regional Educational Laboratory	a	Missouri	OE
60	1,710	Southwest Educational Development Laboratory	a	Texas	OE
61	1,707	Coordination Center in Early Childhood Education	a	Illinois	OE
62	1,685	Far West Laboratory for Educational R&D	a	California	OE
63	1,680	American Institutes for Research	c	Pennsylvania	DOD
64	1,613	Institute of Medical Sciences	c	California	HEW
65	1,454	Learning R&D Center	a	Pennsylvania	OE
66	1,404	Retina Foundation	c	Massachusetts	HEW
67	1,390	Educational Development Center	a	Massachusetts	OE
68	1,359	Southwest Foundation for Research and Education	c	Texas	HEW
69	1,350	Mathematics Research Center	a	Wisconsin	Army
70	1,207	Public Health Research Institute of New York	c	New York	HEW

71	Center for R&D for Learning and Re-Education	a	Wisconsin	OE
72	Analytical Services	a	Virginia	AF
73	Cerro-Tololo Inter-American Observatory	a	Chile	NSF
74	Salk Institute	c	California	HEW
75	Wistar Institute	c	Pennsylvania	HEW
76	Hudson Institute	c	New York	DOD
77	Space Radiation Effects Laboratory	a	Virginia	NASA
78	Eastern Regional Institute for Education	a	New York	OE
79	Stanford Center for R&D in Teaching	a	California	OE
80	Center for R&D in Higher Education	a	California	OE
81	Mid-Continent Regional Educational Laboratory	a	Missouri	OE
82	Appalachia Educational Laboratory	a	West Virginia	OE
83	Southwestern Cooperative Educational Laboratory	a	New Mexico	OE
84	Regional Educational Laboratory for the Carolinas and Virginia	a	North Carolina	OE
85	R&D Center in Teacher Education	a	Texas	OE
86	Atomic Power Development Associates	c	Michigan	AEC
87	Center for Study of Evaluation of Instructional Programs	a	California	OE
88	Upper Midwest Regional Educational Laboratory	a	Minnesota	OE
89	R&D Center of Educational Stimulation	a	Georgia	OE
90	Fels Research Institute	c	Ohio	HEW
91	Southeastern Educational Laboratory	a	Georgia	OE
92	Center for Study of Social Organization of Schools and Learning Process	a	Maryland	OE
93	Michigan Cancer Foundation	c	Michigan	HEW
94	Palo Alto Medical Research Foundation	c	California	HEW
95	Policy Research Center	a	New York	OE

Note: The table values for the numbers in the left-most printed column (1,200; 1,180; 1,179; 1,169; 1,131; 1,074; 1,041; 999; 995; 938; 938; 896; 862; 820; 820; 815; 809; 800; 790; 699; 670; 614; 610; 608; 587) correspond to rows 71–95 respectively.

Rank	Federal funds, 1969 (millions)	Institute	Type	State	Main agency sponsor
96	$ 564	Blood Research Institute	c	Massachusetts	HEW
97	537	Lowell Observatory	c	Arizona	NASA
98	519	Center for Advanced Study of Educational Administration	a	Oregon	OE
99	511	Boyce Thompson Institute for Plant Research	c	New York	HEW
100	500	Center for Educational Policy Research	a	California	OE
101	488	Arctic Institute of North America	c	District of Columbia	DOD
102	457	North Star R&D Institute	b	Minnesota	Interior
103	456	Haskins Laboratory	c	New York	HEW
104	449	Gorgas Memorial Institute	c	District of Columbia	HEW
105	436	Marine Biological Laboratory	c	Massachusetts	NSF
106	390	Central Atlantic Regional Educational Laboratory	a	District of Columbia	OE
107	385	Michigan-Ohio Regional Educational Laboratory	a	Michigan	OE
108	379	Research Foundation of Children's Hospital	c	District of Columbia	HEW?
109	346	Rocky Mountain Regional Educational Laboratory	a	Colorado	OE
110	320	South Central Regional Educational Laboratory	a	Arkansas	OE
111	320	Pacific Northwest Research Foundation	c	Washington	HEW
112	280	Institute for Medical Research and Studies	c	New York	HEW
113	241	Cooperative Educational Research Laboratory	a	Illinois	OE
114	205	Hanford Occupational Health Foundation	c	Virginia	AEC
115	204	Scripps Clinic and Research Foundation	c	California	AEC
116	169	Bureau of Social Science Research	c	District of Columbia	HEW
117	166	Carnegie Institution of Washington	c	District of Columbia	NASA

118	National Opinion Research Center	c	Illinois	HEW
119	National Planning Association	c	District of Columbia	HEW
120	Institute of Gas Technology	c	Illinois	DOD
121	Institute of Public Administration	c	New York	DOD
122	The Brookings Institution	c	District of Columbia	NSF
123	Western Behavioral Sciences Institute	c	California	DOD
124	Friends of Psychiatric Research	c	Maryland	HEW
125	New Jersey Mental Health R&D Fund	c	New Jersey	DOD

* a: R&D center; b: applied research institute; c: other nonprofit institute.
SOURCE: NSF 1970*b*.

Index

This book was set in Vladimir by University Graphics, Inc.
It was printed on acid-free, long-life paper and bound by The
Maple Press Company. The designers were Elliot Epstein and
Edward Butler. The editors were Nancy Tressel and Cheryl
Allen for McGraw-Hill Book Company and Verne A. Stadtman and
Dennis Wynn for the Carnegie Commission on Higher Education.
Alice Cohen supervised the production.